# VINTAGE DOCTOR
*Fifty Years of Laughter and Tears*

*Miles Hursthouse*

SHOAL BAY PRESS

First published in 2001 by
Shoal Bay Press Ltd
Box 17-661, Christchurch, New Zealand
Copyright © 2001 Miles Hursthouse

ISBN 1 877251 08 9

Cover photograph by Michael McArthur

All rights reserved. No part of this publication may be reproduced,
stored in a retrieval system or transmitted in any form by any means
electronic, mechanical, photocopying, recording or otherwise,
without prior permission from the publisher.

Printed by Rainbow Print Ltd, Christchurch, New Zealand

*DEDICATION*

To my wife Jillian for helpful advice, assistance, encouragement, proofreading and patience during my work on this book, and to our children, Linda, Tim and Mark for being what they are.

## ACKNOWLEDGMENTS

My patients who placed their trust and sometimes their lives in my care.

My medical, nursing and paramedical colleagues with whom I worked and who helped so much with advice and assistance when problems arose.

Bill Moore, editor of the *Nelson Mail*, who initially edited my manuscript and who encouraged me to publish it.

My publishers, Shoal Bay Press. David Elworthy's letter of acceptance gave me an unforgettable adrenalin rush, while Rachel Scott and Ros Henry had the unenviable task of moulding my work into a workable length, which they did with great skill, sensitivity and feeling.

# PROLOGUE

*ONE OF THE SADDEST DAYS* of my life occurred at Wellington Hospital in a large ugly room containing a number of so-called 'iron lungs'. Most of these were old models that had been donated to the hospital 20-25 years earlier by Lord Nuffield, following a disastrous epidemic of poliomyelitis, then commonly called infantile paralysis.

These old wooden machines were about the size of a large coffin. Underneath was an electric motor driving a large crank that worked a bellows on the underside. It was a noisy piece of equipment that made a constant grinding, wheezing noise while working, which it had to do 24 hours a day.

A patient paralysed with polio and unable to breathe was put into this box for anything from a few days to some weeks until they could breathe again, lying face up with head protruding from one end. Foam rubber edging sealed the box around the neck. Along the sides were panels that could be unbolted to allow those attending the 'victim' to insert their hands and arms through rubber seals to help with washing and toilet. The poor patient had to have a small hole made in his windpipe just below the voice box to allow air flow, since nose and mouth could be obstructed. The action of the bellows caused a rhythmic suction and pressure cycle in the cabinet, which made his chest expand and contract, thus effectively giving constant artificial respiration. If the power went off for any reason the pump could be worked manually with a large lever.

There were many disadvantages. For instance, the pressure cycle worked on the abdominal wall as well as the lungs, so the patient tended to swallow air and sometimes belch it out or vomit. The noise was horrific, not only from the machinery, but also from the whistling of the air flowing in and out of the tracheostomy tube in the windpipe. This effectively prevented sleep, which in any case was difficult as the patient was cast, on his back, unable to move or be moved. The only way he could make any attempt to talk was to have a small plug put in the tracheostomy tube so that the air passed through the voice box for a short time.

Those of us who had to work with these machines hated them because of the misery associated with them. I can still hear the awful cranking, grinding and whistling as I write this 47 years later. But they worked – mostly.

In 1952, while I was working as a house surgeon at Wellington Hospital, there was a nationwide epidemic of poliomyelitis: we saw up to a dozen or more suspected cases a day. If spinal fluid showed the typical changes of polio they were admitted into a special ward, which gradually became so busy that house surgeons had to be taken off other duties to look after them. My friend Owen Prior and I were landed with this job and it kept us busy and exhausted, rushing down to Casualty to do lumbar punctures on all suspects, then arranging admission if they were positive, and attending all the in-patients.

The worst cases were those who became increasingly paralysed as more muscle groups were affected. The paralysis was accompanied by severe muscle pain and tenderness so that inevitably we had to place some patients in iron lungs to keep them alive. This was a dreadful time for them and their morale needed constant boosting, with someone sitting at their head talking quietly, just having a hand on them, attending to their wants or perhaps giving them sips of water – a 24-hour-a-day job with high risk of cross-infection. There was no immunisation in those days and several house surgeons contracted mild polio infections with muscle weakness, though no serious cases occurred among the staff.

One day I was called to Casualty to see 'Isobel', a young woman in her thirties who had a slight headache and stiff neck. A lumbar puncture showed a heavy lymphocyte infiltrate in the spinal fluid typical of polio, so I admitted her and watched her closely.

'Isobel' had been playing vigorous sport a day or two previously. We had found that heavy exercise in the early stages of infection was often associated with severe paralysis and this proved so in her case, with rapid onset of excruciating pain and total paralysis of her legs. When the paralysis moved up to involve her abdomen, chest and arms, we had to put her into an iron lung. Her spirit was wonderful and she was dearly loved by all the staff, who realised the seriousness of her case and kept her company the whole time. I spent countless hours at her head, encouraging her and trying to give her strength. Eventually the condition peaked and we were optimistic that she would improve slowly in the next few days.

At that time I was involved in setting up a general practice in Nelson and had to fly over to see a doctor who had offered me a partnership. I left early in the morning after seeing 'Isobel' and telling her to hold on as I would be back that afternoon. She seemed in fairly good shape.

When I got back from Nelson I went straight up to the ward and found her resuscitator empty and silent. She had died. I was devastated and unashamedly wept for the loss of this lovely and brave young woman.

# 1

*I WAS INTRODUCED TO* this world in a house in Hastings, New Zealand, on 27 October 1919. I am told I was born with a 'caul' (in unruptured membranes for the technically minded), which at that time was regarded as an omen of good luck – or at least the promise that I would avoid death by drowning. (I have so far avoided the latter and have certainly had my share of the former.)

My older brother Dan, with whom I retain a lifelong close rapport and friendship, preceded me into this life by a bit over three years.

Looking back at the family history it is interesting to ponder that we would not have existed were it not for the interventions of various notable Maori at different stages in the family history. One of our forebears, the Reverend John Hobbs, my great-great-grandfather on my mother's side, came to New Zealand with Samuel Marsden in 1824 as a missionary helper. He later became a Wesleyan leader and was very involved with Maori, using his influence to encourage the Hokianga tribes to sign the Treaty of Waitangi. He later fell into life-threatening disfavour with some Maori but was saved from harm by the chief Tamati Wakanene, one of the signatories to the Treaty.

My paternal grandfather, Charles Wilson Hursthouse, became involved with the Maori tribes of the King Country when he was, in conjunction with John Rochfort, surveying the main-trunk railway line. He was at one stage imprisoned in a rude hut with his assistant, Bob Newsham, by the Hauhau fanatic Mahuki and his sub-tribe. These folk were dancing around and had actually got to the stage of building a gallows to hang grandfather and his mate. They were saved by a rescue party led by Wetere Te Rerenga, chief of the Mokau sub-tribe, apparently keen to atone for their part in the murder of the Reverend John Whiteley.

We are grateful to Wetere Te Rerenga and Tamati Wakanene for our family's survival!

There is an interesting footnote to my family story that I did not discover until comparatively recently. In the early 1890s, while Grandfather Charles Wilson Hursthouse was working in the King Country, he developed a liaison with a lovely young Maori woman, Te Rongo-Pamamao, who had a daughter in 1892. This girl was named Rangimarie Hursthouse. Oral history tells us that the first name, which has a Maori component and a Pakeha component, signified the coming together of the two races in peace.

When Grandfather was on his deathbed he told the Hursthouse family about Rangimarie for the first time and asked them to contribute to her education as she was said to be very intelligent. I regret to say this never happened – no Hursthouse of that generation ever acknowledged her. My father never told me, or anyone else as far as I knew, of her existence. However, at a party in Western Samoa in about 1970 I met up with a cousin of mine, Ted Lattey, who had worked in the King Country bush during the Depression. During an exchange of mutual confidences he told me the story of Rangimarie. I was astonished and immediately made contact with her and her family. She had married Tuheka Hetet and they had had a considerable family but she was subsequently widowed. She and all her family treated me with great courtesy and affection, which has remained between our families ever since.

The remarkable Rangimarie Hetet became known throughout New Zealand and the Pacific for her fine weaving. She received numerous honours from various arts councils and the academes, was awarded an honorary doctorate from Waikato University, an MBE and a CBE, and finally she was made a Dame Commander of the Order of the British Empire.

She was a lovely gracious lady and I loved her dearly. She died at 103 and I was privileged to be able to speak at her 100th birthday celebrations, as well as to attend her tangi with my family.

My mother Frances Rosamond, known as Jane, was a charming, easygoing, unselfish, artistic woman beloved of all her friends and relatives. She was from the pioneer Nelson Barnicoat family one of whom, her mother Amy, married a Kirk. R.C. Kirk, my maternal grandfather, was a mysterious sort of man who was an expert rifle shot, a national and Australian champion golfer, mayor of Petone and a solicitor in Wellington. Unfortunately in middle age he developed a skin cancer on his ear and medical experts were unable to arrest its progress, despite the removal of his ear. When I knew him, he always wore a black patch over this area. This was intriguing to any small boy, conjuring up images of pirates. He apparently knew that he was doomed, so he concentrated on his golf, to the benefit of that but to the detriment of his practice, leaving the way open for his partner to embezzle funds. Life was difficult financially for my grandmother when he eventually died.

My father was a different type of person, although also from an early pioneering family and with a recorded family history of some 400 years before coming to New Zealand. They were of Dutch ancestry, reputed to have wisely settled in Britain rather than face 'conversion' at the fiery stake when the notorious Duke of Alva was doing his worst at the behest of the King of Spain.

Dennis Hursthouse was the youngest of seven children and became a civil and mechanical engineer. He was 13 years older than my mother, with strong ideas about his place in society. He was a strict disciplinarian, no believer in 'sparing the rod' on his children, and the severity of this was a source of some misery from time to time. His immediate family knew him as an unforgiving man who took offence at seemingly simple statements, and all the accounts of his contemporaries and co-workers seem to agree that his temper was uncertain and his manner aggressive.

He travelled widely around the world in the pursuit of his profession and did a lot of training in the US, reading widely and studying engineering principles until he died at the age of 103. On his 100th birthday he received Letters Patent for a new design of flood-gate control of rivers! Also on that day he was delighted to be given an electronic calculator and could hardly believe the simplicity of obtaining arithmetic and trigonometric data.

My first memories are of standing up in my cot playing with my mother and beating the uprights of the cot door, and also of being forced to sit on a potty daily until the appropriate result was obtained. This seemed to me not only cruelly restrictive, but a stupid waste of time and I soon learnt to propel myself around the house while seated thereon. I can clearly remember following our lovely old charlady, watching her at work.

The next thing I remember is being forced to go to Mahora School in Hastings at the age of four. Perhaps I was a nark at home or something, but it seems quite extraordinary that I should have been sent to school so young. I can remember sitting on top of a rubbish bin at school howling my eyes out until my mother came and took me home again, where I stayed for another year.

Primary schooling at Mahora School was a good time on the whole. There was a good swimming pool and large playgrounds. We had a fine headmaster, Mr Chaplin, but one particularly brutal teacher, of whom more later. A Maori teacher, Mr Priestley, arrived after a few years and was wonderful at teaching us Maori and other New Zealand history as well as many Maori songs. A love of Maori music has remained with me. We sat at two-seater desks and one of my longstanding desk partners was Jimmy Tahau, whom I remember with affection. I cannot recall the slightest racial discrimination at that school.

The strap was used extensively for punishment of minor or major misdemeanours but there was little pain in this and no rancour, except where it was administered unjustly. I seem to have had a weekly whack on the hands and my parents once offered me a goodly financial bribe if I could go a week without this. I do not remember ever claiming the reward. I remember resenting getting the strap only twice. The first time was in standard two when a bee stung me in the ear, which made me yell loudly. The teacher, Miss Bullen, asked me why I sounded off and obviously did not believe me, so hauled me out and whacked me. The other occasion was when one of our lifelong friends and neighbours appeared as a 'pupil teacher' in our class. I called her 'Susie', which I had always done, and she took me along to the headmaster's office where I was strapped for giving cheek. It is interesting to me that I have never resented the headmaster whacking me for that but have always remembered Susie with a sense of grievance.

The only really nasty incident I remember was when we were having open-air English lessons out in the tarsealed quadrangle with a large, tall, crew-cropped, humourless master who shall remain nameless. A perfectly nice Maori lad made some sort of error and the master was so wild he grabbed him and dragged him at high speed across the tarseal to his office to whack him. The boy's knees were torn and bleeding and we were all appalled. I don't know where the subsequent complaint originated – we were too scared to speak out – but there was a brief inquiry and the master was sacked. I was frightened to see such a display of violent temper and my memory of it remains vivid.

I skipped through all the primers in the first year and went into standard one part way through, most distressed at being taken away from my friends.

We lived about a mile away from the school and until I managed to get a bike I had to walk. As an animal lover I was hurt and bewildered when I said 'Hello' to a cocker spaniel in a gateway on the way to school and was bitten on my hand for my courtesy.

When I did get a bike it was a monster of a thing. Its front brake consisted of a pad pushing down onto the tyre and a fixed-wheel drive, so that rear wheel-braking was effected by trying to stop the pedals turning. I got pretty adept at this and in time could lock the back wheel. I had one awful spill going to school on this bike. We always rode (illegally then, as now) on the footpath as the roads were all shingle. I was speeding along the footpath and swerved to cross the small concrete bridge over the gutter onto the road, but I misjudged. The front wheel hit the free edge of the bridge, bringing the outfit to a dead stop, wrecking the front wheel, and propelling me over the descending handlebars onto my hands and knees in among the gravel. It made a terrible mess of elbows and knees, with scars apparent to this day. I had to return home for first aid, which consisted of washing out the gravel and applying horribly painful iodine. It all took weeks to heal, with the bandages having to be soaked off and renewed every day.

I made another serious mistake one day. I absentmindedly set off with my beloved gollywog in my hand and only realised his presence when halfway there. I was mortified and secreted the poor fellow under my shirt as I ran home to put him away. I quake to think of the humiliation if I had arrived at school with him.

Looking back I realise that the Depression must have been in full swing, and lots of kids were barefoot at school. We were wild that we were not allowed to go barefoot too.

There was very little bullying at Mahora and we had (mostly) great teachers and varied courses, including woodwork and vegetable gardening. I hated history (except New Zealand history) and to some degree geography, but I guess this was due to the way these were taught in those days. I made some lifelong friends at primary school but had an academic enemy in Stanley Watkinson, nicknamed 'Skinny'. He and I were good friends but bitter rivals for high places in the exams and he pipped me for dux, much to my fury. We went on to high school together and continued our friendship and our battle. I was deeply saddened to hear that after we left school he was killed in the battleship HMS *Hood* when she was destroyed by the Germans in World War 2.

I was in standard six, aged 11, on the first day of school in 1931. It was 3 February and at morning interval one of my mates in the class below asked if he could buy some of my previous year's textbooks, so I hopped on my bike and shot home to get them. My mother had just given me a glass of milk and a bun when to my utter astonishment she seemed to take leave of her senses and grabbed me to try to throw me out the door.

It was the beginning of the Hawke's Bay earthquake, in which 257 lives were lost, two towns virtually destroyed and countless homes made uninhabitable. We rushed outside onto the lawn where I was thrown to the ground. I crouched like a dog and howled like one too, while I was drenched with water from a neighbour's water tank, which fell off its high stand and burst. Our chimneys, and radio mast with stays, fell in heaps around us. The din and chaos were appalling.

My mother held on to a garden fence and managed to stay upright. When the first major shock was over we checked to see that the kitchen fire was out and the gas ring not burning, then rushed down the drive to wait on the footpath. All the chimneys in our house had been demolished, and some of the roof destroyed by falling bricks. From the front gate we could see clouds of dust over the town centre. The post office tower with town clock was gone, as were most of the upper storeys of the Grand Hotel in the main street. As we waited there were further jolts every few minutes, during which the telephone and power lines would swing wildly like skipping ropes between the poles.

After a short while we saw my father coming down the road, pedalling wildly on his bicycle. He had a large engineering workshop on the King Street/Avenue Road corner with a lot of machine tools and heavy equipment. The front wall was brick and the rest was corrugated iron. He told us the whole front wall had disappeared except for a small section in the centre where the workshop clock hung. All the bricks from the wall had been flung out onto the road, thankfully sparing the lives of the workmen and office staff, as well as major damage to machinery.

We three waited in the street, looking anxiously for my brother Dan, who was at Hastings High School a mile and a half away on the other side of the shopping centre. Knowing that the high school was built of brick and probably therefore seriously damaged or destroyed, we were relieved to see him come pedalling down the road, looking not the slightest perturbed. He had had to ride through the main street on his way home and said he had to pick his way through the rubble from destroyed buildings. He was amazed at the goods lying on the road among the bricks and mortar and spoke with envy of some lovely cameras …

With the family assembled we took stock of our situation. The house had no chimneys and was a terrible mess. All our china, glassware and ornaments were smashed or damaged. The pantry was ankle deep in a mass of preserved jams, jellies, bottled fruits, curry powder, milk, cream and every other sort of food, fresh and dried. We attacked this first, with buckets and shovels, finding to our joy that many of the last bottles and containers to fall had landed in this goo intact. Ceilings in some rooms were broken where bricks from the chimneys had come right through.

By that first evening, martial law had been declared. A hospital marquee had been set up at the racecourse, and the shopping centre was cordoned off to keep people out of the way of rescue teams and to prevent looting. The weather remained fine, windless and warm, which was just as well, as most people could not stay in their houses and there was no gas for cooking, no water supply, and no electricity.

We set up two tents on the back lawn and built a nice fireplace out of fallen bricks from the house. The next-door neighbours had an artesian well – quite a common feature in those days – and we were able to use this supply, but all water had to be boiled as the sewers had all been smashed in the ground. We were also invited to wash in their outside wash-house tubs. A close friend, Mr Gill, got out of his office safely, then went back to try to rescue his office girl, who had not come out. They were both killed by falling debris. His wife and small son were staying with us for refuge and comfort.

At about 9pm the small boy, my brother and I lay awake in our beds in a largish ridge pole tent while the three adults were sitting around the fire. Suddenly there was another devastatingly violent quake. It was terrifying, especially in the dark. The ground buckled so much that our tent came right down onto the ground and the ridge pole hit my brother on the forehead. We could all feel the canvas on our faces, after which it sprang up again into place – not one guy rope or peg had been pulled out. It was all too much for the bereaved Mrs Gill, who screamed uncontrollably.

My father somehow got his car, a Chevrolet tourer, out into the road, packed all our bedding and us inside and headed south out of town. There was a lot of oncoming relief traffic and I remember we dodged around road blocks, avoiding cracks in and debris on the road, and eventually arrived at the Waipukurau racecourse, about 30 miles south of Hastings, where we all lay down in our blankets on the thick pine needles under the trees and slept until dawn.

We returned to Hastings the next day and started cleaning up as best we could. There were hundreds of aftershocks every day for a while but we got used to them – we thought. Dad had a lot to do to make his workshop secure and clean it up, but before he could do this he had an urgent cablegram from the United States firm for whose engines and orchard materials he was a New Zealand agent. They requested that he arrange publicity photos of their products in the midst of the devastation to show how rugged they were. So with some help he placed engines, spray pumps and belting in among the piles of brick on the footpath and road, with a few strategically placed signs beside them. He then arranged for a professional photographer to take pictures which were duly sent to the US.

It was apparent after some days that children were very much in the way in Hastings and Napier. No schools could open, there were no proper toilet or bathing facilities in the town and adults were fully occupied in caring for the sick and injured and cleaning up the mess. For these and no doubt other reasons an evacuation procedure was put into effect, and refugee trains took children off to other centres. This was all very exciting for us. We were given labels showing that we were refugees, as well as small ID cards declaring this status. (This card gave us free access to all sorts of things, such as transport, movies and other entertainments. The rule was that you could not get anything free that caused a financial loss to the donor, such as food.)

Dan and I were evacuated to our grandparents' house in Petone, where we often went for school holidays and were always made me very welcome and comfortable. For about a week I had earthquake nightmares every night awakening to feel them, I imagined. Dan used to hear me from the next room and come in to reassure me. But all in all we had a great time with our refugee cards, going to pictures, the zoo and some shows that were on, taking buses, trains and trams all over Wellington.

After some months of this we were sent home. The town had been tidied up but remained devastated. We spent a lot of time helping Dad rebuild the chimneys of our home as all skilled labour was in high demand to get industry on the move again. I seemed to spend whole days in the weekends doing nothing except chip the mortar off bricks with a cold chisel and hammer.

# 2

LIFE EVENTUALLY RETURNED TO NORMAL. Our time outside school was mostly fun. I was mad keen on all animals but we were not allowed a dog or cat. I had one of the latter for a short while but it was destroyed by my father while I was at Sunday School one morning. I was pretty upset about that. However, there were plenty of other animals. I kept pigeons for some years and bred from them, making some good pocket money selling the offspring. After they had been sold at the Saturday auction some of them used to come home again and were never reclaimed so the best of them were sold several times! One day one returned with a shotgun pellet in one leg. Alarmed I made enquiries as to who was buying my pigeons at auction and found to my horror that it was the local gun club. I never sold another bird.

I also had some bantams, which were great fun. The wee rooster, Little Mister, became such a good friend that he used to fly down the drive when he heard me coming in the front gate on my bike, and sat on my handlebars as I went to the back of the house. His little lady was demure and pretty and seemed to endure frequent marital relations. I got the idea that it would be fun to raise bantam chicks, so I used to put the eggs aside for about 10 days, eating the oldest each day and adding the latest to the end of the row so I always had 10 eggs in reserve. When she became clucky I would put her in a nest with these 10 eggs and watch the babies hatching out three weeks later. The newly hatched bantam chicks were absolutely fascinating and the parents were wonderful at shepherding them around the garden, finding them particularly juicy morsels to eat.

Guinea pigs were another source of interest. We started off with Annie and Ginger, keeping them in a hutch with a largish wire-netting yard and a waterproof box at the end. We used to move the whole caboodle around the lawn and I was amazed at their ability to perpetually eat to the exclusion of all else. In this latter assumption I was greatly in error as I went out one morning to find several small new guinea pigs. They would start eating grass shortly after birth and keep going all day. In fact guinea pigs seemed to be singularly lacking in spectator interest. After repeated batches of babies had exhausted all available recipients of gifts we liberated them in the country. I suppose they were taken by predators but I never thought about this as a child.

We lived in a nice old wooden house with pleasant neighbours, and with lots of large empty paddocks nearby where we could fly kites and lie in the grass watching skylarks to see where they descended so that we could find their nests. Tree climbing and bird nesting were great sport. We used to climb up to the nests and take one egg – but only if there were more than one. It was very competitive as we vied to get the most unusual egg. I was puzzled and still am why a blackbird's egg was pale blue with light brown streaks, while a thrush's was dark blue with black spots. I remember how hard it was to find a skylark's nest, especially one with eggs.

We used to indulge in harmless pranks at times. One of our favourites was to make a small parcel neatly wrapped in brown paper and put it on the footpath outside our front gate with a fine cotton thread attached. This was held firmly through the fence while we watched for gullible passers-by through a knot-hole. Sure enough someone would spot the parcel and always glance around before stooping to pick it up. Before they had a firm grip we would pull on the thread and snatch the parcel away. We found that there were three possible reactions. Some just laughed and occasionally shook a playful fist in our hidden direction; some scurried away guiltily without glancing back. A few were obviously furious at being duped and abused us loudly or shook an angry fist. It was great entertainment.

We always had an elderly car, the first one I remember being a small AC open two-seater. There was room for the driver and one adult passenger with the smallest child (me) squeezed in between them. Dan sat on the floor on the passenger side with his feet outside on the running board, the door having been removed. The roads were all gravel and some were pretty rough. Dogs were a problem because the car went so slowly that they could run faster than we could drive and they would try to get at Dan's legs and ankles. This was not much fun for him so we always carried a container of suitable-sized stones to pelt the dogs with. The result was that our progress was a real circus event since our going on the offensive seemed to stimulate more farm dogs to join in the fun.

Sometimes we would have a picnic in the country, usually at a beach or river. Dad fished at the beach, especially Clifton, and I seem to remember he always caught plenty of snapper. He would swing enormous sinkers round and round his head, finally casting the line out beyond the breakers before leaving it propped on a long stick to keep it away from the waves. One day while he was preparing to put his second line out he asked me to hold the first line, which I did by foolishly winding the string in a complicated fashion around and between my fingers. In a short time I found myself being pulled against all my strength down the beach and into the water, yelling my head off. Dad and some other fisherman ran down and grabbed me. After getting the line free they hauled in a biggish female shark with a host of unborn baby fish inside. I was fascinated.

My father was keen on all sorts of fishing, especially trout fishing at Taupo. He went there regularly with friends from the early 1920s, always coming home with a large supply of smoked trout. In the late 1920s we started going there as a family for Christmas holidays, usually camping in the local camping ground, and we were introduced to trout fishing, both with fly and trolling in a borrowed dinghy. We always caught plenty of fish and didn't think much of any fish under about 6 pounds. We got on well with the local Maori, who were great friends and taught us a lot about fishing.

In the late 1920s Dad bought an acre of land in Heu Heu Street, two blocks from the main street of Taupo, for about £35. It was covered in broom and had a small gully as well. Over the next few years we cleared the broom and planted masses of trees, such as silver birches, many of which are still there. We built a bit of a shack with a lean-to and a concrete floor in which the adults could sleep and we could all eat. The young slept outside in tents and it was all very snug and comfortable. Down in the gully Dad carved out two large niches from the pumice soil and made one of these into a toilet and the other into a smokehouse for the fish. We spent many happy days and weeks there over the years. Dan and I were most upset when Dad sold the property 20 years later without giving us a chance to buy it.

Dad decided to build a launch to use on the lake and set about this in his workshop, employing the local carpenter, blacksmith and engineer when they were short of work. It was a 21-foot V-bottom launch and was coming along nicely until the 1931 earthquake shook it off its cradle, leaving it lying on its side in among open drums of grease and lubricating oil, which had emptied their contents onto the floor.

It was pretty heartbreaking but eventually the work started again and it was finished off with an old Chevrolet motor. Lake Taupo was out of the question by this stage, for economic reasons, and unfortunately the lovely inner harbour at Napier had disappeared after the earthquake. So we took her to Napier's Port Ahuriri on a railway truck and prepared to lift her into the water with suitable ceremony. Alas, the spreaders holding the lifting rope slings away from the hull broke with a loud bang and she got an almighty squeeze, which did her no good at all. When she was put into the water she leaked like a sieve and we had to take turns at pumping her for hours until the wood swelled and she sealed a bit. We did have a lot of fun with that boat but she had trouble after trouble, even catching fire from an electrical fault one day. So Dad did a deal and sold/swapped her for some more land at Taupo.

One of these sections was in what is now the best part of town, overlooking the lake, and the other was on the foreshore with natural hot water below the then Terraces Hotel. Both were sold at bargain-basement prices a few years later.

Our out-of-school time in those days seemed to be largely unsupervised and we did get up to mischief now and then. As so many boys have done, Dan and I started to make gunpowder out of the usual ingredients. The lax state of supervision in those days is typified by the fact that we could walk into hardware shops in our early teenage years and buy fuse in any length with no questions asked! I remember Dan's first test explosion. He bored a large hole in a lump of hardwood, filled it with gunpowder, put in the fuse, rammed damp paper in firmly all around and then lit the fuse while we ran for cover. The success of the manufacturing process was dramatic. The explosion split the hardwood with such force that a piece of it flew up and broke the radio mast stays, bringing the whole wooden mast down around our ears.

Dan's next development was to add to the basic formula some potassium chlorate, despite dire warnings from friendly workmen that this was dangerous stuff that could explode with the slightest impact, such as a light smack with a hammer or an accidental blow. We decided the best way to test the result was to drop it into the water from the middle of the Havelock North bridge. So we biked out there, lit the fuse and dropped the bomb. The resultant underwater explosion was spectacular and as far as I am aware has remained an anonymous event until now.

Well, the gunpowder saga came to a dramatic end one day. Dan, with the newly developed and very unstable formula, was asked by a friend to blow up some large tree stumps for his father. The contract was accepted. Dan duly drilled his first hole and put in a hefty dose of powder, followed by a length of fuse. He rammed it all nice and tight with moistened wads of newspaper, using a length of steel rod but quite forgetting that a percussive blow could set off the unstable potassium chlorate – which it did in spectacular fashion. Our lifelong friendship could have ended at that point: the rod shot out with violent force and may well have impaled him had he been in its path. As it was, the explosion split the log and covered the skin of his face and hands with powder burns. He came home in a terrible mess and would have got into deep trouble and suffered heavy punishment from Father had we not covered up with all sorts of excuses such as bicycle accidents.

There was a sequel 66 years later when I was relating this story to his astounded family at his 50th wedding anniversary. He left the room, reappearing a few minutes later with the old tobacco tin that held the gunpowder, as well as the 'recipe', dated March 1932.

I suppose Hastings was a pretty dull place for young people but we made fun for ourselves by heading off on our bikes to outlying areas and the hills above Havelock North. We thought nothing of riding up to 30 miles in a day to go fishing at Napier port breakwater, or to the beach at Haumoana to try to catch kahawai in the river estuary. When travelling the 13 miles to Napier we always tried to get a tow from a car for part of the way. (It must be remembered that cars were very slow in those days, usually touring at about 30mph, with some older vehicles and trucks quite a bit slower.) The trick was to see a vehicle coming up from behind and judge whether its speed was suitable. If it was, we would pedal like mad as it drew alongside and grab hold of some projection – usually the 'dumb-iron' part of the soft-top supporting mechanism or a tail light, which was often quite high up. In the case of a truck, always a good catch, it was the left rear corner of the flat tray. Then, by leaning away from the vehicle and hanging on like grim death, steering with one hand, one got an exhilarating ride. Some vehicle drivers hated us doing this and tried to make us let go by weaving across the road or steering into potholes in the gravel surface, but others would see us preparing for a tow and slow down a bit to allow us to connect up. It was hard on the arms and we usually gave it away after a few miles. Nowadays I wonder that we survived at all.

One of our favourite exploits was to puff up Te Mata Peak so we could enjoy the death-defying ride down again. Not only was the road extremely steep but it was unsealed and bumpy with some very sharp bends. Our bikes had only a rear-wheel brake, which was operated very effectively by back-pedalling, but of course it relied on the chain staying on the sprockets, which it did not always do since we were not always too meticulous in keeping the chain fully adjusted and firmly tight. It would sometimes jump off, leaving one with no brakes whatsoever. We usually tried to put a foot on one of the tyres to slow it – without much success.

The most dramatic incident for me came when I was belting down from the peak and attempted a sharp right turn into the beginning of Simla Avenue. I tried to slow down but there was no one home in the braking department so, yelling my head off, I ploughed straight ahead across a grass strip and into a fence which was just the right height to stop the bike but allowed me to fly over the top into some nice long grass on the other side. There was no personal damage, apart from the usual skinned knees and elbows, but the bike had a seriously bent front wheel.

As I have said, Dan and I often visited our maternal grandparents in Petone, separately or together. This old home was an exciting haven for us.

Getting there was an adventure in itself as we had to go by train from Hastings, leaving at about 8.45am. We could never afford to travel first class so the seats were pretty uncomfortable and often it was very cold, although some weird metal chemical containers gave off a slight warmth. We used to try to pop into a vacant first-class carriage but we must have stuck out like sore toes and were usually shepherded back to our own seats by the guard. I always tried to con the engine driver into letting me up onto the locomotive but was always refused.

A train journey was a special event in those days and your close friends would come to see you depart. I have two outstanding memories in this regard, both of which taught me lessons. The first was when our local vicar came to say goodbye and offered me a florin as a present. Having been brought up always to show polite reluctance in the face of such generosity, I protested and said I could not accept it. To my horror, he did not repeat the offer but stuffed it back into his pocket! This taught me to be careful about refusing generosity. On the second occasion a sort of uncle by marriage came to see me off and pressed half a crown into my palm as the train started to move off, thus preventing any chance of a pseudo-polite refusal. This taught me to try to make it easy for people to accept gifts.

The train always had to stop at Woodville, where we disembarked and boarded another train to travel via the Wairarapa to Petone. The trip from Woodville to Wellington was exciting as we had to go over the Rimutaka Range, which entailed stopping at the foot of the mountain and changing engines to Fell locomotives, usually with one at each end of the train and sometimes another in the middle. These small engines reminded me of steam tugboats shoving big ships around. They were quite small but underneath they had a big gear wheel that engaged with a toothed rail in between the two ordinary railway lines, and by this means these small engines could haul a biggish train over the mountain without wheelspin.

It was a winding track with lots of tunnels and if you put your head out of the window on some of the curves you could see the whole length of the train as well as the smoke- and steam-belching locomotives. Over the mountain these engines were replaced with a conventional locomotive and it was all straightforward to Petone station, where my grandmother always had a taxi waiting.

These beloved grandparents lived in a largish two-storeyed house one block off the main street. To children it was an absolutely fascinating place as it occupied half a city block with enormous trees, a tennis court, an outside wash-house with loo, a tricycle house that contained a large adult tricycle with enormous wheels, an outside laboratory, chookhouse, small orchard, stables, motor garage and gardener's cottage, all joined by immaculate gravel paths. Inside the house was a large room with all sorts of fishing rods, guns and rifles – even a couple of revolvers. What a paradise for schoolboys.

My grandfather died in the 1920s, after which the house was run by my grandmother and her single sister, Rosamond Barnicoat, always known as 'Aunt'. They really were a couple of characters. Grandmother was a dithery, impractical sort of person who seemed to do the more menial jobs while the practical, thin aunt cooked and generally ran the house. There was no electricity until 1950: lighting was by gas lamps (which we boys were allowed to light) and cooking was done on a coal range.

Upon my arrival at this lovely old home my grandmother would throw open the door with the greeting, '*Here* he is!' Aunt would go to an enormous amount of trouble to arrange trips to factories and workshops for us and this quaint old lady with pinned-up hair, prim little face and long dark brown or black dress used to accompany us with every evidence of interest while we were taken around the Hutt railway workshops, the Petone woollen mills, the Gear Meat Company engine rooms, the W.D. & H.O. Wills cigarette factory and so on. She also made a point of getting permission to take us over some large overseas ships, including once some battleships of the US Navy that were visiting Wellington, and always we made a trip to the zoo.

Aunt was world travelled and a talented artist who left us a collection of her watercolours. But she inhabited a past era and her Victorian mannerisms used to put us into fits of giggles. Whenever she was surprised she would say to my grandmother 'Oh, Amy, I simply can't conceive!' And if she disapproved of somebody or their behaviour she would say, 'Of course, he is not at all gently born.' When she was very ill and had to be taken away in an ambulance, to die shortly afterwards, she refused to lie down on the stretcher in the back and insisted on sitting up front with the driver.

I have all sorts of memories of that home. On the other side of the road was a large empty paddock in which Worth's Circus used to set up. One day a baby elephant got loose and investigated with his trunk the tempting hand-hole in Grandmother's large, solid front gate, managing to unlatch it and get into the garden. Everyone was running all around trying to catch the wee fellow, who thought it was a grand game.

My bachelor uncle John also lived there with the two old ladies. He was reclusive but seemed to like my company. A fitness freak, he rowed competitively with the Petone Rowing Club and had lots of lovely exercise gadgets, including a rowing machine. I used to spend hours on it, and am sure my love of messing about in dinghies stems from this. Uncle John did some sort of medical degree in the US but gave it away for marine engineering. In his later years he used to be the engineer on the Wellington–Day's Bay–Eastbourne ferry and I loved going with him on these boats, the *Cobar* and *Muriwai*. I would get down into the engine room to watch the large reciprocating steam engines and all the signal process and valve handling when we came into the wharf.

One day a woman at Eastbourne tried to drown herself off the wharf and Uncle John leapt into the water and rescued her. For this he was presented with a Royal Humane Society award. It is sad and ironic that he drowned himself at the same spot when he was an old man living by himself. I never knew him to be cross or unpleasant to us kids and we were able to repay him in some degree in later life. When we were married and had homes of our own he would come and stay with us: I wish I had known how miserable he really was.

The Harding family of Petone were great friends. Dr Harding and his wife were wonderful to us kids and gave us presents that lasted all our lives, including beautiful leather-bound books that we still have. I seemed to live at their place when I was at Petone and they were always good to me. One of their unforgettable acts of generosity was after the Hawke's Bay earthquake, when they sent up to Hastings a large hamper of lovely food that they had just put together for a holiday they were about to take. In the throes of the Depression they could ill-afford this – general practitioners were having a harsh time with few patients able to pay. (I remember the Hardings used to be given all sorts of produce in lieu of fees. People would also come to do odd jobs around the house.)

One of the sons was to have a profound influence on my life. Jack Harding became a doctor like his father and he and his wife were very kind to me in my teen years. He used to take me on his visiting rounds and I waited in his car while he went in to see the patients. (I forget if it was Jack or his father who had been to the Hutt Hospital for an amputation operation and took the amputated limb, wrapped up, for destruction in the Wellington Hospital furnace. He stopped en route to visit a patient and while he was inside someone saw the parcel on the car seat and stole it.)

I was fascinated with the medical life and Dr Jack Harding always answered my innumerable questions about medical matters with great care and honesty. It was at this adolescent stage of my life that I decided that I wanted to practise medicine and I never deviated from this ambition. I was thrilled to meet Jack again 20 years later when I was working at Wellington Hospital as a house surgeon. By then he was an eminent paediatrician.

My grandmother was also a wonderful woman, full of caring love for her grandchildren. After she had a stroke that left her seriously paralysed, she was moved up to a hospital in Hastings so my mother could visit her easily. One of the last times I saw her before she died was when I took my new fiancée to see her, having given my bride-to-be a small bunch of violets (about all I could afford). After I had proudly introduced her, my grandmother said to my mother, 'Couldn't he have given her a better bunch of flowers?'

Grandmother and Aunt were a pair of staunch Christians whose influence on our lives was considerable. Everyone who knew them remembers them with the greatest affection. Of my relatives who have died, I realise that those who are remembered with the most love and affection nearly all died leaving little in the way of material wealth, but an enormous legacy of happy memories, gratitude and love. This is what endures.

# 3

*IN 1932, AGED 12, I STARTED* at co-educational Hastings High School. For the next five years I had some wonderful teachers and enjoyed most of the work, especially science, maths and languages. But I regret to say that I also suffered some miserable times through the incessant bullying, month in, month out, of a few overgrown imbeciles who could not accept that some pupils actually enjoyed learning.

I was younger than average at high school and quite small. I have never forgotten Stratton Morrin and Bill Howard as the ringleaders of a group who used to wait for me in the cloakroom and beat me up several times weekly. I am amazed in retrospect that my parents did not ever suspect or know of this – but of course I never told them. I still sometimes fancy meeting up with these two in these days of my retirement when I am so much stronger and fitter.

Another infamous bully was a chap called Kidd, who was keen on attacking studious types. I was going home after school one day when I saw him beating up a friend of mine who was not very robust. I intervened and he then took off after me. I managed to butt him in the stomach and bring him down but he got hold of me by neck and legs with his knee in my back, bending my back so far that there was suddenly an audible crack that scared even him. I was in agony for a long time and have permanent damage to my lower back.

As I grew older and presumably wiser I was better able to avoid the known bullies. So, with that unpleasantness dredged up – and reburied – I must say that the schooling there was great, with many of my teachers I remember with great affection: S.I. (Jonah) Jones, Charlie Aitken, B.I.F. Fulton, Tommy Atkinson and Mousie Mathieson. The headmaster, W.A.G. Penlington, was a talented man who was held in high regard by all his pupils. We did not have much to do with the women teachers but I will always remember 'Ma' Steele, who was a real character and quite uninhibited on stage playing her cello.

Wrestling was a craze in those days. Matches were broadcast on the radio and there were a number of notables in the sport. George Walker I remember, and also Lofty Blomfield. Although there was some showmanship in these bouts it did not reach the ludicrous proportions of later years, as seen on television. Lads such as I used to listen avidly to the bouts and try to emulate some of the holds – the 'Boston Crab' and others. Once put into one of these holds, one's opponent was defeated. The sport became such a craze at Hastings High School that at intervals and lunchtimes, as well as after school, the grounds would be littered with pairs of boys wrestling vigorously.

Occasionally there were some semi-serious injuries arising from overuse of some of the holds such as the 'arm bar', in which the victim's arm is held behind the elbow while the wrist is pulled backwards to try to over-extend the arm. But injuries were surprisingly few, I suppose because each of us knew that if we overdid it, someone was likely to do it to us in return! It was all good fun and must have developed us well physically. It certainly made a mess of our clothes.

Father had a well-equipped engineering works in Hastings and I was fascinated by this, often calling in there on my way home after school. His employees taught me a great deal about engineering, machining and the handling of tools – even electric welding. The smithy's forge, blown by an electric motor, was fun and I made lots of iron things, even cold chisels, which I tempered and still have. But some machinery was out of bounds, such as the power hammer and power saws.

I had my uses around the place. There was a large single-cylinder industrial engine with a big flywheel lying around that I loved starting and hearing run for a few minutes – I got it down to a fine art. One day the workshop manager was trying to sell it to a local farmer and, seeing me (aged about 12) he said, 'Miles, show us how easy it is to start this engine.' Luckily it performed as usual and the man bought it.

My mother was in charge of the women's page of the local newspaper, the *Hawke's Bay Tribune*. I was interested in the way the written word eventually became the printed word and haunted the print factory. The staff were all amazingly tolerant as I wandered around and asked countless questions, following the written copy from reporters' desks through subeditors' hands to the linotype operators and onwards to typesetting, to the making of the half-drum-shaped affairs that were bolted onto the actual press, and to the press churning out the completed newspapers. I especially loved the linotype machines and their operators, who typed so rapidly and apparently easily in an era when the keys had to be struck with some force. Every now and then one of the operators would make me a small lead piece with my name on it. The incredible complexity and ingenuity of this machine is fascinating.

My interest in engineering has continued throughout my life and I have a well-equipped workshop at home.

Almost all my close friends from those days lost their lives in World War 2. Julian Cotterill was a great guy but mercurial in temperament. One day he rode down the drive alongside the bike sheds at high speed but an idiot who wanted to tease him to make him lose his temper (which was always spectacular) was unwise enough to stand with arms widespread in the driveway. Julian just pedalled harder than ever and took the obstruction head on with such force that it broke his handlebars right off – doing no good to either the cyclist or the obstructor. No wonder poor Julian was killed early in the war. I tried to weld his handlebars for him but my father was furious at this, and rightly so, I realise in retrospect, as it was vital to have a professional repair of such an important part.

Another close friend for many years was Jack van Asch, who came from a well-known Hawke's Bay family. He and I were as different as chalk from cheese but had a tremendous relationship. Jack was poor at school academic work, a nuggety, powerful young man, while I was the just the opposite at that stage. He was brilliant at radio building and development: he just knew how they worked and even built a quite illegal transmitter at one stage. He used to listen to radio stations all over the world. He also sold me my first motorcycle after he left home to work on a farm, but more of that later. Jack also introduced me to smoking a pipe, which we borrowed from his father's collection. We were both violently ill and his father was highly amused, having observed the whole process from afar.

Jack and I used to meet on our bikes on the way to school each day but for some reason one day we fell out and stopped meeting. Unbeknown to us our mothers put their heads together to end our stupidity. My mother told me that Jack wanted to meet me at the corner one morning on the way to school, and Jack's mother told him that I wanted to speak to him. It worked and we remained great friends until Jack was also killed early in the war. I have always missed him greatly.

I was a keen Boy Scout, finding the weekly meetings great fun and most educational. We were taught lots of skills, such as rope work (splicing and knot-tying), that have been very useful for all my life, especially when camping or boating. I also went to a number of memorable camps.

Photography became a passion and I learnt to develop and print my own films and plates. My first camera was an old quarter-plate box camera – enormous, heavy and expensive to run, but with which I took a number of memorable photos, developing the glass plates and printing them myself. I have had a series of cameras since and retained an interest in the hobby but do not try to process the complex colour films now used.

At one stage Dad thought it would be a good idea to rent some paddocks close by and run a cow and perhaps some sheep. The latter venture was very short lived as he had absolutely no idea how to manage them, and after he tried to slaughter one he rapidly sold the lot. He came home one day with a brown paper parcel containing a brand-new, heavy, hardwood mallet. I asked him what it was for and he said he did not believe in killing sheep without stunning them unconscious first. Unbeknown to him I had several times visited the local freezing works and seen sheep slaughtered professionally, but wisely I kept my mouth shut. I was prohibited from watching this first production of mutton so got a ladder and peeped over the roof of the chookhouse at the circus that eventuated. Dad caught a sheep in the cow bail shed, gave it a mighty blow on the head with his new mallet, then let it go to turn and pick up his nice sharp knife. The dazed sheep saw the writing on the wall and took to her heels. This happened twice, so he eventually resorted to killing one by the usual method, but then made a beeline for the house and the whisky bottle.

The acquisition of a dairy cow was a different matter altogether. I was sent a mile or two away to lead back our first and only cow. We named her Rosie and she was a dear old thing. Very shrewdly, Dad straight away taught Dan and me to milk, and this we did for as long as we had Rosie. For a start Dad milked in the morning while we boys took the evening milking week and week about. We became pretty adept at this, with rapid development of hand, wrist and forearm muscles as she was a great provider.

It was our job also to put the milk into large pans and skim the cream, as well as make the butter from the surplus cream. We had plenty of cream with our porridge and puddings from then on.

Rosie mysteriously (to me) went dry after a trip away and then, equally mysteriously, produced a calf. Watching this process of birth was also strictly forbidden so once again I had to resort to the ladder against the chookhouse to keep myself informed. When we lads left home, which we did fairly early on, Dad lost interest in his farming venture and Rosie was made redundant.

When I was a senior high school student I had a nasty accident. By this time in our lives most of us had reasonably good bicycles and mine had three speed gears as well as double headlamps. I could go like the clappers, especially with a tail wind. One night I was coming home from my friend Philip Whitlock's home when I charged straight into the back of an unlit dark van parked on the roadside, my face taking the full force of the collision. A man in a nearby house heard the crash and came out to help me – my bike was smashed badly and my face felt peculiar. He took me to an outside pump and pumped water over my face, then took me home. My parents had visitors and when I walked in there was pandemonium as I had put my teeth right through my bottom lip, cut my top lip, broken off two top front teeth at gum level and another half off. I felt awful and there was blood everywhere. When I saw myself in the mirror I was heartbroken as I had just finished several years of getting my protuberant front teeth straightened with plates and wires, and the dentist had made a great job of them.

They called the family doctor, Sandy White, who, with no anaesthetic, sewed up my badly lacerated lip inside and outside while I sat in a chair. I never forgot this and never could understand or forgive such brutal management, particularly of a shocked 14-year-old. When I became a doctor myself I kept this in mind and never sewed up any injuries without anaesthetic, even when the patient was either drunk or nearly unconscious.

Afterwards I faced the trauma of the dental repair with, eventually, the loss of three upper front teeth after troublesome infected crown failures.

My friend Philip Whitlock and I became interested in motorbikes and Jack van Asch, who had by now left school, had one for sale. It was a monstrous thing and we decided to buy it, but did not mention it to our parents as the transaction would have been vetoed. We were 14 years of age. The machine was a 600cc P & M Panther – hand gear change, of course, and with acetylene lights. I think it was a 1928 model. It went like the clappers, threw us on several occasions and got us into serious trouble with our parents who each were given to understand that the machine belonged to the other joker.

Needless to say we had no licences and did not even contemplate such a matter. At holiday time we used to take turns having the bike and one day we went about 30 miles along a bad road to a farmhouse where Philip was going to stay. There was no pillion seat and no proper footrests so it was not very comfortable. We also had no easy means of stopping the brute and often used to put a hand over the air intake to stop the engine. We roared up to the farmhouse, the engine running very fast – probably in retrospect due to a sticking throttle cable – and I put my hand over the intake, unwittingly allowing the motor to suck in raw petrol and squirt it out into the hot exhaust. You guessed it: it erupted into flames in front of the startled host and hostess on the front verandah. Somehow we doused it and, since it managed to start again, I rode it home.

Being quite small for my 14 years I found kick-starting a 600cc bike difficult, so usually I shoved it along the road in second gear with the clutch lever pulled and then let the lever go when up to speed. Once it took off with such speed that I couldn't hold it and as it shot past me the hunk of bare iron that passed as a footrest caught me on the back of the ankle and threw me. The bike fell spluttering into the grass on the side of the road, which smouldered in sympathy. At this dramatic moment my long-suffering mother, bless her, came out of the front gate and saw the tableau. She didn't ever tell Dad about that one. Eventually, however, Philip's and my parents got together and found out the truth about the motorbike's ownership. Exit one bike.

I had various rides on other bikes for the next year or two, and remember in particular a lovely 350cc ohv Ariel with chrome tank and speedo in the middle. It was, I think, a 1934 job and belonged to Michael von Dadelszen of Havelock North. I can remember seeing 63mph showing on that speedo, and my eyes streaming in the wind as I rode it through Havelock North. No one wore helmets in those days.

My passion for motorcycling grew steadily until I was well into my mid-seventies when various deteriorating joints forced me to quit that sport.

I was also, as were most of us at that time, besotted with flying. Aircraft were few and far between in the early 1930s and we knew all the locally based ones by their registration letters, and most of the visiting ones too. They operated from an airfield at Bridge Pa, outside Hastings, and we often rode there on our bikes to watch the pilots servicing, hand-starting and flying their machines.

We were in awe of these pilots. They looked so glamorous with their leather helmets, goggles and leather jackets, the scarf around the neck with the ends blowing in the wind. They often wore riding breeches and long leather boots too. These august flying folk were very tolerant of us kids and would show us their aircraft and explain all the technical details. So much so that I reckoned that when the time came and I got a chance to fly an aeroplane, I would be able to do it straight off. So it eventually proved to be when the opportunity did come many years later, but that is another story for later.

At about this time Sir Charles Kingsford Smith made the first crossing of the

Tasman in his *Southern Cross* Fokker, three-engined monoplane. While in New Zealand he visited various centres, including Hastings, and took paying passengers. My father was totally and vehemently opposed to flying but was happy to come out with his wife and sons to see the machine, as well as an air display arranged for the occasion.

I remember that whole day with vivid clarity, including a parachute jump by Scotty Fraser, who was killed shortly afterwards at Rongotai airport when his parachute failed to open; 'Mad' Macgregor, who flew a Gipsy Moth inverted close to the ground round and round the airfield; and someone else who did a loop in which his wheels brushed the ground at the lowest point.

I was determined to have a flight and managed to talk Mum and Dad into lending me the money. A 10-minute flight in *Southern Cross* cost 10 shillings – a fortune to a lad in those days – but one sat in a large cabin and could not see much. Also available were flights in a Waco cabin bi-plane owned, I think, by either Fraser or Macgregor. This flight lasted 15 minutes or more and cost 7s 6d so I settled for that and got to sit in the cockpit. I can remember every detail of that trip. My only regret is that it would have been a very historic thing to have had a trip in the 'Old Bus' with 'Smithy'.

I promised myself I would eventually learn to fly.

I was up to sit matriculation after three years at high school but was deemed too young so I had to stay in the fifth form for another year. I was fed up but looking back I think it was probably a good thing, as I consolidated a lot of academic work, particularly in maths and science as well as Latin, which was essential in those days for a medical career.

It was a good year, with lots of tennis and bike rides all over the district, and I sat the examination with satisfactory results. In those days we were excused further schooling after our exams until the end of term as long as we put in an occasional appearance. Most of us took on some sort of work to get a bit of ready cash and I worked in the orchard of a family friend who was also my godfather, thinning apples and doing odd jobs. I earned enough money to buy my first fishing rod: a split cane fly rod with two tips that caught me a lot of fish, and which I still have.

My ambition to become a doctor was firmly entrenched but there seemed to be little possibility of its ever happening. Times were tough economically and my elder brother had first call on any parental funds. I was very unhappy at home, with my father's domination and violent temper, and was determined to get away. Eventually my father decided that I should undertake a career in law.

I returned to do a sixth-form year with about 10 other pupils. Very few students stayed on at school after the fifth form in those days, because of economic circumstances and the cost of university education. I also enrolled as an extra-curricular student at Victoria University to take some subjects for the LLB degree. I had a lot of advice from a former Hastings High School head prefect, Gavin Donne, who had done precisely what I was doing a year or two earlier. He went on to a distinguished legal career and I was delighted to meet him many years later when he was Chief Justice at Apia in Western Samoa.

I started off with four university subjects – jurisprudence, constitutional history, English Stage I and Latin Stage I. It was too much on top of the advanced mathematics that the school insisted I do, especially as I had no tutor for the law subjects and had to do them straight from textbooks. It was a hard year and I did not seem to do a great deal other than study, although one rather bizarre incident sticks in the mind.

I was studying hard in the upstairs library on a sports day not long before my exams, when a fifth former, who was getting sports gear from the storeroom next door, kept deliberately and provocatively rattling the library glass door each time he passed it. I eventually went out and remonstrated with him, but when I turned my back he lashed out with his foot and kicked me in a very vulnerable area, which was extremely painful. In reflex I swung round and belted him with my fist, which had all my considerable tennis practice behind it, thus laying open his cheek in spectacular fashion with plenty of blood.

He went to a doctor who stitched him up. But later that evening my father asked me what had happened at school that day and, as he probed, I realised he had heard about and wanted to know details of this incident. I told him exactly what had happened. It turned out that the victim's father had rung my father and told a story of brutal assault by me, claiming recompense for the medical fees. However, he didn't get them I am glad to say. What's more, he was bigger than I was too.

Eventually I dropped my two law subjects, but I sat stage one English and Latin in October that year, aged 16, and managed to pass them both, leaving school with those and a Higher School Certificate.

Then came the problem. To continue my studies I had to head to a university centre, but where was the money to come from? A part-time job as a law clerk in an established firm paid the appalling wage of 15 shillings a week at a time when board with meals cost 26 to 30 shillings a week. So we looked to government departments and eventually I was offered a job as a cadet in the Land and Deeds Department in Auckland for the comparatively magnificent starting wage of about 45 shillings weekly. While I was working I was to study for the law degree my father had decreed. Board was found for me at a hostel in Grafton Road called Trinity College, so off I went very happily by train to Auckland in December 1936.

# 4

TRINITY COLLEGE WAS A PLEASANT brick building with a sunny enclosed open area with outside seats. It was a Methodist theological college with about one-third of the rooms occupied by divinity students ('divs', as we called them), while the remainder were available for university, training college and technical college students. It had a great atmosphere and we all got on well, with a lot of quite harmless fun which in the end was, unfortunately, to result in my expulsion.

We had nice rooms and I suppose my main claim to fame there was that my roommate was destined to become Chief Justice of New Zealand. It makes me smile to see him looking so stern and solemn on the TV screen today and to compare this with some photos I have of him eyeing up an attractive waitress in our dining room, and also of both of us dressed up to kill, wandering around the Auckland Domain on a Sunday afternoon. Ron Davidson was good company and a dedicated law student (obviously).

One of the traditions at Trinity College was to let off steam by organising a 'blacking'. This consisted of bursting into the chosen victim's room and holding him down while smothering him with black boot polish. It was applied with a brush to the skin surface of his whole body, except for face and hair. We were all fighting fit so the whole process took a long time, and was very noisy. There was no animosity involved and some of the attackers would even try to help one remove the worst of it in the shower – it was not easy to clean your own back. I can still remember my own experience as a victim and it was great fun.

However, the tradition fell into disrepute when it was decided to 'do' an extremely large and strong fellow – he was 6 feet 4¾ inches and built in proportion: a daunting prospect. One amateur scientist, who knew a bit about chemicals but not enough, suggested that we paint him with silver nitrate solution, which every young chap should know turns black in the light. But those involved did not know it was also corrosive. The resultant blisters on the less accessible and more vulnerable areas of his anatomy caused quite a sensation, even to the medical students amongst us.

Another little trick that was traditional was to drop water bombs from our rooms on the first floor (which overlooked the footpath) onto unsuspecting amorous couples who loitered in the shadow of the wall at night. There were none of these modern plastic jobs - we made our own out of good stout paper and ruined many a happy moment, I am sorry to say. There was occasional return aggression from an angry male, but we were well used to fighting and enjoyed a bit of activity.

The divs were by no means a meek and mild group themselves. The college's principal was somewhat dour and, there did not seem to be a great deal of room in his life for horseplay, which of course made him a prime target. He held a regular prayer meeting in the common room for all the divinity students and any others who were so inclined, and these sessions involved quite long periods of silent prayer. There was a piano in this room and one div one day set an alarm clock to go off during the meeting – secreting it in the works of the piano. The ensuing cacophony apparently wrecked the atmosphere of the silent prayer more than a little and there were disciplinary results. The culprit went on to become a leader in his Methodist Church.

We were quite an assembly of different races, with Fiji Indians, one Swede, several Maori and one Chinese among us. We did a lot of singing in which we were led by several of the divs, some of whom had magnificent voices. Maha Winiata was a dab hand at the ukulele too. Sometimes in the late evening when we were sick of study we would go off in a large group singing as we marched down to the Friendly Inn in upper Queen Street, where we could get a good cheap pea, pie and spud. This introduction to the night life of Auckland gave me my first encounter with Worcester sauce, which I had never seen before and which I soon realised is a necessity for the consumption of a meat pie.

Trinity College fielded several rugby teams. Some were quite good, others extremely poor. I regret to say that my team (third grade open) was in the latter category, despite the best efforts of our coach, Jock Bartrum. The only outstanding abilities I can recall were those of Andrew Deoki from Fiji, a fleet-of-foot winger. I think he was probably the only one to ever score any points in our matches, which were always played on the worst and most distant fields. Quite the worst of these was at Freemans Bay, where we played on a field near the gasworks. The whole of the red muddy ground seemed to be permeated with the smell of stale coal gas.

During that first year in Auckland my dear old Mum and her mother came up to see me and stayed a while in a private hotel. This was quite an undertaking as they were by no means young, and it was an expensive and arduous trip by train from Hastings for my mother and from Petone for Grandmother. But we had a great old time seeing all the sights and it helped me to settle in a bit.

While they were there we met up with the Tennent family, with whom we had longstanding family connections. They had three girls and one boy and lived on a farmlet on the hills out from Papakura. The father was agricultural editor of the *Weekly News* and a pleasant and jovial man. My first meeting with them was via the youngest daughter, whom we met for coffee one morning in the city. This sophisticated young city woman bowled me completely and I was staggered to find that she was younger than me. Armed with this slight edge I felt able to develop our friendship considerably, and this lasted for many years.

A few months after I had come to live in Auckland I developed appendicitis and was admitted to Auckland Hospital to have my appendix removed. I had a miserable time in a large ward with seriously ill people all around me: one died in the bed next to me one night. When I was discharged I could hardly walk and was told to have a further two weeks off work and play no tennis for six weeks. The Tennent family kindly offered to have me out at their place and the father picked me up in his elderly car. It was an excruciatingly painful and long ride to Papakura in a vehicle which had hard springing and no upholstery left in the rear seat. But they were great to me and I had a happy time recovering. After that it was 'open home' for me out there and I spent a lot of weekends with them.

One day Mr Tennent told me he had bought an old motorbike several years previously, to use the engine for a water pump, but had never taken delivery of it. He said I could have it and gave me a note to the little old garage in Karangahape Road to authorise delivery. I found the place and there was a 1928 350cc Douglas twin-cylinder machine. It had no electrics except the magneto but had non-working acetylene head and tail lights. Warrants of fitness had not been invented in those days so the condition did not matter. We hauled it out from under a pile of old junk, put some air in the tyres, fuel in the tank, and pushed it out into the road and down the hill. To our mutual astonishment it fired up and ran beautifully.

Petrol cost 2 shillings a gallon and I was usually able to afford only a quarter or at most half a gallon at a time. However, I used this bike extensively to ride in and out from Papakura and I also explored the Waitakere Ranges from time to time. My school friend Julian Cottrell, who had also somehow finished up in Auckland, had a powerful 500cc bike. He led me into one or two adventures, notably an occasional visit to Mt Eden, where we rode our bikes in and around the crater on the rough grass and sheep tracks.

I am afraid that this bike was responsible for some slight but temporary coolness between myself and the senior Tennents. They had a grass tennis court that needed mowing most times I went out there and usually the grass was very long. The only home mowers in those days were hand ones, which made for a tedious job, so one day I hitched my Douglas up to the mower and had one of the girls hold and steer it while I towed it around the lawn. But the poor old mower was not engineered for this sort of thing and suffered severe bearing and other mechanical problems as a result.

One of my close friends at Trinity College was Colin Brown. He was a large, attractive man who was at teachers' training college. We got around a lot together and when I introduced him to the Tennents he fairly promptly fell in love with Marion, the middle daughter, who was a few years older than him. From then on he saw her at every possible moment, including at night. He used to beg or borrow transport of any nature and head out there after dark, often climbing up the fire escape to the top storey of the Tennent house and Marion's room. The permissive society had not at that time been 'discovered' so this was a pretty daring and advanced form of courtship, but knowing them both very well, I hasten to say that I am sure that it remained confined to levels of behaviour deemed acceptable at that time.

This led to a troubling situation. Colin and Marion decided to get married but because Colin was under 21 the marriage required parental permission. So he faked his age upwards. They asked me if I would go to the Registry Office as a sort of best man and witness. This I agreed to, with some misgivings as the Tennent family had been very good to me for several years. And so they were duly married in an office virtually next door to my place of work.

Of course the happy couple were not content to hide their bliss away indefinitely, living many miles apart, and finally told Marion's parents – who were rightly upset at the secrecy of the affair, as well as the fact that they would have liked to have had a formal wedding for the first of their daughters to marry. They were also hurt at my part, and my silence over the whole thing, and wrote me a letter saying so. I felt very ashamed when I got this letter, which effectively severed their relationship with me. I still wonder what I should have or could have done to be loyal to everyone.

To end that story, as soon as Colin and Marion had their first baby the family was reconciled. I still have contact with Marion, but Colin died some years ago after a rotten illness.

The old Douglas motorbike lasted for years. From time to time I sold it or pawned it to get some ready cash, but I always managed to get it back and it never let me down.

Looking back on my Trinity College days I realise that quite a lot of our behaviour would nowadays be quite unacceptable and would get us into trouble with the various local bodies and perhaps the police. But I am also quite sure that none of our pranks and practical jokes were motivated by innate 'badness' or evil. Like most young people at the time we were just thoughtless and somewhat selfish in our outlook. But I cannot help wondering whether the young adolescent and teenage minds of today are equally harmless or whether there is a more sinister type of bad behaviour developing. Certainly we could not afford motor vehicles except for an occasional clapped-out motorbike, nor could we afford alcohol except on rare occasions such as a university capping parade. Any other form of drug-taking was quite unknown. Still, it all came to a sticky end for me.

One balmy Sunday evening late in the year, when the divinity students and some others were at church and we others were feeling a bit like spring lambs, we put on a spontaneous performance of *Romeo and Juliet*, with of course some university-type modifications. The college was right on the edge of the footpath and in the centre of this frontage was a bow-shaped window off the central staircase. Being the most innocent and feminine-looking of the group, I was cast in the role of Juliet and dressed up accordingly, with certain essential anatomical alterations and exaggerations.

We thought we would be perfectly safe with this performance, being the only ones around, but we did not count on the principal being at home in his house next to the college. At the height of my masterful musical monologue, to the great interest of passersby, with my lover Romeo down on his bended knees on the footpath imploring me to let him come in, who should come along with a dramatic sense of timing but the top man himself.

He was absolutely livid and I copped most of his wrath. I can hear him now, bellowing at the top of his formidable voice, 'MILES HURSTHOUSE!' It certainly brought proceedings to a rapid halt and my mates disappeared like snowflakes in the summer sun. He said he would ring my parents at once, asking them to remove me. I knew what the outcome would be, and so before the official axe could fall I resigned.

A Hastings school friend of mine, Bruce Oliphant, was also at law school and we decided to go boarding together. We found nice digs away down Grafton Road close to Mt Eden gaol. The Scottish landlady was past the first flush of her youth and very strict. The house and our rooms were spotless and her meals good on the whole, but she was suspicious of young folk and treated us warily.

This poor lady used to get 'bilious attacks', which I now realise must have been severe migraines, and would retire to her room and apply wet-packs to her forehead. For some strange Scottish reason these packs were first thoroughly soaked with vinegar. The smell would permeate the whole house so that we always knew when she was having an attack. I still think of her when I smell vinegar.

Mrs W's propensity to feel insulted when no insult was intended caused my rapid expulsion from this place also. One night at dinner I noticed a large gloomy portrait in an oval frame. I am sure it was the curved glass and poor lighting that gave rise to my grave error because I can honestly say I spoke in all innocence. Trying to make conversation, which was never particularly easy with her, I pointed to the photo and said, 'What a fine-looking gentleman. Who is he?' A shocked pause and she said, 'That is my mother.'

She said she had never been so insulted in all her life and asked me to leave forthwith – and my loyal mate Bruce decided to leave with me. We realised we would be better off in a larger, more impersonal institution, so we checked into the YMCA hostel in Wellesley Street, near the art gallery, as permanent residents.

This was great. We had a large comfortable room and mixed with young men from all walks of life. There was a gymnasium where we could work off steam at any time, a dining room with first class meals, and it was handy to our places of work and the university. There was also a billiard room that we could use if ever we had a little spare cash. I loved to watch the experts playing.

I had had a strong Christian upbringing and went to church regularly, but always seemed to have questions about some aspects of Christian belief. In Hastings I had attended Sunday School and later Bible class every Sunday. It was expected that one would be confirmed after a few years of Bible class but at that age I just did not feel ready to make that sort of commitment. I told the vicar how I felt – he was very good and did not put any pressure on me.

The vicar regarded me as a bit of scallywag at times, I fear, as we used to get up to some pretty weird pranks. One Sunday after Bible class a mate and I climbed up the church tower when the main morning service was about to start, and intermittently held on to the bell rope so that the poor fellow who was trying to ring it regularly found that he was producing a somewhat jazzy tolling. We escaped by climbing down the ivy on the outside of the tower but the vicar knew who it was and told our parents, with unpleasant results. Ho hum. That lovely tower was destroyed in the 1931 earthquake.

In Auckland I finally felt ready for and undertook confirmation, after which I assisted at communion services for many years at St Matthew's Church in Victoria Street. A peal of eight bells was played each Sunday morning and evening for an hour before services and also sometimes during the week at lunchtime. It was lovely to hear them in the city parks while having a sandwich.

I eventually met up with the chief bellringer and soon joined the team, which was great fun. We had all the sequences for the different rounds and chimes up on a board on the wall of the belfry and had to learn these by heart. We also used to practise with tuned hand bells on the roof of the bell tower during services and became very proficient. I did this for years.

As a sequel to this, when I lived in Nelson many years later the Newman family presented a peal of eight bells when the new cathedral tower was built. These were to be rung by one person from short ropes gathered together in a small area but there was no one at that time able to ring them so I asked permission to do so. The workmen were on the job when the bells started pealing for the first time and I remember their amazement. I had a great time and continued as bellringer for a few weeks until a permanent arrangement was made.

My job at the Land and Deeds Department was enjoyable and interesting. As a cadet I was the lowest of the low in the pecking order, while the head of the office was the rarely seen District Land Registrar, Mr Keeble. Our head clerk, 'Ocky' O'Connor, was a short, somewhat rotund man who trained us exceedingly well in sensible office procedure. Our office hours were strictly 8am to 4.35pm Monday to Friday, and for the first year or so, another four hours on a Saturday morning. The chief clerk would not permit anyone to leave the office at the end of the day unless their desk was immaculate.

Initially I was put to work as a filing clerk. Of course in 1936 there were no photocopying or electronic facilities and all the precious original legal documents such as memoranda of mortgage, transfers, leases and transmissions were filed according to a registered number in large metal shelves under the eagle eye of Mr Culpan. He had been in this department for many years and his greatest fear, with justification, was the accidental or careless misfiling of a document – usually due to its being caught in the pages of another document.

The office was inundated daily with law clerks from other government offices and legal firms who needed access to documents to obtain the particulars for pending transactions. These chaps would present us with the numbers of the required papers and it was our job to fetch these and note down to whom they had been issued. If the file or document was in use in another part of the office we had to keep the number in our heads until it was found, so one interesting spin-off from this work was that I learnt to remember numbers, even very long ones. For years after this I used to register automatically the number plate of every car I passed on the road, until the next one appeared. My friends and family used to test me but they never caught me out.

After a while on this work I was put onto entering details of transactions onto Certificates of Title. We had to cultivate a special type of handwriting for this and had to use classical old-type pens with specially issued nibs. The ink, in the inkwells on the desks, was of a special type to last for ever. This was quite hard work as the heavy volumes of certificates were stacked under the long steel desks. Some of these were very old and of animal parchment.

In time I graduated to running my own little department, entering in a ledger and filing new documents for solicitors to uplift when fully processed. I enjoyed this work and it taught me a very useful skill – to be able to read upside down. This was easier than continually having to turn around the large heavy book the solicitors had to fill in. This skill turned out to be quite useful, especially in the army for reading papers on officials' desks when standing before them.

One day I had to locate a document that was not in its final resting place. Whenever this happened I would have to go through the various departments to track it down, and often came to the bottleneck of uncompleted work on the desk of one of the Assistant Land Registrars who was notoriously slow. His name was Harry Osmers and this characteristic of his was to have a profound and lasting effect on my life and career, for which I am eternally grateful to him. He was heavily involved in the territorial army and, I think, held the rank of colonel. The 'terries', as they were called, were held in low regard by most of our acquaintances.

One day several searches ended up in the enormous pile of unsigned documents in Mr Osmers' office. We chided him as much as we dared, as he was a pretty exalted person in our hierarchy, and he said it was no problem – he could get them all done in two hours. We laughed at this impossible claim, but Mr Osmers was adamant. Well, he said, he would have a bet: if he could get them all done in two hours we would join the territorials. We agreed.

The beggar then commandeered a whole lot of office staff to get out the big books for him, open them at the right place and put them away after he had checked and signed them. He flew through the work. It was the only time we ever saw him move at any speed. When he had the job done, well inside the time, he called us three cadets to his office and said, 'Off you go to the army recruiting office – they are waiting for you.'

It is hard to imagine now just how innocent – and ignorant – we were of any threats to world peace, even though by now it was early 1939 or so. So off we went to the recruitment office, thinking it all a bit of a joke, but when we arrived we were signed up on the spot. Given the choice of which unit to join I opted for the coastal artillery regiment. I was interested in shooting and in the mechanics and ballistics of every sort of firearm, and there was the added attraction that 'coastal artillery' must mean that there would be beaches in the vicinity.

We went back to the office having honoured our contract with Mr Osmers and wondering what the next step would be. We rapidly learnt: we were soon called up to a training camp at Hopu Hopu near Ngaruawahia. This was the most ridiculous and wasteful event I had ever seen.

First we were taken to the quartermaster's store for an issue of army clothing. There was absolutely no attempt made to try to match sizes and none of it even remotely fitted – we all looked ridiculous in our gear. Our boots were big, black, heavy and hard and because wearing them was compulsory at all times we all got blisters smartly. Accommodation was in enormous huts filled with beds of wooden slats covered by thin straw palliasses. We had to live out of one kitbag and leave the bed every morning in perfect condition, blankets folded and everything accurately aligned. I guess it was good for us.

Training in the old style started immediately. This also did us no harm, and introduced us to the soon apparent army motto of the old, bad-tempered, usually dumb and sometimes sadistic senior warrant officers: 'Yours is not to reason why, yours is just to do and die.' We survived our time there, but I doubt whether any of us really enjoyed it or learnt anything much – apart from a fairly low opinion of some of those in charge.

After that we were obliged to go about once a month to a regular unit for a weekend or an odd day's training. With the rank of gunner, I was allocated to Narrow Neck's Fort Takapuna. This was armed with 4-inch calibre naval guns, two from outside the domain museum forecourt and the rest from the scrapped HMS *New Zealand*, I seem to remember. I loved these guns and training on them, little realising that shortly I would see more than enough of them.

These training days were good fun, with intelligent tutors and pleasant surroundings. We were sensibly indoctrinated with good discipline, had tons of exercise and I am sure I was a better person for it.

Up until this time my jobs at Lands and Deeds had entailed being on my feet all day, and this was quite tiring. So it was great when I was promoted to looking after the cash book: I actually had a desk and niche of my own behind the main counter. It was interesting and challenging work, especially balancing the book at the end of each day – without the help of a calculator!

Of course all this time I was also studying for my law degree. University work gave me an awful shock after high school. While I liked the university life and activities, the lectures were often well beyond me and my most hated subject at school, history, predominated in that first year in the form of constitutional history and Roman law. I did my best for a long time but had not really matured enough by the age of 17 to tackle that type of teaching. Lectures were mainly after work in the evening and I was usually starving when I got there and, always late for dinner at the college. I battled on but failed my term exams over and over again.

I had never been keen on law anyway – it had all been my father's idea – and soon resolved that somehow I just had to get enough money to study medicine. One of the medical students at Trinity College was our rugby coach, Jock Bartrum, a very nice man who was in his sixth and final year of medical study at Auckland Hospital and a great source of information. When asked the cost of medical training he said it was £120 a year for the first five years and £100 for the sixth year. This answer stuck firmly in my mind as a goal. To give an idea of the magnitude of this sum, my salary at that time was £115 a year, from which I paid £70 for board and lodging, leaving a paltry £45 a year for clothing and all other necessities.

Despite this formidable obstacle I was determined to save this enormous amount and fulfil my ambition. When I got my pay every two weeks I paid my board, then put aside one shilling and fourpence to allow me five of the cheapest brand of cigarettes a day. I allocated a small extra amount to enable me to buy a cheap lunch and go out to the pictures and use trams occasionally, and I saved the paltry sum that was left.

The opportunity for me to go to medical school arrived in a way I could never have anticipated.

We had all heard vague stories of Jewish persecution in the late 1930s but the general feeling among my contemporaries at the time was that those who were fleeing Germany were being disloyal to their nation and folk. How little we knew, and how ashamed and red-faced we were when the truth became known. However, even to us it was becoming obvious that Germany seemed hell-bent on plunging the whole of Europe into chaos.

One Sunday night we were told to expect an important radio announcement so we sat up and played cards in the common room where there was a radio (none of us at this stage of our lives owned such an apparatus). At midnight we heard Britain formally declare war against Germany, followed immediately by confirmation that New Zealand was also in a state of war with Germany. Then to my utter and complete astonishment the announcer said: 'The following military units will report for immediate duty…' and named among them was the coastal artillery regiment I had joined.

First thing next morning I put on my uniform, leather bandolier across one shoulder, packed my kitbag and walked to the Land and Deeds Department office, where I was greeted with great astonishment. The head clerk asked what the devil I thought I was doing and when I said I was off to the war he told me to go home and come back properly dressed. However, I had heard that callup announcement, so off to the ferry for Fort Takapuna I went.

If anyone had told me then that it would be five years before I would wear civilian clothes again I would have thought they were quite mad. On 4 September 1939 I was only 19, and such a thing was inconceivable.

officers and other ranks, so we were sent off to other units around the country. No soldiers were permitted to go overseas until they were 21, which is why we were sent to other home defence units, even though they were crying out for volunteers to go overseas. I was posted to a 4-inch gun battery at Battery Point near Lyttelton – which would mean my first trip to the South Island.

While in Auckland I had friendships in varying states of progress with several young women whom I saw when on leave as and when they had some free time. I have to say that no firm commitments were given to any of them, but nor did I give any of them any indication that there were others … This was to lead to some embarrassment. When I left Auckland railway station one evening in April 1940 on the Limited Express, several young women lined up to say goodbye and each looked daggers at the others. I didn't quite know how to handle it, so I settled for giving each of them a goodbye peck and leapt onto the train to wave from the safety of the carriage window. Whew!

My new posting was at Battery Point, a mile or two from the port of Lyttelton towards Sumner. I soon discovered why I had been sent to this unit.

A little earlier there had been a serious tragedy caused by incompetence. A fishing boat, which sailed regularly in and out of the port, tried to come in under the cliffs close to where the guns were sited, probably in order to avoid reporting to the examination vessel. The examination vessel requested a warning shot across his bow, which was duly fired, but it hit the fishing vessel amidships right on the water-line. These warning shells were filled with a non-explosive material such as pitch, so there was no explosion when they landed, but they weighed 30 pounds and packed quite a punch. The fishing boat was sunk on the spot and the skipper killed by a fragment of the engine torn off by the shell.

There was – and is still – a lot of ill-feeling about this tragedy, so when I landed at the battery, having undergone extensive training in a similar unit, we embarked on a major training programme. I am happy to say that the steady training in gun drill gradually produced a high degree of efficiency on the guns and command posts.

Battery Point was an awful site and morale was pretty low at times. For a month or two in the winter it got absolutely no sun, so that if it was frosty the whole place became icy and if wet it became a quagmire. The accommodation for the men was the usual sort of barracks – but they were in almost perpetual shade. We officers lived in 'PWD tents'. These were a well-known phenomenon of the post-depression years and consisted of ridge pole tents boarded up the sides and ends for about two or three feet with wooden door and floor, as well as a single electric light. There was no heating, so you can imagine how cold it was. Some time later a building was erected for the officers and moving in was like entering paradise.

We had mostly young soldiers, aged about 17 to 21, and most of the senior officers were ex-World War 1 chaps – good people but not nearly vigorous enough to control this exuberant bunch. The few newish young officers like me faced a steep learning curve. The watch and duty routine was much more tiring than it had been in Auck-

a day was plenty for a few cigarettes and the occasional trip into town, so I put four shillings a day of my pay directly into a bank account.

After a few months of army routine I was selected with about a dozen others to undergo an officers' training course at a permanent army camp next door to our artillery unit. I was the youngest of this bunch and probably also the most naive, but it was an excellent experience, vigorous and comprehensive, even though as 'gunner', the lowest of the low, I really got the push around.

We were occupied every day from first light until dark and sometimes during the evening with lectures, intensive drill, bayonet practice, gas drill, physical training and cross-country route marches using compasses and map reading. It was great. I realise now that they were terribly short of territorial (as opposed to permanent army) officers and were really pressurising our course.

Physical training was vigorous. Before breakfast we went for a run with full battle dress, rifles, packs and sometimes wearing gas masks as well. A session always ended with a swim at Narrow Neck beach.

Lectures covered every imaginable subject such as military law, weapons, general behaviour, troop management and so on. Later in the course we even had training in correct behaviour in an officers' mess and at formal dinners.

For training in the use of gas masks and protection we went into the camp hall where we put on our masks and other kit, after which they released tear gas into the room. We soon learnt the hard way to keep our anti-gas equipment in good order.

There was a somewhat amusing sequel to this. The walls of this hall were lined with a pinex type of material that must have absorbed the tear gas, unbeknown to the authorities. Next time the hall was used to show a film, the warmth of the assembled company made the walls weep out the chemical and everyone was so severely affected by tear gas that the show had to be abandoned.

Permanent army senior NCOs (non-commissioned warrant officers) ran the course and it seemed at times that these people, knowing they would never reach officer rank themselves, were hell-bent on taking out their frustrations on us before we outranked them, but we took it all and mainly enjoyed it for the few months it lasted.

After four months of this intensive training we sat various exams and most of us were recommended for a commission. While awaiting the formalities we were given the rank of sergeant, which had certain advantages. Our pay was increased, and we lived in the sergeants' quarters where we had single rooms and a decent (non-crowded) dining room, as well as a small bar where we could get a drink. After a few weeks in limbo, our commissions were gazetted in Parliament and we each received an impressive page of parchment which, in lovely flowery script, told us that King George VI had trust and confidence in us and we were hereby granted the rank of 2nd lieutenant as an officer and gentleman ... I can remember the thrill of it even now, not to mention the enormous jump in salary.

It was always awkward for newly commissioned officers to remain in the unit from which they had come, as the armed forces strictly forbade any familiarity between

morse and flag, this being a request for us to fire a shot across its bow to make it turn back.

The first British shot of World War 2 was said to have been fired shortly after the official declaration by Wellington Fort Dorset gunners who put a 6-inch shell across the bow of an incoming freighter that did not stop for examination. We had a few warning shots at various vessels with our 4-inch guns, but this was costly and wasteful so it was decided to use a machine-gun instead when possible.

All vessels, no matter how small, had to report for examination before passing into the harbour entrance. This applied to pleasure craft too, which caused quite a bit of fun. When the fine summer weather came, the yachting and pleasure boating fraternity of Auckland presented no end of problems. Myriad small craft would stooge in and out all day and it was hard to keep track of them all. It was quite hilarious to see the skippers' reactions if we were forced to deliver a machine-gun wake-up call. The change from relaxed serenity to violent heave-to manoeuvres was a startling sight.

Our unit was divided into four 'watches'. At any one time one watch was on night gun duty and another was training at the guns during the day and asleep on call at night. The third watch spent the day doing all the chores in the kitchen, latrines and surrounds, as well as formal parade ground training, while the fourth group had leave for the day and part of the night. The powers-that-be never seemed to realise that those who were up all night needed to sleep afterwards and no allowance was made for this, which was stupid as we were all pretty young, mostly teenagers.

Most amusing incidents, I find on looking back, were associated with someone's discomfort. There was one awkward fellow in our group who always bungled everything and was liable to turn the wrong way when the squad had to change direction, causing chaos. He distinguished himself one day on sentry duty when along came our colonel in his chauffeur-driven car. Our man did one thing correctly: he recognised the discreet signal the driver gave him as to the rank of his passenger.

As the car slowly approached, the sentry proceeded to try to present arms (a tricky manoeuvre that required good hand-foot co-ordination and one he had never mastered). First he dropped his precious rifle to the ground with a clang. When he bent over to pick it up, his tin helmet fell off with its edge striking his foot, causing a good oath to escape. But, with rifle and helmet on the ground, the sentry remained undaunted, stood up and saluted, this latter being a heinous offence when not wearing a hat. Thankfully the colonel could not help but see the joke and kept a straight face as he was driven safely past.

But all in all it was a happy, well-disciplined unit and we had lots of fun. In our off times we would go swimming at the beach next door, or head into the city to see friends or have a bit of a booze-up. I remember we were certain the war would end soon and we would not even buy season tickets for the harbour ferry. Little did we realise.

I was better off financially than I had ever been. I was paid seven shillings a day for seven days a week. It was tax-free and clear profit, as uniform and underclothes were supplied and I was being fully fed and housed. I had glimmerings of hope that I might be able to save the £700 I needed for my ambition to train as a doctor. Three shillings

# 5

*AMID THE CHAOS ASSOCIATED WITH* the start of World War 2 it took quite a while to gear up the administrative machinery of the New Zealand Army. The natural good humour of New Zealanders and their ability to make fun out of any situation relieved a lot of the stress.

Those of us who had been called up so peremptorily were herded into rooms to have medical examinations. These were very perfunctory and one would have had to have been seriously mentally or physically disabled not to have passed. The word soon spread among the troops that there was an eye test as well as a test for colour blindness. The charts used were in full view of everyone and so were soon memorised by those who knew they had problems.

Our first accommodation was in a big building with large rooms equipped with comfortable beds, a good communal toilet and shower/bathrooms, as well as dining rooms serving good food. Up until then it had housed the Royal New Zealand Artillery. These professional soldiers were the cream of the permanent army, in the opinion of most of us, and we held them in high regard.

One of the spin-offs of the general chaos was that if one were feeling a bit off after a night out, one could fairly safely sleep in for a while because there was no roll call and they did not seem to have time to inspect all the rooms each day. In fact, things were so chaotic at the beginning that if we were not actually manning the guns we used to wander off into town whenever we felt like it.

Naturally this idyllic, unmilitary state of affairs did not last long and builders soon put up a series of large barrack-type huts. There was an RNZA corporal or sergeant in each hut to teach us the ropes, and gradually we got sorted out into army routine.

Our battery was an 'examination battery' and our purpose was to monitor all shipping coming through the Rangitoto channel to Auckland Harbour against enemy submarines, torpedo boats, raiders or armed merchant ships. Our primary job, 24 hours a day, was to man the 4-inch guns and associated searchlights. We also had a few machine-guns – old Lewis guns, which were pretty good on the whole. While an incoming vessel was undergoing examination we had our guns, one of them loaded, trained on the vessel at the water-line amidships.

Anchored in the channel near Rangitoto was a small Royal New Zealand Navy vessel with signallers on board, which was known as the examination vessel. When an incoming vessel had been cleared the examination vessel either hoisted a flag or sent a lamp morse signal with code letters, which were changed daily. If the incoming vessel failed to report or stop, the examination vessel would send us the figure '2' by land because of a shortage of manpower. We seemed to be chronically short of sleep and there were no recreational facilities. The only telephone was strictly for the use of office staff only – anyone else had to walk into Lyttelton while on leave to use a phone.

I made some good friends in Christchurch, among them Andrew Todd, a bombardier in our unit. I ignored the 'non-fraternisation' rule as far as he was concerned: he was a kindred spirit in every way and I have a lot to thank his family and friends for making my stay down there more bearable. I enjoyed outings with them on my day off, as well as occasional sorties to the local nightclub, the Winter Garden. Our alcohol consumption on these nocturnal excursions was notable at times, I must say. Andrew remained a good friend until he died some 20 years later.

I realise now how incredibly naïve I was during my time at Battery Point – about the war and especially about security. Most of us were still in peace mode mentally and we were very young, but I still find it hard to believe the gross breach of security I committed one day – though in self defence I have to say that at no time were we given any instruction not to talk about military installations.

One of the senior NCOs showed me some photos of our guns and searchlights, as well as the layout of our camp. I think he had taken them before the outbreak of hostilities. I thought these would be a great record of my stay there so I asked him if I could borrow the negatives, took them into the Kodak shop in Christchurch and ordered a set of prints. Now, I can hardly believe my own stupidity. Well, quite rightly, Kodak staff threw a fit when they saw the photos and got in touch with army headquarters in Christchurch. I was 'asked' to see a senior officer at HQ.

This was a memorable interview with a Colonel Queree who questioned me at great length. He made me realise my gross irresponsibility, but obviously saw my youth as the problem and handled the whole thing so well that I always had great respect for him thereafter. I had the opportunity to get this message back to him many years later when I met his daughter, who was a physiotherapist at Wellington Hospital while I was employed as a doctor there.

The Wellington–Lyttelton ferry, *Rangatira*, was kept in service during the war and miraculously was never attacked en route, despite the fact that enemy ships were in the vicinity from time to time. After the war I read the diaries and log of a German raider captain who laid mines just outside Lyttelton Harbour at the time we were there. He was unable to penetrate safely inside our searchlight beams, but after working out our routine he came in close to the outer limit of the beam and dropped his mines near the harbour entrance.

The ferry always travelled at night and moved fast. Her record crossing was about seven and a half hours: an average speed of over 20 knots. There was, of course, a total blackout on board and we would be alerted as she came out into the channel so that we would have our gun crews and searchlight crews on full alert. We would train one searchlight on the harbour entrance and the other would sweep the whole channel in from the entrance. We could never light up the ferry herself. Because of the speed at which she travelled through the unprotected water she used to arrive far too early for passengers to disembark so they used to hang about on board until 7am.

On one trip it was exceedingly foggy and she overshot Lyttelton Harbour entrance and went aground on rocks. There was no significant damage and the passengers were all brought in by lifeboats and rescue craft. As the fog lifted it was quite a sight to see them come up the harbour in their dozens.

Virtually every young soldier at that time was desperate to turn 21 so he could serve overseas and in common with the rest I eagerly awaited my own 21st towards the end of 1940. When the time came I was casually invited by another officer to come for a drink at the Governor's Bay Hotel, some distance away at the head of the harbour. Upon arrival I found all the other off-duty officers and a few senior NCOs waiting to give me a 21st party. It was a beaut thing to do and a total surprise, as was the lovely large decorated birthday cake, made for me by the proprietor's wife.

Of course I expected to be drafted for overseas service immediately after this and daily awaited notice to this effect. No such letter came. Instead of being sent to the Middle East I was kept on at Battery Point for a time then sent to Dunedin's Taiaroa Head where defences were being prepared. This was the most awful place and quite unfit for troops – in terms of both living conditions and service from headquarters.

At Taiaroa Head a 6-inch disappearing gun was being restored but was not in working order when we were there. It was situated near the top of the grassed rocky headland near the albatross colony. The colony was fenced off and out of bounds, but the caretaker would allow one or two of us to go in occasionally to see these magnificent birds, who seemed not at all disturbed or frightened by us. There was only one pair of the birds during our stay, but they had a chick – I think the first to be hatched there. I also understand that this bird is now the senior resident there.

Down at sea level at Harrington Point, a little way up the harbour, in a cave dug out of the bank, was an ancient piece of artillery that really was a museum piece. This was a 12-pounder, an old field gun from the last century. It was mounted on wheels, had open sights, fired one shot at a time and had the most extraordinary means of absorbing the recoil when fired. Underneath the gun was a large sort of spade with teeth on it. This was connected to the gun itself by a hinge and held in position by a large spring. The idea was that when the gun was fired the spade would dig into the ground while the gun would lurch or bound back against the force of the spring. The gun was manned 24 hours daily by a few men from our unit. There was no electric power for these men, no facilities of any nature and the cut surface of the cave-like shelter was earthen and reduced to mud in the winter. They had an alarm to be sounded in the event of attack so that we could reinforce them by going there in our old truck – about a 20-minute drive!

This magnificent artillery outpost was Otago Harbour's defence against high-speed torpedo boat attack: thank goodness I never had occasion to see an attempt to fire the gun.

The whole Dunedin establishment consisted of one officer, two sergeants, a few bombardiers and about 50 troops. We were given public works tents to live in once again. There was power in the mess hut only, basic latrines, no hot water, mud underfoot, and no heating for anyone. My quarters were a tent about 100 metres up the road to the lighthouse on the outermost point on the headland. All our water had to be brought from Dunedin by truck. We had a Ford V8 truck on which was lashed a 200-gallon steel tank, and driving this vehicle with a fully laden tank of water out to Taiaroa Head along the winding harbour road was a hair-raising experience.

While we were there we had appalling southern ocean weather with gales, snow and fog. The foghorn in the lighthouse sometimes sounded all night, making sleep impossible. Morale hit rock bottom despite all my efforts. I let the troops off as much as I could, since we had only one small (probably useless) gun in working order, and they used to go to dances at, I think, the Kaik. But I could only get away myself if both sergeants were left on station. And this was the main problem.

One of my sergeants was 'Doc' Grundy, whose assistance at this time made him a close friend. The other was a permanent Royal New Zealand Artillery man who shall remain nameless. So bad were our conditions that I was warned by one or two worried men that there was serious talk of rioting, with the men all going absent without leave. They quietly advised me to sleep with my loaded revolver under my pillow, which I did, in my isolated small tent.

I tried to head off the trouble. I applied to HQ in Lyttelton for better food supplies, more waterproof clothing, heaters, power, better amenities and so on, but none of my requests or requisitions were acted on, despite repeated communications. Eventually I did the unforgivable and went over their heads, making a special trip into HQ in Dunedin, where I saw the colonel in charge and told him our troubles. He immediately attended to our most urgent needs.

My word, this brought action, in the form of a personal message to get in touch with our Colonel Lyons at Lyttelton. What did I mean by going over their heads to get stuff? When I told him how often my requests had been ignored by the quartermaster in Lyttelton he immediately backed down and attended to our deficiencies as best he could.

But morale remained bad. One night we heard a rifle shot from the direction of Harrington Point, so we sounded the alarm, piled a crew into our small truck and made a hair-raising fast trip on the awful road to the site. We found that the man on sentry and lookout duty had deliberately put his hand over the muzzle of his rifle and pulled the trigger. Poor young man. It wrecked his hand for all time, of course, and put him in the way of severe discipline for a self-inflicted injury.

In another incident I was personally attacked violently by the permanent army sergeant. Leave passes were filled in by the sergeant (we shall call him X) with the allowed dates and times of leave, then given to me for signing. I noticed that X had filled in his own pass for the whole weekend, which was neither permissible nor practicable, given our shortage of NCOs. He knew this, but I guess he thought I would sign the forms without checking. I told him it was not on, altered the entries to give him one day's leave and left it at that.

The contingent went on leave to Dunedin as arranged, but when the truck went to pick them up on the Sunday morning X was not at the rendezvous. After waiting for a while they telephoned me and sought advice. I made inquiries and was told an address where he might be, so rang the Dunedin military police and asked them to accompany the truck driver to that address and bring X back to Taiaroa Head if he was there. He was – in bed with a woman – and was brought back under escort. Upon his arrival I had a formal hearing of the matter in the presence of the other sergeant, Doc Grundy, and I told X off in no uncertain manner for his actions. He suddenly came at me, his arms swinging violently and face distorted with rage. I ducked his haymakers, charged him head-on low down and brought him down with a tackle. After a violent struggle and a lot of noise he was subdued by Doc Grundy and other soldiers who came running.

Physical assault of an officer by a non-officer, or vice versa, is a serious matter in the armed forces so the matter was out of my hands. The man was almost uncontrollable in his violence and was eventually admitted to hospital for psychiatric care. He was in disgrace and his career was terminated.

Another unpleasant incident, about which I have wondered ever since, involved a brake failure in our light truck that could easily have sent me over the cliff.

From our administration building at the top of the hill the road went on down the hill for about 150 metres to the lighthouse perched on top of a sheer bluff. We used to park our light Ford V8 pickup alongside the building at the top of the hill, having turned it off the road and parked at right angles out of the way. The heavier truck was kept down the road by the lighthouse.

One day I backed the light truck out as usual and turned, but when I put my foot on the brake the pedal went to the floorboard. There was no one home in the braking department and I was running backwards towards the bluff and the drop onto the rocky shoreline. I put the handbrake on at once but it would not hold. I vividly remember my mind going into hyperdrive. I opened the driver's door, leaned out and steered the vehicle to run back into the front of the big truck, which was parked near the bottom end of the road just above the cliff edge, hoping that it was parked in gear with handbrake on. I had decided that if it moved backwards I had a moment to fall out of the door before both vehicles went over the cliff. We crashed into the front of the truck ... and stopped!

We took the pickup into Dunedin to have the damage repaired, as well as the brakes, which were found to have a broken – or cut – hydraulic hose. It was an almost new vehicle and no explanation was ever forthcoming for the defective hose.

I think morale gradually improved as time went on but it was a dreadful camp with disgraceful facilities. All efforts to improve it were blocked by army quartermasters and petty officials at their worst. Later, when we heard about the fall of Singapore to the Japanese and the gross inefficiencies of the British there, I used to think that the people in charge must have been like those who were meant to be in charge at Taiaroa Head.

My replacement as officer in charge, when I left Taiaroa Head, was an older man who had much more experience than I. His report after a short while highlighted the deficiencies and I believe steps to improve the place were taken soon afterwards. For me it was back to Battery Point with its watch-keeping and lack of sleep.

One very unpleasant and sad incident marked this period. I was not in camp at the time as I was on afternoon leave, but heard the details when I got back.

We had a permanent army ex-World War 1 senior warrant officer who had always acted as though he was in a guards regiment. He was not particularly bright and he was always quoting 'the book'. If it wasn't in 'the book' then it was not permitted. One day some of the men had committed some misdemeanour sufficient to arouse his wrath. He made them dress up in full battledress kit with boots, gaiters, rifles and packs, then made them run along the parade ground, down a flight of concrete steps to the barrack huts, along to another flight of steps and up these to the parade ground again – round and round at the double until the men were exhausted. If any of them flagged he would roar at them and make them do extra laps.

He forgot or ignored the fact that some of our troops were there because they were medically unfit for overseas service. One young gunner in particular was known to all of us as a rather frail man and was always managed accordingly. Sergeant Major O. bullied and hectored this chap so mercilessly that he collapsed and later died.

I have always wished that I had been in camp that day as I am sure I would have put a stop to it, which the officer on duty did not have the guts to do. The sergeant major, after the resultant inquiry, was disciplined and became a broken shadow of his former pompous self, but that did not bring the lad back to life. I have always felt bitter about this incident.

In late 1941 I was given some leave and went up to Hastings to see my parents and friends. One day a telegram came ordering me to report back for immediate duty. It was 7 December 1941. No reason was given or evident but the news about the bombing of Pearl Harbour was soon out. I was ordered back to Wellington to train on anti-aircraft guns at Mt Victoria.

At Mt Victoria we were accommodated luxuriously in what was formerly the Karitane hospital or the nurses' home thereof. We had no night duty but underwent an intensive daytime training course in anti-aircraft artillery work. Once again I found it extremely interesting, learning to direct guns accurately at aircraft while allowing for their speed, direction and changes of altitude.

When it was judged that we knew enough we were sent to Trentham military camp to await transport to our future destinations. As was the norm when going overseas, everyone was dropped one rank, so that my then rank of full lieutenant was reduced to that of 2nd lieutenant, but we did not complain.

After the usual vaccinations and multiple delays we were eventually scheduled to depart. None of us had any idea where we were going or to what sort of unit, but presumed we would be in the Pacific area.

The day we were due to leave we had an 'open' day at the camp, when our next of kin were invited to come and spend the day with us. This was a pretty gloomy affair for most of the relatives – the early euphoria and temporary glamour of war had well and truly worn off. I have a photo of my parents with me on the railway platform and they both looked pretty grim. I had concocted a code to be used if I were taken prisoner of war and gave them a copy.

The train trip was most uncomfortable, with hard second-class seats. All the windows were blacked out and at each stop, of which there seemed to be an endless number, military police were on the platforms to see that none of us peeped out. This might have allowed those outside to see who were in the carriages or to what unit we belonged. I found it almost impossible to sleep in my seat so found my way to the luggage van where I made a nest of kitbags and had a pretty good few hours' snooze. We travelled all night, arriving on the wharves at Auckland after a trip of 20 hours.

Alongside the wharf was an enormous ship, HMS *Ascania*. She was a former luxury cruiser of the Cunard Line taken over by the Royal Navy and fitted out as an armed merchant cruiser with about eight 6-inch guns. Her sister ship, *Athenia*, had been torpedoed and sunk in the Atlantic early in the war while carrying nurses and civilians.

My accommodation was a beautiful mahogany-panelled four-berth cabin with shower, toilet and wash basin. Two other officers, Jim Bidwill, from the Wairarapa and Bunty Harper from Auckland, shared it with me and we three were to form a long-lasting friendship. There were 200–300 troops aboard as well.

After we had settled in the officers were mustered and told that we would be allowed ashore until 11pm but were honour bound not to mention to anyone that we were from a ship, nor that we were on our way overseas. Nor were we to communicate with any of our next of kin, wherever they might be – not even if they were in Auckland. It was made plain to us that breach of these rules could endanger the whole ship and any others if we were in convoy. No one except officers were allowed ashore and there was no communication from ship to shore. I went to a movie.

Early next morning we left Auckland harbour and were soon in the open sea where we joined up with the *Monowai* and *Wahine*, with whom we proceeded in convoy. After a day or so it started to get a bit rough and before long it was unbelievably rough. Eventually the storm proved too much for our companion ships both of which had to turn back: the *Monowai* had her bows stoved in, while the *Wahine* suffered a condenser failure and ran out of fresh water for the boiler(s) and troops. We proceeded alone. Our ship was by far the largest but it got bad enough to put all passengers, except for five of us, off their tucker.

None of us had the slightest idea where we were going except that it was in a northerly direction, and none of the crew would tell us. But after four days we arrived one morning at a small harbour in a hilly country, which we shortly found out was Suva in Fiji.

I had always loved the sea and boating but had never been away on a ship before, so even a brief, stormy four-day trip was a wonderful adventure to me. I had loved every minute of it and was sorry to leave the *Ascania*, which I never saw again. I hope she survived the war with her crew.

# 6

MY FIRST AND LASTING IMPRESSION of Suva from the ship was one of greenness – quite a different green from New Zealand's. It was also warm. We were taken to the military headquarters of the New Zealand 3rd Division and met the officer in charge, a short, wiry, fit-looking older man, who briefed us on life in the tropics. He warned us about sores: in particular the likelihood of infection occurring in small cuts and abrasions, and strongly emphasised the need to keep ourselves fit.

Suva was hot, sticky and little loved by New Zealand troops. I was relieved when postings were made known that I was being sent to the western side of the island, which was much lonelier, but also less humid, as all tourists now know. I was transferred to the then Fijian Defence Forces and sent to a coastal defence unit at Momi Bay, about 15 miles east of Nadi. So much for my special training on anti-aircraft gunnery! The road was terrible, with shocking dust and massive potholes, but I was fascinated by the countryside, strange plants and birdlife, as well as the different types of housing and people.

I liked the Fijians and with their help, as well as that of local resident 'European' officers I learnt to speak Fijian reasonably well. This was a great help as we had about 120 Fijian troops, many of whom could speak little English. As well as ethnic Fijians and a few Indian Fijians our unit had a bunch of Australian, New Zealand and local white officers and some white NCOs.

Momi Battery had two medium-range 6-inch guns mounted in a large concrete emplacement with massive roof and side walls, sited on top of a hill about a mile inland from the coast. The position was chosen to guard the main entrance through the coral reef, through which ships had to come to get to the harbour at Lautoka, some distance further up inside the reef. The usual naval examination ship sat near the entrance, following the same routine as used in New Zealand. There were mines moored all around and occasionally a large fish would bump one of them with a massive explosion and spectacular results: a whole fleet of local canoes and boats would put to sea to gather the harvest of dead fish that floated to the surface.

We had to make our own fun at that place because we were so far away from the other units and from town. We did manage to get an occasional concert together, using some of the talent in the unit. We somehow acquired an old piano, which was wildly out of tune and with many notes not working at all. Our engineer officer was Harry Dudfield, who I think later became a Member of Parliament in New Zealand. Harry was a man of many skills and ideas. He pulled the piano apart, mended everything he could see that needed it and tuned it by ear, using a large crescent spanner on the string adjustments. The piano worked well from then on.

Harry also introduced another wonderful idea. From our camp we could walk for a couple of miles down to the sea, going from barren hill country through sugar cane plantations and finally along a track through the mangrove swamps on the edge of the lagoon. The lagoon in our area was only about knee deep, but unspoilt and full of all sorts of sea life including sea snakes, bêches-de-mer and coral. About a hundred metres out this inner reef fell away in cliff-like fashion, with deep water from there out to the main reef, on which the Pacific Ocean pounded incessantly.

The coral on the shallow inner reef was not particularly wonderful but when we swam off the outer edge we could see the wonderful colours and marine life of the outer surface in the deep water. But it was tricky swimming off the edge of the reef into the deep water as there was usually a slight swell, and getting back in was equally hazardous. At all costs you had to avoid coral scratches, which were a devil to heal and could be painful for weeks.

Well, Harry Dudfield, our local Crocodile Dundee, invented a snorkel! The device was unknown to us in those days, but Harry, like all of us, was frustrated at not being able to get a good prolonged look at the coral at the outer edge of the reef in the deep water, so he adapted a gas mask to use as a snorkel. He removed the canister from the end of the hose and tucked the free end of the hose in behind the head harness. It was not perfect – the end of the hose did not have much freeboard as it was not long enough, so the slightest wave flooded down the tube, which was not fun when breathing in. But it was vastly better than nothing and, as everyone had a gas mask, there was no shortage of supply. We had a great time snorkelling around the outer coral reef.

Unfortunately the salt water did the gas masks no good, especially the metal valves. When these valves eventually corroded and seized up, the owner would appear at the quartermaster's store with a doleful face and show it to him, tut-tutting about how hard the tropics were on the gear.

The irrepressible Harry Dudfield also made a lovely box kite and it flew beautifully in the almost constant trade wind there. One day he decided it would look lovely at night with a light inside it, so he rigged this up with a small kerosene lamp and also painted swastikas on the side. He then launched it and got it to a great height before an alert was actioned by a lookout. Phones buzzed, aircraft were scrambled, and they were sure that the invading light was centred somewhere near our area. But by this time the kite was down and no one, naturally, knew a thing …

There was a lot to see on land as well and we were always made welcome at Momi village a mile or two away, usually with a kava ceremony. Nadi itself held little attraction, although the New Zealand infantry battalion was based there in their (to us) luxurious living quarters with their apparently endless supply of beer and other grog.

On one notable occasion a number of us descended on these poor infantry fellows and had the most enormous party, managing to drink them dry – even their after-dinner liqueur supplies. Somehow one of their lovely armchairs subsequently found its way into our truck that night and finished up in our camp. No one claimed responsibility but next morning the brigadier's staff captain appeared in his own vehicle and took it back. Ah well, it was worth a try.

Somehow we acquired a motor launch which even came with an elderly grizzled Fijian, who could speak no English but who had an endless smile and knew the area and channels like the back of his hand. The craft was about 20 feet long and had a small cabin. It was powered by a single-cylinder, four-stroke engine that could only be started by grasping the large flywheel and attempting to spin it over by hand after setting the throttle and choke correctly, or after pouring some petrol into the spark-plug hole. We never found one European who could start that engine but our Fijian skipper did it every time. There was no gearbox or clutch so any manoeuvring involved a lot of stopping and starting. With such a sophisticated piece of marine equipment our horizons were widened considerably and we could do some serious fishing, having lots of fun on our days off.

Scattered at intervals along the outer reef and several miles from the shore were small islands, sometimes only a few hundred metres in diameter and covered with palms and other foliage. From where we were these looked beautiful so a group of us planned a trip one leave day. However, this outing was to prove a little more eventful than we had hoped. The island we chose was a fair distance away and there were too many of us to use our small launch, so we scrounged a ride with the naval examination vessel, which duly dropped us off and arranged to pick us up again late afternoon.

We had a great day on this unspoiled island with its beautiful beach. There were masses of fallen coconuts, and lots of palms and undergrowth to provide shelter from the sun. We swam, lay about and did some spear fishing, although this latter was smartly aborted when Jim Sherratt from Poverty Bay spied a dorsal fin gliding slowly and inexorably towards him. His speedy escape to the beach showed us why he had been a rugby rep!

Come late afternoon we began to worry when there was no sign of our launch back. We waited and waited, as the sun went down and the air became cool. We had no warm clothes. Eventually, in pitch dark late at night, and to our huge relief, the boat managed to navigate through the coral and pick us up. It turned out that she had been ordered unexpectedly to Lautoka, but had no means of communicating this to us.

But our troubles were far from over. Unable in the dark to pinpoint the spot on the shore where our track from the camp came through the mangroves, the navy just dumped us where they could. In the dark we floundered through the mangrove swamp and mud, disturbing all sorts of splashy nasties in the process, until we eventually came to some barbed wire. We squeezed through this, with much cursing and discomfort, when suddenly we were surrounded by US marines in full battle kit with levelled, loaded carbines. They took us to their headquarters in a tent further inland, where we were taken before their very angry West Point regular army colonel, who told us it was only our Kiwi cursing that had made them realise we were not a small Japanese commando invasion force coming ashore. When he heard of our abandonment by the navy he was sympathetic, giving us some good American tucker and then sending us home in a command car, much the worse for wear after our 'day off'.

The US Air Force was active in the region and my passion for aeroplanes took me to the Nadi base to see a bunch of P39 Bell Airacobra fighters. They were beautiful aircraft, with streamlined fuselages made very slim by having the 12 cylinder Allison engine amidships, with a shaft to the propeller coming forward underneath the pilot.

The men there got to know me and even let me do the start-up of one of the aircraft one day for its routine warm-up. They were apparently tricky to fly and lethal in a spin, as one RNZAF senior pilot found when he tried one out, finally burying it close to the main street of Nadi with fatal results.

The main air base was heavily used by B17 Flying Fortresses and B24 Liberator bombers, which we used to watch heading off on bombing missions to the Solomon Islands with a full load, wondering how on earth they were going to get airborne. There were also a number of very fast B26 Martin Marauder medium bombers there. They were reputedly quite dangerous to fly and were spectacular to watch, often with condensation trails coming off their wing tips.

One day, when I was on duty at our battery, I arranged for the Airacobra squadron to make a mock attack on our place. They did this with great vigour, causing a few of us to hit the deck as they flew low across us. They came in from the sea at ground level, straight at the guns, while another bunch came from the hills behind us up the ridge on which the barracks and administrative buildings were sited. It showed huge deficiencies in our defences, resulting in many changes and repositioning of lookouts and anti-aircraft defences.

We saw no enemy aircraft or other enemy activity there, but I was on duty the night the Battle of the Coral Sea started. We were all put on a high state of alert and stood by listening to all the messages coming through. It was apparent that these massive invasion forces were heading our way (and not too far off at that), and also heading towards New Zealand and Australia. It was a close thing.

When the war in the Pacific changed from being defensive (against advancing Japanese forces) to offensive, US armed forces of all types arrived in Fiji in large numbers. I was sent back to Suva, where I joined a unit with long-range 6-inch guns at Flagstaff, overlooking Laucala Bay flying-boat base at Suva Point.

This unit was on a hill so it got a fair bit of breeze to keep one cool, and it was situated among trees, which helped provide camouflage. We turfed the land that had been cleared around the gun emplacements, and planted all sorts of vines for further camouflage. The guns themselves were sophisticated and modern high-angle jobs in turrets, with excellent range-finding and fire-directing equipment.

The Fijians seemed to love regimentation and were great at gun drill. The shells weighed exactly 100 pounds each and had to be manhandled from magazines to guns, then hand-loaded into the breeches of the guns. This was no problem to the muscular Fijians, who tossed them to each other as though they were footballs.

Morale was good and I can remember some happy times, including Christmas dinner when all the officers, NCOs and other ranks of all the nations in the unit joined together for a feast and an evening of song. There were perhaps 200 ethnic Fijians, about a dozen Fiji Indians, perhaps 20 Australian and New Zealand officers and NCOs and a few local white officers. I shall never forget the camaraderie or the singing: the voices boomed out like a mighty organ from the open-sided thatch-roofed building under the palm trees.

The huge number of US armed forces almost overwhelmed the town of Suva, changing the whole social fabric of the place because of their different social customs and lavish spending. A gradual change appeared in the attitude of the local population, with massive increases in prices and financial reward expected for every small service.

There was also a large increase in drunkenness and fighting in the streets at night. The US and New Zealand/Fijian forces had to share the provision of military police at night, since neither was permitted to arrest soldiers other than its own. We would patrol the streets of Suva with a significant force of US military police in one of their open trucks. If and when we found any drunk, aggressive or otherwise disorderly soldiers of any race we were supposed to take corrective action, each nation to deal with its own soldiers.

We New Zealanders were sickened at the behaviour of the US military police during these patrols and hated having to go out when our turn came. It showed an incredibly wide gap between the two countries. As you could expect, if we came across one of our own troops misbehaving we would usually manage to correct this with a sort of rough Kiwi humour and a minimum of force, with the latter being used only as a last resort. In serious cases the offender might be taken off to camp and locked up.

But when the US military police came across one of their own soldiers who was either drunk or disorderly in some way they would leap off the truck and attack the individual viciously with batons before hurling him roughly into the accompanying 'paddy-wagon'. At times the attacks were so sadistic and vicious that we felt quite sick to see it, and it caused serious antagonism between us.

There was also a massive increase in venereal disease among the local population, where this had been almost non-existent prior to this time.

However we had our own place in the community and our own well-trained, well-behaved units. We had sufficient personnel to make our watch duties pleasant, with night duty being split into two halves. As would be expected in Fiji, the long hours of night would be full of music. There was always someone who could play a ukulele or guitar and the strumming would start up at any time, with deep soft voices joining in the song from the various lookouts on guns and in the command posts.

On free afternoons I used to walk down to Suva Point to swim and walk along the beach. There were often Fijian women net fishing in the area and I used to chat to them and watch them hauling in their catches. One day when I was walking back I met an American soldier on horseback going in the opposite direction. We stopped for a chat and I admired his horse, to find that he was about to move on to Guadalcanal and wanted to sell it. We haggled a price and I became the proud owner of a bay stallion. He was used to being ridden bareback so I made a bridle from some rope and a rope noseband that tightened when I pulled on the reins – there was no bit. Named Viliame, he was quite good to ride and I had immense enjoyment from him. He rarely strayed since he was passionately fond of bananas and knew that he would get the occasional one given to him if he stayed in the vicinity of the officers' mess, where we always had a bunch hanging.

One day some of us were reclining in our chairs having a drink in the mess, when Viliame appeared looking hopefully at me for a banana. I picked one from the bunch hanging from the rafters and took it to the doorway, whereupon one of the officers said, 'I bet you can't get him to come up the steps and get it.' With this challenge I told them all to keep absolutely still so as not to give him a fright, and coaxed him in. Viliame slowly came up the steps and right into the room, where he towered above the reclining officer who had made the challenge. I gave Viliame his banana.

Unfortunately, at this stage one of his shod feet slipped slightly on the wooden floor, which was conscientiously oiled daily by the staff. This sudden movement right beside the said officer made him start suddenly and this was too much for Viliame, who panicked and tried to get out in a hurry, attempting a 180-degree turn on a slippery floor. All hell broke loose, with flailing feet, splintered floor and scattering bodies as poor Viliame staggered all over the show, then shot out the door at high speed, leaving behind a torn floor and pale army officers. Thankfully all was forgiven and the damage quite repaired.

An Australian officer lent me a saddle and bridle so that on my leave days I could go for long rides. Viliame was not shod, but the same man offered to shoe him for me if we could get some nails. I could not find any in Fiji, so wrote to my parents and asked them to send me some, which they did. After this I could ride him almost anywhere.

One day Viliame disgraced himself by finding a nice little mare belonging to one of Suva's most eminent women, who kept a stable of equally eminent horses which she used to graze on army land adjacent to our area. She was outraged when she found the mare to be pregnant and complained to the police, since all stallions were supposed to be licensed and registered – presumably to stop the development of a herd of brumbies.

I had a visit from the civilian police and officers of the Department of Agriculture who, I must say, were somewhat amused at the whole episode. However, the law was the law and they said that Viliame would have to be put down or castrated. We chose the latter, although I suspect that poor Viliame might have chosen the former if he had known what was going to happen. The operation was carried out outside the officers' mess under local anaesthetic after Viliame was tied and thrown. His progeny was a lovely foal and I have a photo of the little chap.

I was very fond of that horse, and I like to think it was mutual, but one morning when he did not come when called, which he normally did, we went out looking for him. The party of searchers – Kiwis, Fijians and Americans – stopped in our tracks when we found him shot dead near a US army camp about half a mile away. Everyone was upset and I was devastated. I realise now that I became a bit depressed for a while: I did miss him so much. I guess some trigger-happy sentry let fly after hearing some nocturnal prowling. I like to think it was that and not something more malicious.

Being now based near Suva I met up again with my friends Jim and Bunty. By this time Jim's undoubted social talents and connections had brought him to the attention of the Governor-General and his staff and he was asked (directed) to be an aide-de-camp to the Governor. Jim filled this role with distinction, while Bunty and I got some spin-off, since Jim made sure we were on the invitation list to many of the parties at Government House. Since booze of all types and female company were in short supply, we relished these outings.

One of the highlights of camp life was the intermittent arrival of a shipment of beer, usually Australian, though there was never enough to go around all the units. We always ran out long before the next lot came so this was an important occasion. However, as a coastal defence unit we were in a privileged position, having the secret information as to when the ship would arrive. Naturally this meant we were always first in the queue at the wharf with our truck and a team of willing loaders!

I learnt a lot at Flagstaff battery, especially about human nature, and quite a lot about myself. Up until this time in my life I had a fairly simplistic view of my job, whatever that happened to be, and I took little notice of what others thought or felt. I don't think I was arrogant, but realise that I used to persist along a course of action if I was sure it was correct, ignoring the feelings of others on the way.

There came a time when we got a new commanding officer. He was a Kiwi whom I had known slightly in Auckland where he had been a senior teachers' training college student. He had a fearsome and ugly countenance and we thought he would make a good CO. (In fact he proved to be a dud, but this is another story.) I soon fell foul of this man and he awaited his opportunity for revenge. Thus occurred a series of events that were to have a profound effect on my life, my attitude and my personality – for better or for worse.

Life in the armed forces was ruled by a large book called the 'King's Regulations', which covered every aspect of what was right or wrong, allowed or disallowed. As an officer and a keen reader I read it carefully from cover to cover. I found it useful when dealing with minor infringements by troops, but my knowledge backfired.

In the officers' mess, theoretically, all officers were equal, although normal courtesies were always observed to one's seniors, just as they would have been in civilian life in those days. Our rations and meals were pretty deadly, with a lot of tinned bully beef and dalo (a root vegetable) with which we became pretty disenchanted. One evening at dinner there was a bit of the usual grumbling about the tucker, whereupon our new colonel, Butch, as he was known, announced that he would introduce a levy on us to buy extra supplies.

I demurred and, quite respectfully, pointed out that the King's Regs specifically forbade this. The colonel pulled rank and shut me up. After dinner I stupidly trotted off and got my copy of the Regs, and showed the colonel the specific relevant clause and regulation. The stunned silence that followed should have warned me what an enemy I had made. He blustered and said again that he would run the place as he thought fit and that was that. But it was stored away for later.

The next chapter in this wee affair once again showed my ignorance of the need for people to keep face. On a hill about a mile behind and above our guns was a command/observation post containing sophisticated equipment to control our guns by way of a beautiful instrument called a Depression Position Finder (DPF). This system had never been used because they had never managed to get the DPF calibrated and working correctly. This intrigued me and I used to get the key to the building and go up there on leave days for a walk and to study the DPF.

One night it hit me with a flash what the trouble was. Without telling anyone, I got some tools and went up again at the first opportunity. I made the necessary adjustments, did tests, and found that everything checked out correctly for the first time. This meant we could now hook the whole system up and would have a much more efficient and accurate long-range gun battery.

I went back to the camp and told some of the others about it, including the colonel, who received the news without comment. A few days later I was officially summoned to the CO's office and I really copped it. No one, but no one, in the army was ever permitted to adjust, tinker with or do any work on anything mechanical or instrumental unless he was a qualified artificer. This was of course to stop 'butchers' getting at things and wrecking them and was a fair enough rule. The experts had tried to fix the DPF and failed, whereas I had done it … I could not win. Once again 'face' was lost. No matter what good had been achieved, I had done wrong, and we all knew it.

I got a terrible ticking off, was threatened with court-martial, and virtually sent to coventry by the hierarchy and a number of my contemporaries. Butch had got his own back for his loss of face due to my tactless behaviour in the mess. Looking back I have often wondered if he and others had realised what I was up to on my leave days, and let me get on with it so that I could give them something with which to hang me (as well as perhaps having the DPF fixed)!

I had a bit of a bad time for a while, not helped by the fact that I managed to contract dengue fever about then, and this laid me low for about a week. Then one day another officer, quite a bit older than I was, had a yarn to me. He said that since I was reasonably intelligent, why did I not use my intelligence to make people like me, and not to offend them? In essence he advised me to disregard other people's stupidity – to keep my mouth shut at these times.

I thought long and hard about this wise advice and decided to keep silent when off duty, except when asked questions. It was a real eye-opener and a time of considerable learning for me. Over the years this policy became such a habit that I became lazy as a conversationalist, not bothering to chat to anyone except close friends. It also tended to make me more reclusive, always tending to look for activities that I could do unaccompanied.

At about this time all officers in our regiment had to sit an examination on gunnery tactics and equipment – which was right up my alley. I was particularly fascinated by a wonderful piece of complicated equipment known as a Fire Direction Table, which was used to correct the angle and direction of the guns sights after allowing for wind direction and speeds at different heights, barometric pressures and air temperatures. (This was all in pre-electronics days!) I had studied this machine extensively for my own interest.

One of the exam questions asked candidates to explain the workings of this machine, which was a gift for me, and the other questions were all a piece of cake really, so my exam results checked out well.

I presume it was this result, plus my new policy of keeping my mouth shut, that had me promoted to the position of Battery Commander shortly after. I enjoyed this work very much and got on well with all the troops. However, I guess it was my interest in machinery and instruments that occasioned my next move, which was a transfer to headquarters to take charge of all the weapons and equipment for the whole regiment in Fiji.

Still attached to the Fiji Military Forces, I noticed that the New Zealand 3rd Division, of which I was a member, was gradually moving off without me, heading north to various areas closer to the Japanese. HQ would not release me despite my various attempts: I had made myself too useful in the engineering and stock departments. I even tried to get out into the Fleet Air Arm – because of my interest in flying and boating, I thought it would be great to combine these two. But once again they would not approve my release. Perhaps I should have made myself more objectionable. Life at regimental HQ was pleasant enough, with no night duty or watch-keeping, but I was restless and hated to see some of my old mates moving north without me. However, I was promoted to the rank of captain. This was a welcome financial boost to my goal of studying medicine, and I was also sent home for an extended leave.

We arrived at Auckland late afternoon and there was no transport to Hastings until the next day so I booked in to the Station Hotel. I filled a bath with hot water, ordered a long, cold beer and lay there for a long time.

I was not impressed with the apparent change in young New Zealand women at first reacquaintance. When I checked in, the receptionist asked if I had any American cigarettes and coolly asked for a carton – clearly with no intention of paying for them. There is no doubt that many of our younger women had become gold-diggers after the visit of large numbers of well-heeled US troops.

On the train next day I had the luxury of a sleeping car to Palmerston North, from where a connecting train to Hastings was scheduled. I had hours to wait so when I saw an army truck lurking around the station and found that it was headed in my direction, I scrounged a lift. More troubles … ! The army runs on tracks like a train and does not countenance any deviation: apparently there was a flap as I did not board the Hastings train. I was enjoying a great welcome home when an army official rang up to tell the family I was missing. He was very put out to hear what I had done and I abandoned my newly acquired tact, telling him I was on leave and would travel as I wished.

I had a great thrill that night, as I lay in my bedroom with windows opening onto the front verandah, when, quite late, who should come in through the window but my older brother Dan. He had heard I was home, wangled leave from his unit (NZ Dental Corps) at Harewood RNZAF base, and got home as fast as he could. He also had just been promoted to the rank of captain, and as we both were of similar appearance and build and rank there was potential for a lot of confusion when we got among the local female population. We exploited this to some advantage and had a lot of fun.

After Dan had gone back to his unit I met up with old friends who were home on furlough from the Middle East. My lifelong friend John Maclean was back with a decoration, while Cyprian Bridge was home minus a leg. So we three got together, with John's friend Doug Hawkins and proceeded to let off steam.

There was a number of girls whom we knew well and we partied long and often. It was all quite harmless but a bit noisy for other occupants of the houses we frequented. One night in Napier, at the home of a well-respected and busy doctor, father of one of the girls, we moved the piano into the kitchen, whence we proceeded to belt the daylights out of it and sing uproariously. Suddenly the lights went out as doctor father turned off the mains. I was staggered when his daughter coolly went to the switchboard and turned the power back on again. However, it put a damper on things and we gave up. I guess we were pretty selfish, but we had this tremendous urge to let off steam – especially the chaps who had had a bad time in the Middle East.

Eventually my leave ran out and I received marching orders to head off again to Auckland and wait at Papakura military camp, where I met up with a few other officers heading back to Fiji. We were somewhat startled to find that we would be travelling by US warship – either a corvette or destroyer. The US navy has no alcohol aboard its ships but we smuggled a goodly supply aboard to partake surreptitiously in our cabins behind locked doors. Those in command would have had to be quite moronic not to know what was happening, but they never said a word.

Back in Suva I was stationed at Regimental HQ in charge of all technical equipment, except electrical and searchlight material. It was a cushy job and I became increasingly frustrated – as well as feeling guilty that so many of my mates had moved on. But for me it was not to be. I became ill with a renal infection, which plagued me off and on for several weeks until I was admitted to a US base hospital.

I languished there for several weeks, becoming increasingly depressed as the other New Zealand troops were taken from Fiji to move north. Eventually, after a lot of pain and absolutely no treatment, a urological surgeon arrived to investigate me, which he did very thoroughly, using no anaesthetics in the process. He diagnosed a severe infection of the whole urinary tract. I now know that this was an acute pyelonephritis, and it may have contributed to a kidney stone I developed many years later. Back then antibiotics were almost unknown, having been developed for general use only a year or two earlier, and they were reserved for front-line injuries because they were in short supply. However, since I was not getting better, the surgeon obtained permission from the US to treat me with sulphanilimide, the first of the sulpha drugs. The infection cleared up in about 10 days, but the side-effects were unpleasant, the worst being loss of energy and general nausea.

I was kept in hospital for a while until one day a nurse came in and told me to get cracking, get dressed, get packed. I was to be taken to the wharf to catch a ship back to New Zealand. At last I was leaving for good.

I presumed that I would return to active service after my sick leave and was absolutely shattered when I was told this was not to be. I was given three months' leave and posted to the reserve.

Rehabilitation for returned servicemen was in full operation at this stage (1944) but when I was interviewed they threw their hands up in horror at my stated intention to undertake medical training. They tried to persuade me to go back to my aborted law studies but I made it plain that I was going to medical school. Eventually they agreed to grant me the bursary available to 'civvies': about £115 pounds a year. I was back on the road to health and happiness.

My friend John Maclean was also out of the army, home from the Middle East and having discharge leave. He and I got pretty fit playing a lot of tennis and golf. Transport was a problem since petrol and tyres were in such short supply that none of our parents was keen for us to use their vehicles. So one day I went along to a local garage, Ross Dysart & Maclean, and asked Andy Dysart if he had any old vehicles going cheaply. He took me into a back shed crammed with old bombs and showed me a 1928 Buick three-seater saloon, with a dicky seat in the back for another two if need be. He had it hauled out and put in some petrol and a battery after which, to the astonishment of everyone, it started readily. He sold it to me for £30 – a song even in those days. It was in beautiful condition, with good tyres, upholstery and instruments, and looked extremely elegant after a few polishings.

My friends and I used my new car a great deal, but petrol was strictly rationed and, since Buicks were not famous for economy anyway, I decided to convert her to run on diesel or fuel oil, making the necessary modifications to the manifolds. I also fitted a small one-gallon tank onto the scuttle with a tap, which would change over from this tank to the main tank. I filled this latter with fuel oil – cheap and unrationed – while the small tank had petrol in it. When starting, the tap was set for petrol, but after running a short while to get warm, it was changed over to the fuel oil in the main tank. An extension of the jet adjustment ran into the driving cab so that the driver could make appropriate alterations while driving.

It worked like a charm, to the amazement of my father, who was entirely sceptical of my mechanical expertise. But it got so hot and efficient at times that the engine would run on like a diesel when the ignition was turned off. I reckon Mr Buick would have been shattered to know the loads that his lovely old engine was submitted to with this conversion!

When I finally left to take up civilian life elsewhere I reluctantly sold the old girl, affectionately named by my friends 'The Dieselbug', the first of a long line of lovely motor vehicles in my life.

The soonest I could enter medical school was February 1945, some seven months away. But I found that if I went back to work for the Land and Deeds Department, I would be employed with the seniority (and pay) I would have earned had my service not been uninterrupted by the war. Furthermore, my superannuation fund had been kept up all the time I had been away. So, after four years and 10 months in uniform, I went back to work in the Wellington office of that department.

While I was working there an old friend from the Auckland office, Ralph Goodwin, came into the office. I hardly recognised him: he was gaunt and emaciated. Ralph had been a prisoner of the Japanese. His teeth had been knocked out for the gold in them and he had been starved almost to death. He finally made his escape by walking across the insulators of an electric fence and swimming across the harbour. He then walked across China for several months, blind at one stage from beriberi, a vitamin deficiency disease. It was wonderful to see him again.

A bonus for me of these few months in Wellington was participating in a scheme set up by Shell Oil to offer free coaching in science subjects by the company's scientists to returned servicemen. At that stage there were about five times as many applicants for medical school as there were vacancies. Applicants were judged on their marks in the first year, known as medical intermediate, for which the subjects were physics, organic chemistry, inorganic chemistry and zoology. I had only ever done physics at school. My appointed tutor thought I should concentrate on the chemistry subjects and came to tutor me twice weekly at the house, setting me 'homework' and tests. This grounding proved invaluable in the following year when I started at university and I was able to write and tell him with thanks of my examination marks.

But the Land and Deeds department itself was a pretty dreary place, with lax discipline, sloppy time-keeping, prolonged morning and afternoon tea breaks. People read the paper thoroughly every morning before settling down to work. I was glad to leave after about six months – with a goodly lump sum of withdrawn superannuation in my bank account.

# 7

*THERE ARE OUTSTANDING AND MEMORABLE* moments in everyone's life. One of these for me was my first day at Otago University. I shall never forget the thrill that was the beginning of the fulfilment of a lifelong ambition.

I managed to get accommodation with a family by the name of Johnson, in the nearby suburb of Opoho. From there it was a pleasant walk downhill and through the Botanic Gardens to the university, but a bit of a hike at the end of the day, when I usually took a tram. The Johnsons were very good to me, giving me a nice room and ideal study conditions. Alf Johnson was a manufacturing jeweller and some years later he designed and made an engagement ring for my wife-to-be. Their daughter Alma became a well-known TV personality.

I met up with several other ex-servicemen who were to become life-long friends. I worked hard at my studies, but we ex-soldiers also played hard when we cut loose for special occasions. Keith Simcock, John Wray, Brian Booth and occasionally a younger friend, Owen Prior, and I played golf on Sundays. This was quite a chore as the Dunedin city fathers (and presumably the mothers) at that time did not allow public transport to run on a Sunday morning except that which was needed to get people to church. This meant a lot of walking to get an early start at Balmacewen Golf Course and it was eventually a considerable stimulus to our getting our own motorbikes or even push-bikes. But we had a great time playing nine holes in the morning, lunching at the club and then playing a further 18 holes in the afternoon. The first year we were preoccupied with getting a place in medical school – even the returned servicemen, who had been told they would have some priority. We realised that there were hundreds more hopefuls studying like mad at the other three main centres, all with the same ambition.

To my huge relief when the results were posted I found that I had passed my medical intermediate with four As. Another chap, Derek North, at Auckland University, did the same. He and I became close associates and friends during the rest of our training, although he was younger and far brighter than I could ever hope to be. He eventually became a Rhodes Scholar, Professor of Medicine and also Dean of the Auckland Medical School.

At the end of that first year I went back to Hastings. My parents had sold their home in town and moved out to the small coastal resort of Te Awanga, a few miles from Cape Kidnappers. Travelling to and from Hastings was difficult, being limited to an infrequent bus service, so I put an advertisement in the local newspaper: 'Wanted, old motorcycle, any age, make or condition.'

I soon had a telephone call from a grocer who said he had an old Douglas lying in the shed which I could have for £7. When I tried to beat him down he replied, 'Listen, this bike is so good that you only have to put your leg over the saddle and it will start!' It proved to be an ancient belt-drive EW model with no clutch, two-speed gear and hand-pump lubrication of the engine. He was quite right in that with a little fuel in it and a bit of a shove – it had no kickstart – it went off in grand style.

It had no lights, practically no brakes and no warrant of fitness (which was not required in those days), but it was dead reliable and never let me down on any of my frequent 10-mile trips to Hastings or elsewhere. I even used it to go along the beach the five or six miles to Cape Kidnappers. It would be worth a packet nowadays. It so happened that my friend Jim von Dadelszen, who was also just out of the army, acquired an identical machine, so we had lots of fun together, as his family had a holiday house at Haumoana nearby.

I had come to realise that I was going to need more funds for my medical course than I had budgeted for, so as soon as I had recovered from the hard year's study I looked around for a job. I saw an advertisement for someone to cut thistles at a seemingly good hourly wage so I applied and was given the job on the spot. Next morning at an early hour I beetled along to Havelock North where I was presented with an enormous paddock, probably of about two acres, completely covered with tall scotch thistles. I was given a grubber, the means to sharpen it, and told to grub them all out. I had no idea how to tackle this, but I decided to start in one corner, work a line through to the middle and then outwards from there. It was mid-summer, hot and dry. I very soon mimicked the weather in these two aspects and was glad of a large bottle of water. Well, the cleared area became larger each day, and my shoulders and arms did the same with the exercise. I became very fit indeed and did not mind working alone.

Since then, whenever I have been faced with a long and tedious task, I have often thought of that thistle paddock and said to myself or to my family, 'Start at one corner of the thistle patch and just keep going.'

However, destiny, fate, luck or whatever intervened before I had completed the job. I was asked to a cocktail party one evening and met Kathleen Beamish, daughter of Noel and Margaret Beamish, old family friends from Whana Whana, some 30 miles west of Hastings.

When I told Kath I was thistle cutting she suggested I come rabbiting on their property instead – there was good money to be made. Later that evening her father rang and offered me a job. There was to be a basic wage, a bounty for each rabbit killed, free board and lodging, horse and materials supplied, one and a half days off per week and no restrictions on work hours. I took the deal. My father thought I was mad, saying that Noel Beamish, albeit a good friend, had a reputation as a tough taskmaster. In fact he was a strict boss, and a perfectionist with farm work, but he was scrupulously fair. He was exceedingly good to me and I became very fond of him, admiring him greatly. Noel had three daughters and one younger son who was at Massey University.

I gave my thistle patch owner notice and travelled up to the Beamish's farm, Awapai. The farm was 4000 acres or thereabouts and carried many thousands of sheep, several hundred cattle and uncountable numbers of rabbits. There were also some deer and pigs in the outer reaches.

We had known the Beamish family for several generations since the patriarch, George Beamish, had married my grandmother's sister, Great Aunt Maude Humphries, after his first wife died. George had three sons, two by his first wife and another by his second wife, this youngest therefore being a cousin to my father. These three Beamish brothers farmed adjacent farms of about the same size. All had served with distinction in World War 1, two in the army and the youngest, Harold, in the Royal Flying Corps. He was an early New Zealand ace. All three were decorated for gallantry.

We knew these families well and often had holidays on their farms. The youngest Awapai daughter, Marion, was a crazy one on horses and taught me to ride.

The reason for the massive population of rabbits was the shortage of labour during World War 2, as well as a series of seasons favourable to their breeding. Low rainfall allowed them to propagate happily and profusely in the under-runners (small underground rainwater channels typically on sloping country), which normally flood with a decent fall of rain. There were certainly zillions of the little beggars and in the evening one could sit on any small hilltop and shoot about a dozen or so before moving to another area. They were nearly as bad as in Central Otago at that time and several stations had to be abandoned because of rabbit depredation, one noted one being Big Hill, close to this region.

I was lucky to be accommodated in the main house in a former farmhand's room and I also ate with the family. One must remember that because of the manpower shortage Mrs Beamish did not have the benefit of the usual gardener, cowboy or various other odd-bod farmhands – and she was not one to let an opportunity slip by. I soon found that instead of being put out forthwith as a rabbiter, I was instead put to raking the extensive gravel drive, cleaning the family car (and also the elder sister's if she got her way), grooming horses for various pony club activities and digging and setting up the vegetable garden, which had been virtually abandoned for years. I was interested although totally inexperienced in gardening, so did not really mind, but it meant forgoing any rabbit bounty. Mrs Beamish was keen on peas and insisted on many plantings of long rows. I put the usual labels at the ends of the rows and was a little embarrassed when one of the family members read these labels aloud: 'peas', 'More peas' and 'peas again'.

I was also put to feeding the chooks and horses when the family were late back from town. I caused a bit of a crisis on one or two occasions when I let the rooster loose among the hens, and also when I let the calf I was supposed to feed out with the cows, which caused them a lot of disturbance and unbalanced the milk production for a while.

My instinct for self-preservation prevented my telling them that I had extensive experience of milking cows, and since they naturally did not expect a 'townie' like me to know anything about it the girls continued to do that chore. Several years later, when I finally terminated summer employment with this family, I quietly milked the cow on my last day there without telling them. When they went out to do it later they were puzzled that they could not get her into the milking bail. The penny only dropped when they saw the bucket of fresh milk in the dairy at the house and they realised they had missed countless opportunities to exploit this skill of mine!

A major event in my life occurred one day when I was planting peas when one of the daughters, Jillian, just back from town, passed by and stopped for a chat. I can see her now in her lovely yellow dress, laughing and loving life. She was the middle one of the three sisters, studying for her Bachelor of Music at Canterbury University, and was known for her sunny nature and total lack of malice. I married her many years later and she is just as sunny now, 50 years later, as she was when I was planting peas.

My employer soon realised that even though his gravel drive was in good condition, the garden was weeded and there were all sorts of veges planted, both he and I were being exploited by the womenfolk around us and that his rabbits were continuing to breed happily. So he finally sent me out rabbiting. I have never been sure whether he or Jillian was responsible for the next arrangement, but she was sent as my assistant.

Rabbiting in those days was mainly accomplished by poisoning with strychnine. I will not go into the morality of this now, and can only say that the only other way to mass-destroy rabbits at that time was a more painful and slower form of death: phosphorised pollard baits. Strychnine killed them fast. It was mixed thoroughly with apple jam and put into a large 'jam gun', which was like an overgrown grease gun. You carried it by a handle with 10 pounds of jam inside. When you wanted to lay a bait you lowered the gun and pushed the handle down, forcing a measured amount of jam out the nozzle. The most dangerous part for the operators was the mixing of the powder with the jam, as there was a certain amount of dust from the packets of strychnine powder. I hated that part of the job and my boss usually did it except when he was away.

The routine was arduous but was tremendous fun in parts. We had to get up before dawn, usually about 4–4.30am, since it was important to be in the work area before hawks or seagulls could get at the dead rabbits and distribute the poison around the place – not to mention killing themselves. While Jill prepared a substantial breakfast I went up to the stable paddock where I caught, groomed and harnessed a couple of horses. Sometimes I also caught a packhorse and got him fixed up with a pack saddle to carry our skins back.

This family was horse mad and had heaps of them. They competed in all the horse shows and did well. They actually bred a line of horses all of which had musical names stemming from the original dam, Melody. There was Lyric, Banjo, Piccolo, Trumpeter, Guitar and Cymbal, who was a lovely-looking large horse and a champion hack. My horse was initially Piccolo, a nice little mare but bone lazy. She loved her tucker so much that one could leave her untethered indefinitely while working in a paddock and rest assured she would not wander away from the good grass.

She did, however, give me an unpleasant tumble one day when we went through a

*ABOVE:* Tamati Wakanene, one of the signatories of the Treaty, whose influence protected my great-great-grandfather, the Rev. John Hobbs, and other missionaries in the Hokianga in the 1820s.

*RIGHT:* Great Aunt Rosamond Barnicoat, Great Uncle John Barnicoat and Grandmother Amy Kirk, neé Barnicoat, in the garden of their Petone home, where we often went for school holidays and were always made very welcome.

With my aunt Rangimarie Hetet at the Te Kuiti marae during the presentation of one of her many awards.

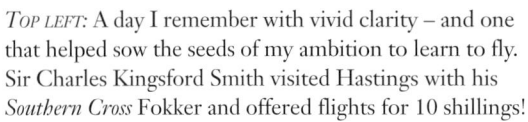

*Top left:* A day I remember with vivid clarity – and one that helped sow the seeds of my ambition to learn to fly. Sir Charles Kingsford Smith visited Hastings with his *Southern Cross* Fokker and offered flights for 10 shillings!

*Top right:* One of my passions was photography and I learnt to develop and print my own films and plates.

*Above:* Father with fish, Taupo 1937.

*Right:* With my friend Bruce Oliphant in Queen Street, Auckland, 1938.

*TOP:* Battery Point, Lyttelton, parade, 1940. It was a bleak and miserable place.

*BELOW:* The 4-inch gun at Battery point being fired in practice.

While I was at Lyttelton I had two very enjoyable duty tours at Ripapa Island, where an ancient 6-inch disappearing gun was being restored. I was lucky enough to be in charge when this museum piece was test-fired – with spectacular results. I have to confess that I don't think the safety of Lyttelton, or the realm, was greatly enhanced by this addition to our defences.

*LEFT:* Gunner Hursthouse, 1939.

*BELOW LEFT:* My friend Jack Van Asch at home on final leave, December 1939. He was killed in action early in the war.

*BELOW:* With Jack Eastall in Cathedral Square, Christchurch, May 1940.

*OPPOSITE:* Snapshots from the war. Clockwise from top left:

With Jim Bidwill and Bunty Harper in Suva, 1942. We styled ourselves 'the three leftovers'.

Our 'commandeered' launch *Iona*, with our Fijian skipper in the foreground.

With my brother Dan. We were home on furlough at the same time in 1943.

With my 1928 Buick saloon – my first car, which cost me £30.

Riding Viliame.

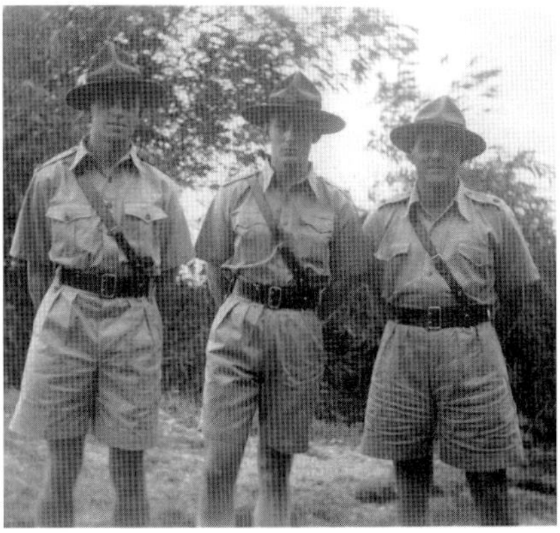
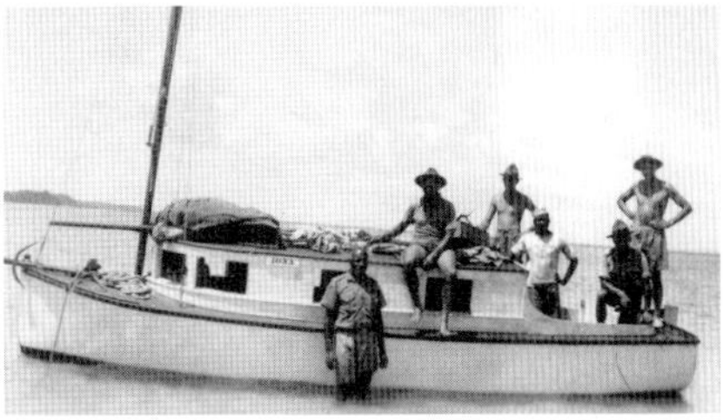
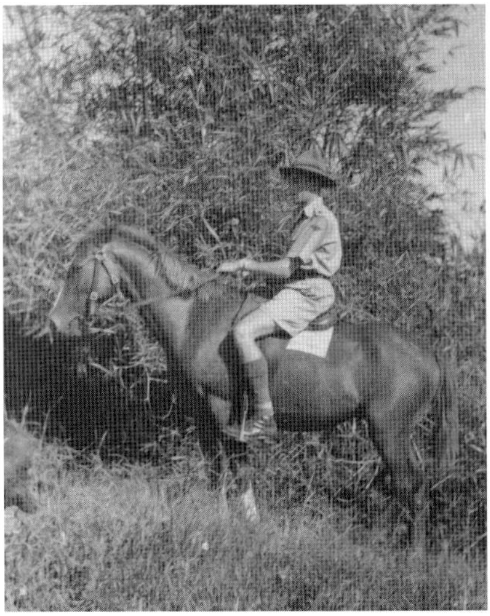
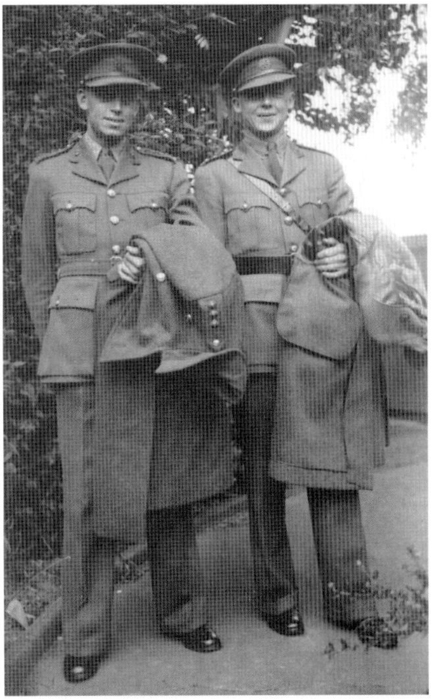
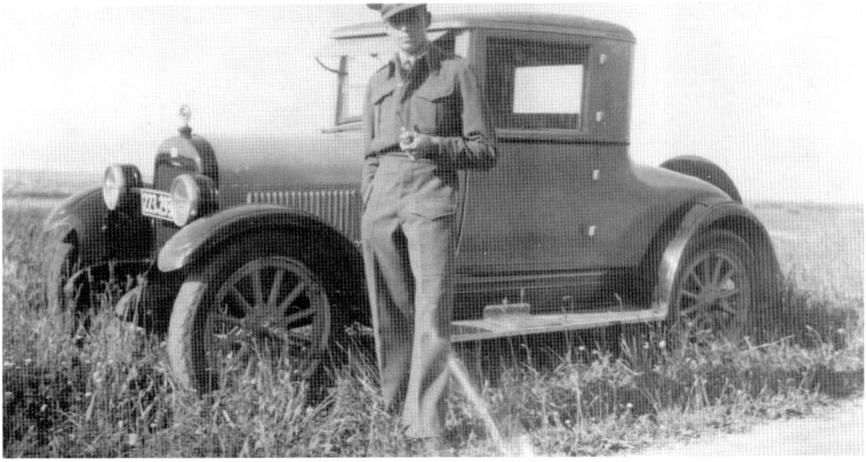

Fellow rabbiters, married on 16 December 1950.

My parents at our wedding.

*OPPOSITE, TOP:* The 1919 Buick tourer (normally used as a farm vehicle) in which we left after our wedding – just as Jill's parents had done. It was driven by the same driver, and towed along behind were a couple of dead rabbits.

*LOWER LEFT:* My Kissel, which I bought for £75. Unfortunately, as an impoverished medical student I could not afford to keep the car – let alone run it – so eventually I sold it for £100. It was unique in New Zealand at the time and I think it has now returned to the United States, where it is worth about $1 million.

*BELOW:* First time in a pilot's seat: returning to Wellington after an emergency flight to Dunedin …

… and my first baby – a whopping 10-pounder delivered at Queen Mary Hospital in Dunedin.

My wonderful 1933 four-valve, 500cc Rudge special. It had been modified for racing and went like the clappers – one of the most outstanding motorbikes I have ever owned.

Our 1932 MG PA, which Jillian and I had great fun with around Wellington. We sold it when we realised that it was hardly suitable as a family car …

… buying instead this 1937 AC 2-litre convertible. It was much too expensive, but we had fallen in love with it.

patch of tall thistles while I was carrying a razor-sharp adze in one hand. She bucked furiously and I became airborne. All that I could think was, 'Get rid of the adze!' If I had landed on it I would have done myself a serious mischief. So I threw it away from me and landed flat on my back in the patch of thistles – winded, prickled, but otherwise unhurt. This was one of the occasions when Jill's sunny nature asserted itself and she roared with laughter, which was not appreciated at the time.

After breakfast we would head out with lunch and tea as well as our poisoned jam, jam gun, adze and wet-weather gear. We wore shorts and heavy boots at all times. The boss set the area for us to work over and getting there usually took up to an hour of steady riding uphill. It was absolutely beautiful on most occasions, with the sun rising over the lower hills, casting shadows on the rolling farmland.

The horses were well trained, as could be expected from the Beamish family, so that when one came to a gate the horse did everything except unlatch and relatch it. It always positioned itself so that one could reach the latch and when the horse heard it being undone it either pushed or pulled the gate open, went through, swung around and shut it, then got into position so that the rider could replace the latch.

The designated area might be up to 200 acres, to be done over several days. First we assessed the lie of the land to make setting and clearing the lines as easy as possible. I would lead and dig with the adze a spit/clod of earth every six long strides. Jill would follow me with the jam gun and squirt a dollop of pure, *un*poisoned jam on each small patch of fresh earth. Rabbits have to be tempted and will not take the poison if it is put out the first time. We found that 600 spits were enough the first day. The second day we would go out again and rebait our first lot of spits with more jam, dig a fresh 600 and bait those also with unadulterated jam. On the third day we would put *poison* jam on the first line, rejam the second line and dig a further fresh 600 sods, putting pure jam on these, and so on.

From then on, each day was arduous and long. We would go out just before dawn, pick up dead rabbits all along our poison line (usually 200–300 on a 600-spit line) and carry them in a sacking bag slung over a horse to a pre-chosen skinning area, usually in the shade. After a while I could pick up the corpses without dismounting, by leaning right out of the saddle, but one needed a special horse for that, as well as long legs.

When we had picked up all the dead ones – always close by the poison bait, showing the speed of death – we set about skinning them. With razor-sharp knives and time-saving techniques I was able to skin 120 rabbits an hour while Jill could do 100. Then the carcasses were buried. We had to trample them well down so that scavengers would not dig them up. Our boots used to get pretty grubby doing this, so blowflies were an unpleasant problem when we sat down for a cuppa or lunch after skinning and burying. Jill estimated more than 300 blowflies on my boots and lower legs on one occasion. Dinkum!

After dealing with the dead catch we would then dig and jam another 600 spits, rejam the previous day's line and poison the line which had already been baited with jam for two days. It does not take a brilliant mathematician to work out that we covered a lot of ground in one day, and all of it hill work, so we got fit – very fit.

*VINTAGE DOCTOR*

After the field work we would pack our skins into a bag and ride back to the house, usually reaching there about 5.30pm, with time for a bath before dinner. After dinner we would go out to a shed and put the skins onto stretching wires, then hang them up to dry. This was our daily pattern while fine weather lasted. It was a great life.

We had quite a scare one day. We carried our poisoned jam in a large tin with the lid firmly pressed on, and strapped this across the front of our saddle. We sometimes used a large bay horse called Billy, who was a good jumper but also pretty stupid – I called him William Twerp Beamish. One day we were picking up carcasses when William Twerp took off for home without permission – and he moved fast. I was worried sick about the 20 pounds of poison bait on his back and chased him on foot, also at a gallop, trying to follow his tracks and watching carefully for the tin of poison. There was one stream to cross and I knew he would jump it rather than walk through. I had visions of the strychnine landing in the waterway … After some miles I got back to the homestead and there he was – minus the tin of poison. I caught him and backtracked carefully, fearing the worst, but luck was on my side. Back at the stream I found the tin in some low scrub where Billy had landed after jumping. It was intact.

There were some funny incidents, one of which was widely broadcast among family and friends by Uncle Harold Beamish, who was constantly joking and teasing. Our pack saddle had two large steel hooks on each side to hang our bags of carcasses on. One day we faced a particularly long walk back to the depot over tough country and I suggested to Jill that she save her energy by riding back on the packhorse. She did, but when she dismounted her shorts got caught on one of the pack saddle hooks and ripped right up one side. Luckily she was not injured. But when we eventually rode home at the end of the day, Jill with her shorts virtually torn in half, we ran into Uncle Harold and some others, despite our attempt to sneak in without any drama. Uncle Harold thereafter made great capital of the incident on every possible occasion – the more public the better. 'Here was the rabbiter coming home with the daughter of the house with her clothing in shreds …'

We killed thousands of rabbits: the tally on one 200-acre paddock was 2001 rabbits, one hawk, one sheep and one sheep dog pup. I made good money, without which I would never have been able to complete my medical studies.

I returned to that job every summer for several years but we never made a really big dent in the rabbit population. Eventually Noel Beamish brought in more student rabbiters and made us bury all carcasses without skinning, since the skin preparation took a lot of our time. This massive assault was successful and in another five years one couldn't find a rabbit on the property.

At the end of our medical school training every student had to present a thesis on a subject of public health importance. I chose 'The rabbit menace in Hawke's Bay' as my research project and uncovered a lot of interesting facts about land damage, reduced production with consequent lowered incomes and lifestyles, public health risks and a few cases of strychnine poisoning in humans. I will always be grateful for what I learned in the employ of Mr F.N.H. Beamish, who was to become my father-in-law. He was a man of great wisdom and his influence on my life was considerable.

# 8

*IN 1946, 120 SUCCESSFUL STUDENTS* were admitted to Otago Medical School out of 600 hopeful candidates who had sat the qualifying medical intermediate examinations throughout New Zealand. In our year we had 40 returned servicemen and about 80 who came virtually straight from school or from other professions such as pharmacy or dentistry.

It was the first year with a large influx of returned servicemen and became known in that and subsequent years for the dedication and hard work of the students. I think this was because we older ones were realising a lifetime ambition and worked like blazes for it, thus stimulating the younger ones to keep up with or beat us academically. The morale and camaraderie were incredible with lifelong friendships being made. The course in those days lasted four years at Otago medical school, followed by a further two years of compulsory hospital work, which meant that one was with the same group of people for a long time.

On my first day I sat there glowing with pride and pleasure that I had finally made it into that establishment and I can remember in finest detail my first class. It was an anatomy lecture by the then Professor of Anatomy, Bill Adams. He was a magnificent lecturer who always prepared his material meticulously and spoke lucidly at a speed which we could paraphrase in our notes. But he was a tough rooster with a craggy face and could not abide students interrupting him, either by coming in late or by whispering during the lecture. I saw him once just point to a whisperer, command 'OUT!', then wait for the unfortunate to come down from the amphitheatre and leave. Similarly he would refuse entry to latecomers, whatever the excuse. But he was a tremendous force for good, a great teacher and an inspiration to us, and not without his own brand of sometimes macabre humour. When he started teaching us about the internal organs of the abdomen and pelvis he said, 'It is an interesting fact that life's most pleasurable sensations all seem to be associated with the emptying and filling of hollow viscera.'

For the first two years at medical school we studied anatomy and physiology all day, every day. Anatomy is the study of all the body components and how they are made up, while physiology is how the body works – chemically, electrically and psychologically. We had lectures on both subjects in the mornings, starting often at 8am, while in the afternoons from 2pm until 5pm we studied gross anatomy in the dissection room on embalmed human bodies. Sometimes there were also lectures after this until 6pm.

First day in the dissection room was always a shock, even for those who had seen a corpse before. The large room occupied about half the top floor of the medical school. Twenty stainless steel-topped tables were distributed about, each with a naked body on it. We formed ourselves into groups of six, three students either side of a body. One had this same body for the next two years and got to know every intimate detail of it. From time to time one would stop to wonder who or what the person had been, but by and large they were impersonal objects to us.

On the first day we were given a short talk by the senior departmental lecturer about the law in relation to these bodies, which henceforth would be known as 'parts', and the dignity we had to accord them in our work before their final interment. We also learnt that we must keep our scalpels sharp with the stones provided, and were told to keep our 'part' damp by putting wet cloths on it – or wrapping any bits in damp cloth – at the end of each day. This latter instruction led to our team setting an unpleasant record. So enthusiastic were we about keeping our 'part', a severed arm, damp that we overdid the moisture and it became flyblown. This caused a furore and a stern lecture to the whole room.

We each had a book that described in detail where to start and what to look for as we dissected. We would then expose the relevant nerve, artery, tendon or muscle, which we would study carefully in its position and in relation to surrounding structures. Our team consisted of returned servicemen Charles Sorrell (wounded), Keith Simcock (wounded), John Wray (wounded) Brian Booth, a younger Owen Prior and me. We got on famously for the two years in which we spent the whole of every afternoon together.

Our study began at the armpit, which was carefully dissected for inspection of all the nerves, blood vessels and so on. Then the arm was removed and worked on for a whole term while the rest of the body was taken away into storage. A further term was given to study of the leg, then in the final term the abdomen and chest areas completed the study for the first year. The whole of the next year was devoted to study of the head and neck.

Thinking about this two-year training in the components of the body and how they worked gives me a somewhat cynical view of those alternative medicinal practitioners who undergo a brief course in their particular field and think they know how the body functions. Even our two-year apprenticeships in these subjects gave us only the basics, as those of us who went on to do specialist postgraduate studies were to find out.

We worked hard but did have a few parties from time to time. The ones around the annual capping (graduation) time were famous for their alcohol consumption and wild behaviour. One of these was known as 'The Rigger Strings' because it was held at a rowing club. My friend Des and I, both motorbike enthusiasts, had a race one night around the road that encircled the clubhouse. No one seemed to mind – that sort of thing was regarded as good entertainment. It makes me shudder to think how we got away with it – no helmets or protective gear.

This particular function became so notorious that *NZ Truth*, the tabloid weekly that thrived on scandal or sensationalism, sent an undercover reporter to attend and write it up. His identity soon became known after he was plied with a 'few' drinks and this was regarded as quite a joke. But the joke backfired seriously for him, as he had a few too many and inadvertently stepped out of an upstairs window, suffering, if I remember correctly, compound fractures of both legs. That effectively killed any story for *Truth* and very nearly did the same for the reporter.

At the end of each term we had a bit of an examination but these were not regarded seriously. However, the end-of-year ones were a different story, especially at the end of the third year. There was a written paper followed a week or two later by an oral examination before up to three staff members. We hated these face-to-face jobs as there was no chance of hiding your nervousness the way you could in a written paper, and this would sometimes make you freeze up or give silly replies. I guess the examiners were used to this and I also realise now that they mainly wanted us to pass, not fail. The good ones would probe to find out whether an error really was due to ignorance.

During this time I was living with a Scottish family at the end of Cumberland Street, since the Johnson family were not able to have me back after the first year. Mr and Mrs S were exceedingly good to me for a number of years, giving me a comfortable home with a large, quiet room and delicious meals, as well as doing my laundry. But Mr S used to go on the most amazing alcoholic binges for days at a time until he was virtually paralytic and just had to stop to recover, since he had little or no food while the session continued. He was good-natured and often amusing when on the booze but got into terrible scrapes too.

He was built like a bull with enormous shoulders and when sober used to trade in vegetables, which he would buy at the markets and then resell. He came home in a terrible state one day, barely able to speak as his face was dreadfully swollen. It turned out he had been goaded into accepting a bet that he could lift a full sack of potatoes with his teeth, which he then attempted. His shoulders and neck apparently were strong enough but his teeth were not and suddenly several gave way. The poor man was on soup for some time after this.

Apparently several years earlier a man in a pub had boasted that his new car could be driven from Dunedin to Christchurch in a record time. Our Mr S bet a large sum that this could not be done, and so it was set up, with the time of arrival in Christchurch to be recorded by some reliable person.

Off went the car at the allotted time, with our man as a witness. He then became worried as he had such a large sum invested. What if the driver bribed someone at the other end to give a false arrival time? So suddenly he decided to go and see for himself. He rang the aero club at Taieri Airport and asked for a plane and pilot to take him forthwith to Christchurch. Leaping aboard the Tiger Moth or similar aircraft he directed the pilot to go like hell to beat the car. The pilot did his best but clearly it was going to be touch and go and Mr S became very agitated. In his words, 'I tapped the pilot on the head and asked him if he could make it.' But the pilot recounted the episode differently. He recalled being hit a violent blow on the head by his inebriated passenger, heavily enough to make him almost lose control. He immediately did a 180-degree turn and landed back at Taieri, where he handed the unfortunate Mr S over to the police.

The poor man's troubles were made even worse by the well-authenticated arrival of the car in Christchurch within the wagered time, so that he lost his bet as well as being convicted on whatever the police charge was.

These people were good to me and I became fond of them. Mrs S went out of her way to do extra little things, even making me a birthday cake when she heard that my birthday was coming up.

Needing transport I once again bought an elderly motorcycle very cheaply. It was a 600cc side-valve Ariel with a hand change, no rear springing and flat out at about 60mph. It got me around Dunedin okay and took me up to Hastings at the end of my second year in company with my friend Keith Simcock, who had a 250cc two-stroke Velocette. Together we did ourselves up in all sorts of gear, loaded luggage in sacks on the tanks in front of us and headed north. We stopped in Christchurch, then rode through the Lewis Pass to Maruia Springs, where we persuaded a pair of most inhospitable and strange females to allow us to stay in the hotel for the night.

We then travelled on towards Nelson, from where we could get a ferry to Wellington, but it poured with West Coast rain so we stopped for the night in Murchison. Next day was beautiful and we headed on to Nelson in perfect summer sunshine. As we came around the waterfront we stopped to gaze at the sparkling sea and harbour entrance with the mountains in the background, and I said to Keith, 'I am going to live here one day.'

Back in Hastings I used the bike to commute to my rabbiting job, finally selling it at a handsome profit before returning to Dunedin by public transport for my next year's studies.

That following year I bought a wonderful 1933 Rudge special, a 500cc four-valve job that had been modified for racing and went like the clappers. I have had many motorbikes but that Rudge was outstanding in two respects: it always started easily even after being left out for days, and it handled beautifully on the gravel roads of that time, even crossing the ridges of gravel left by cars without any bother.

In the years after the war tyres were in short supply: many of our tyres were bald and some even had the canvas showing through. Because of this, the maximum legal road speed was 40mph. Can you imagine how frustrating this was when coming down the Canterbury Plains on a powerful 500cc bike? One day I was near Oamaru, heading south at a comfortable speed, when I heard a bit of a whine. Thinking it must be coming from the generator I decided to ignore it since I did not have far to go. It gradually got louder until it really intruded, whereupon to my astonishment the front mudguard of a Chevrolet coupé with mounted siren drifted into the edge of my right vision. When the car-mounted policeman said he had had trouble keeping up with me on the winding road I knew I was in for some trouble. I did not have the luxury of a speedometer in those days but he assured me I was clocked at 68mph.

That Rudge lasted me for several years and gave me great pleasure and rarely any bother. It used to hose through the oil but it was so easy and quick to remove the cylinder head and clean out the carbon that it never worried me.

In my third year, I agreed to help with the sale of the annual capping magazine. Our team achieved record sales, but it was pretty tiring and took up valuable study time. The following year I was elected to the Students' Association executive. The president was John Child and an excellent chairman he proved to be: I learnt a lot about managing meetings from him. We all had portfolios and mine was capping. The job of capping controller meant quite a bit of work in the first term of the academic year. The celebrations in May consisted of a procession with collection for charity, sale of the capping magazine, and a capping concert, which ran for several nights.

The capping procession that year coincided with Dunedin's founding celebrations, so a special effort was required. Apart from the usual harmless pranks, such as placing 'OUT OF ORDER' signs on all public toilets in the city, the dental school put on what was probably the best ever entertainment when they made a boat (of sorts), which they towed up the harbour to the wharves and 're-enacted' the first landing in front of a large crowd. Unfortunately, but hilariously, when the lookout climbed the mast and peered around for signs of land, he made the craft top-heavy to the extent that it slowly started to roll from side to side at steadily increasing amplitude, so that the watching crowd roared at the end of each swing. Soon he was unable to hold on to the mast any longer and was flung off into the water, which caused so much hilarity that the leader of the welcoming committee on the wharf overbalanced also and fell down into the harbour, luckily missing all obstructions on the way down!

One of the funniest things I ever saw at a capping concert was an all-male presentation of Swan Lake. In our year we had a self-effacing chap named Willie Morris; with thick-lensed spectacles and a mighty brain he was not noted for his physical prowess. He was the swan and looked very fetching indeed.

Well, at one stage Willie was to fly across the stage and land on a tree stump. For this he wore a harness that was attached to a rope over a pulley, with the end held by a stalwart or two to control his height. At the appropriate moment he was released from a high point back in the wings and swooped across the stage towards the tree stump on the other side. Unfortunately he misjudged his landing and scrabbled a bit before falling off. However, the chaps on the other end of the rope acted with commendable precision and stopped him from falling onto the floor by hauling on the rope. This had the effect of causing him to swoop back across the stage and then fly back towards the tree stump with increasing velocity, colliding with its cardboard trunk with some force and knocking it flying. By this time the audience was in hysterics and Willie was in free flight all over the stage, endangering himself and all other performers. It was time for the curtain to hide the chaos and rescue poor Willie.

This concert was the first ever to have women in it and one of them sang a solo each evening: 'You're Mine Because You Told Me So'. On the night of the last performance one Mike Haggitt came out halfway through the song, walked up to the singer, drew out a pistol, pointed it at her and loudly said, 'I've stood this rubbish for five nights and I can't stand it a moment longer' then pulled the trigger on a blank cartridge. End of song.

Otago University always had a capping band, a brass band that had undoubted appeal and a definite character to its music. People loved it. I managed to arrange a recording of its most famous piece, 'Our Director', even obtaining copyright permission. We had a number of pressings made all of which were sold. I still have my copy.

Professor Eccles, in charge of physiology, was a world leader in research into neuromuscular transmission, which is the way signals are transmitted along nerves and then into muscles to make them contract. A keen teacher, Professor Eccles conducted many interesting experiments, some of them on us! At our practical sessions we had to endure having needles stuck into a muscle, then contract that muscle while measuring the electrical impulse and rate of propagation.

Professor Eccles was a religious man, as we discovered one day when he was conducting a tutorial session about the brain. It seemed to me that with all the functions of the brain there was no room for any metaphysical activity, so I quite seriously asked, 'Does all this mean there is no possible way that there can be a soul?' He was shattered and next day made a point of addressing the whole class to the effect that it was quite wrong to infer such a thing from his interest in and teaching of neurophysiology.

I got on well with him and was fascinated by physiology. Towards the end of this third year Professor Eccles asked me to interrupt my main medical course and take an extra year with him doing research into neuromuscular transmission towards a Bachelor of Medical Science degree and then resume my medical studies. I felt very honoured and, after thinking long and hard, decided to ask the advice of two other staff whom I respected, Dr Aitken of the University Council and Miss Agnes Blackie, a lecturer in physics. They pointed out that since I was already 28 years old, I should carry on with my medical course – I could always go back to research if I wanted to. I took their advice and Dr Eccles was very nice about it.

Some of the other things we had to do in our second and third years would have OSH, ACC and Human Rights campaigners screeching these days, but we didn't mind. The Medical School obtained a decompression chamber from the air force and used it to teach us the effects of oxygen deficiency. I now realise this was fraught with danger. None of us had medical checks before proceeding, despite the fact that a number had been seriously injured in the war and had significant disabilities and nearly all of us were heavy smokers.

The decompression chamber was a large long cylinder with windows through which observers could watch the victims, of whom the chamber took about a dozen at a time. We went in, the door was clamped shut, we sat on benches and watched a large altimeter start to rise as the air was extracted. There was one attendant in with us, who wore an oxygen mask the whole time. We had writing pads and pencils with which we wrote down answers to questions, puzzles and simple mathematical sums as directed while the pressure was lowered.

Fairly soon our reaction times, writing and reasoning skills deteriorated to the point where coherent thinking was not possible. The first of us passed out at about 9000 feet and the attendant hooked him up to an oxygen mask to watch the others falling in heaps. The last reading I remember seeing on the altimeter was just above 10,000 feet, and I recall panicking when the mask was put on as I could not detect any oxygen flow. But I woke up in seconds. Bernie Andrews, always florid-faced, was the last and became more and more purple as he sucked at the air. We all watched fascinated as he struggled to write something, scrawling large patterns across his page. He eventually passed out at about 18,000 feet. I think he would have been a good candidate to go up Everest. This hazardous experiment was conducted for years.

By this stage I had become involved in the local target shooting scene, using army service rifles and with ammunition supplied by the local defence forces. We operated under Defence Rifle rules, which permitted only standard army-issue rifles, with no telescopic or sights other than the standard issue on the rifle, nor any artificial aids such as slings around the arms or elbows.

A team was chosen each year to represent the university at the annual inter-university tournament. We trained at a rifle range near Logan Park where there was a 25-yard range, and went out to a range at Taieri for longer-range practice. We had our own rifles, which we 'tuned up' with new and sometimes heavy-duty barrels, bedded in carefully to avoid distortion as they became hot.

The standard match for defence rifle competition was to have five rounds of 'application', taking one's own time, with the option of up to two rounds to get sighted in, followed by 10 rounds of 'snap', in which a small round target was thrust up for five seconds, then down for five seconds and so on. This was followed by 10 rounds of rapid fire in a limited time – I think 60 seconds – all of these at a range of 300 yards with a bullseye of eight inches' diameter. We then moved back to 600 yards with larger targets for a further 10 rounds of application and 10 rounds of rapid fire.

I was in the rep team for several years and shot in Invercargill, Trentham, Auckland and Christchurch. I trained conscientiously: stopped all smoking, known to affect vision, and practised steadiness by lying on a wooden floor each evening with bare elbows, holding my rifle on a distant spot and breathing steadily for quite long periods. I also got some dummy cartridges and practised every night doing rapid fire.

I had my reward for this at a tournament in Christchurch when I managed to get a 'possible' in the initial application with five bulls, followed by a further possible in the snap with 10 hits. In the rapid I managed to get eight bulls, but dropped two shots to the inner (the next ring outside the bull), thus dropping just two points out of the total possible of 125. This was a record which I think still stands.

I did poorly at 600 yards (and do not to this day know why) but my total score was sufficient to gain me a NZ University Blue to add to the two Otago University Blues I had obtained previously.

As well as shooting I played a great deal of golf and tennis, although not competitively, and these sports plus walking to and from medical school kept me fit.

Fourth-year medicine was regarded as the toughest, but it was also the beginning of our careers proper, as from now on we became involved with 'real' patients at Dunedin Hospital across the road as well as studying theoretical medicine, surgery and pathology. We spent about half of our time going around patients with the senior doctors, learning all about the conditions of individual patients, and the rest of the time at lectures given by eminent medical people. It was unforgettable training. We also assisted at some operations and carried out minor medical procedures.

One day we were having a session from paediatrician Dr McGeorge, on how to conduct a full examination of a child. He told us we should measure the circumference of the skull with a tape measure and that if this was less than a certain figure, we should suspect mental deficiency. He proceeded to demonstrate this on the closest student, who happened to be me. He put the tape around my head, showing where it should be placed, glanced at it, did a double take and reapplied it. The measurement was apparently less than the accepted norm, which naturally caused considerable hilarity in the lecture room.

Nearly all students worried about pathology as it was a complex and extensive subject in which we did not receive the teaching we would have liked. Professor Eric d'Ath, head of the Pathology Department and a very erudite man, taught us medico-legal matters of considerable use later in life, insisting that we attend law courts as observers so that we would learn the procedures and not be intimidated if we were called as witnesses. One lesson was how to conduct oneself when being cross-examined after giving medical evidence. He told us that the opposition lawyer would probably quote from a textbook and ask you to comment. We were to ask to see the book and then check the edition, which would probably be an old one, and then tell the court that it was an outdated edition and not used nowadays. We should also look at the name of the owner in the front of the book to see who had lent the book so as to know one's medical opponent. This was all well and good but he left most of the normal pathology for us to learn by ourselves from textbooks.

There were also autopsies. None of us cared for these but gradually became used to them and certainly learnt a great deal. The pathology museum was filled with what seemed like thousands of specimens of every organ in the body, all showing some sort of disease. Most were ancient and bore little resemblance to fresh specimens, but we still had to try to learn to recognise each one for examination time.

The oral examinations and some of the practicals were a nightmare for me that year as I had been devoting too much time to Students' Association affairs and felt ill-prepared. One of the examiners in the pathology oral was known as 'Smiling Death', which about sums up how we all felt about him. As my time approached I was walking along the street to the appropriate building and I took off my spectacles to clean them. They fell out of my hand onto the pavement, breaking in two across the bridge. I rushed across the road to the hospital Casualty Department where we wrapped some adhesive tape around the bridge and hoped for the best. I then went to the exam room and was ushered into the presence of three unsmiling examiners, who greeted me politely enough and passed me a bottle containing sectioned bone with some sort of greyish tumour material in it.

I was sure I had never seen this before and reckoned they had brought it out of some basement cupboard. I stalled by saying it was a section of bone and they agreed but asked me to describe what was wrong with it. I pushed at the bridge of my spectacles (which I later found out was a tick of mine when nervous) and the plaster repair came unstuck. The specs suddenly fell in two pieces onto the table. I gave a nervous laugh but was horrified to see that not one of them was even smiling – I am sure they thought it was a gag to divert attention. The rest of that interview remains a blur and when the results were posted I found that I had passed by margin of only a few marks: quite the closest I ever came to failing.

However, it was over and I rode north again to my job and my assistant rabbiter. This time I rode up on a 1000cc Square Four-cylinder Ariel. This was a lovely touring bike, very flexible, fast and quiet. It was a 1939 model with the then innovative sprung rear suspension, which made it also pleasant for pillion riders. After the usual enjoyable and financially rewarding summer I headed south again on my Square Four for my last year at Otago Medical School.

This year's study saw the addition of obstetrics, gynaecology and public health. It was a stimulating year for me, especially the time we spent living in at the local maternity hospital, delivering as many babies as we were able and permitted to do. I actually delivered one weighing 10 and a half pounds and have a photo to prove it! It introduced me to the great happiness of maternity work, the occasional sadness of which was not to come until years later.

I was also elected president of the Students' Association, a job I thoroughly enjoyed but which kept me very busy. A new Student Union building was to be built and I had to contribute the student viewpoint while Alan Joel, a pleasant local businessman on the University Council, represented the hierarchy. This took a lot of time and work seeing people, drawing plans and attending meetings, causing me considerable worry as I was busy with other student affairs and meetings, on top of my studies.

It so happened that I had to interview the Dean of the Medical School, Sir Charles Hercus, a gentleman if ever there was. He asked me how things were on the student scene and how I was handling it personally. I told him of my concern at the time I was having to put in and that it was affecting my study time. He asked if I was keeping up with my clinical work in the hospital and attending lectures, and when I told him I was not missing any of this, he said, 'Hursthouse, I consider the extra-curricular activities you are doing a very important part of your training and as long as you are keeping up with your clinical work, you will not be penalised for it.'

His attitude was borne out at the end of the year when we all had to move off to one of the four major-centre hospitals for our last year of training. Wellington Hospital was the only one with live-in quarters for final-year students and there were about eight coveted positions there. It was cheaper than boarding out, but more importantly, one was in a position to see all the urgent cases and assist generally much more than if one were living some distance away. These privileged positions were usually allotted on academic merit at the end of fifth year. I did not hold out much hope because I was about mid-position in class as a result of all my student work, but I was delighted to find my name on the list when it came out.

There were some interesting visitors to meet as president, including the famous acting team of Laurence Olivier and his wife Vivien Leigh, who spoke to a packed meeting in the student hall and captivated the student assembly. Vivien Leigh was intrigued and amused to see that some had even climbed right up into the rafters. She was lovely and certainly one of the most beautiful women I have ever met.

A royal visit to Dunedin was planned for that year, with a ball being one of the functions. Officials were arranging for partners to dance with Princess Margaret, and the president of the Students' Association was to be one of those. My friends, of course, made great play with this, dreaming up all sorts of scenarios, but the visit was cancelled due to the ill-health of the King.

To keep me company and assist with my presidential duties my rabbiting partner came down to Dunedin in the vacations and attended functions with me. On one occasion *Aida* was being performed by an Italian opera company and my generous brother shouted us tickets. That was the night I proposed, and Jillian accepted. We always think of this when we hear the Grand March.

When Jill graduated from Canterbury University with her music degree I was asked to partner her at dinner and the graduation ball. I could not get off to head north to Christchurch until the afternoon because of important lectures and clinics, so hopped onto my Square Four about 1.30pm and set off at high speed to get there and changed in time for dinner and the ball. Unfortunately, en route I was picked up by a traffic officer who clocked me at 87mph and gave me a ticket. (I still managed to get there on time.)

The evening was a great success but I had to leave again early in the morning to attend important lectures after lunch. This time I had a pillion rider, David Frankish, a friend in our year who also needed to get back. We headed off with the bike running like a dream but, horror of horrors, the same traffic cop got me again – this time at the more modest speed of 78mph. Another ticket.

The result of this was a polite but firm letter from the Commissioner of Transport, G.L. Laurenson, which finished up with the following sentence: 'I shall withhold action in regard to these latest traffic offence notices of yours pending word from you that you have sold your motorcycle.' Nicely expressed, I thought.

There seemed to be no room for negotiation, as it were, and I hastened to get rid of my beloved machine. I achieved this through a series of rapid swaps involving other machines, finishing up with an elderly Whippet motor car. I was then able to write to the commissioner and truthfully tell him that I had sold my bike and now owned a car that was incapable of exceeding the speed limit even within the city boundaries! He replied that he was pleased to hear this and that no further action would be taken.

The old Whippet was a great vehicle for Des Hay and me to use pig-hunting, which we did in the hills out towards the coast from Balclutha. On one occasion we came home with two large dead pigs in the back seat, one on each running board and a fifth across the front bumper. We kept some for ourselves and donated the rest to the student canteen.

When the poor old Whippet got sick with a cracked cylinder head I decided to look around for a replacement. I went to a second-hand dealer who showed me around his nondescript dust-covered 'cheapies' shoved away in the back of his premises and suddenly there it was. It was love at first sight. It was a Kissel, an enormous American car: a two-seater, open with no hood and with a dicky seat in the back for two. It had a great long bonnet with a strap around it, two side-mounted spare tyres, aluminium dashboard and floor, leather upholstery and even a lever to bypass the silencer to have an open exhaust. It had a large six-cylinder side-valve engine with a number of interesting features and, for the enthusiast, a Ricardo cylinder head. I remember the Kissels from my childhood days in Hastings when they were marketed by the Hyslop family of Tourist Motors.

The dealer popped in a battery and some fuel and took me for a hair-raising ride over the hill roads. It went like the clappers, but every time he put his foot down hard it squeaked loudly in rhythmic fashion due to a leaking cylinder head gasket.

I bought it for £75, repaired the gasket and had a hood made. Tyres were a problem, though, as they were an odd and outdated size. I drove this great car happily all round Dunedin – when I could afford to put some fuel in the tank.

I think all Otago-trained medical students and new doctors leave Dunedin with mixed feelings. We absorbed a lot of the warm affection over the years from the local population of this great university town.

When my time came I packed all my gear into the Kissel and headed off with a fellow student as a passenger. When I came to completely fill the petrol tank for the first time I was as devastated as the attendant was astonished to find that it took about 20 gallons, but it needed nearly all of this battling north into a norwesterly gale. I dropped my passenger in Christchurch, loaded the car onto the ferry at Lyttelton and sailed to Wellington where Jillian was waiting. At last I could present her with the engagement ring I had had made by Alf Johnson, my first Dunedin landlord.

I regret to say that I could not afford to run the Kissel or even keep it, so eventually I sold it for £100. It was unique in New Zealand at the time and I think it has now returned to the United States. It is worth about $1 million.

# 9

AT THE END OF THE FIFTH YEAR of the medical course it was customary to spend the long summer vacation working as an acting or relieving house surgeon in some hospital. This was a popular move as it was a paid position and most of us opted for work in smaller provincial hospitals.

I applied for and got a job at Hastings Memorial Hospital for the three months before I was due to go to Wellington Hospital for my final year. It was a tremendous experience but an unbelievably steep learning curve. Dr 'Sandy' Whyte and Dr Alan Ballantyne were both astute physicians who were only too keen to pass on their knowledge, as were the surgeon superintendent Dr Len Broughton and senior surgeon Dr R. Cashmore. Many of their teachings have stayed with me.

I remember Dr Cashmore coming in one morning to do the rounds of his patients and asking me for a report before he started. I said, 'The prostate in Ward 2 is bleeding a bit,' and he told me in no uncertain terms that the patients were people, not cases, and made me always know and refer to each of them by name. He was also critical of my keeping a notebook to record the details of each case. He believed one should train one's mind by trying to remember everything about each patient rather than committing it to paper.

This doctor developed serious heart disease to the point where he was liable to drop dead at any time but he continued to operate, with a fully qualified surgeon on standby to take over if necessary. I understand that this did actually happen, while he was doing a caesarean section.

Looking back I see I was given far too much responsibility but I loved the work. I had excellent quarters and senior nursing staff were great at quietly giving advice when I was in doubt. I learnt an enormous amount from them about first aid, suturing and other basic techniques such as intravenous drips.

Dr Broughton was one of those extraordinary people who never seemed to be in a hurry but who could get through the work at an enormous rate when necessary. Such people seem to have an economy of movement to make it possible. He was known for his ability to get blood samples out of those with 'difficult veins', from infants upwards. When all other attempts had failed he was always called for, and never did I see him fail. I asked him to teach me his technique in this procedure, which he kindly did, and it was a great help to me all through my career, especially when I later became an anaesthetist.

My sense of humour got me into the odd spot of bother. The small laboratory was run by a competent middle-aged to elderly technician who took life very seriously, with nary a smile or joke cracked with anyone. One weekend leave I went up to Jill's family farm for a spell, and while there shot for the family pot one of the wild turkeys that abounded on the property. I had taken with me a small blood specimen bottle into which I drained a little blood from the deceased turkey.

Now, the red blood cells of birds are a different shape to human ones, and have a nucleus that humans red blood cells don't, except in the case of rare diseases. I took the specimen bottle back to the hospital where I filled out a laboratory form in the name of Mr Bird, requesting various tests, and with a provisional diagnosis of sickle cell anaemia. Well all hell broke loose, with the lab boss becoming wildly excited about this specimen. Eventually of course I had to own up to my sin, since there was no patient to be followed up. He was absolutely furious and made an official complaint to the superintendent – quite rightly, I suppose ...

Late one afternoon the ambulance came screeching in with a middle-aged man who had tripped and fallen on an open circular saw. His upper leg and groin were swathed in bloodstained dressings. We rushed him to theatre, removed the dressings and found an enormous ragged wound just below his groin with the large femoral artery, which comes from the aorta and supplies blood to the whole leg, fully exposed, happily pulsating and absolutely undamaged at the base of this wound. Whew! How lucky he was. It was only then, when we were able to relax a bit, that I suddenly realised the patient was my fiancée's uncle Leslie. The surgeon did a great job and the patient made an uneventful recovery.

I learned how stubborn people can be. A relative of mine and his wife brought in their infant child who had suffered deterioration in health with loss of weight, loss of attention and some neck stiffness. Tests showed that the wee mite had tuberculous meningitis, a fairly rare and often fatal condition. However, the advent of the drug streptomycin had enabled some of these cases to be cured, including this child, who recovered fully. Investigations showed that the parents milked their own cow, and since they did not believe in any form of pasteurisation they had been giving the milk raw to the infant, despite this being known to be the commonest cause of tuberculosis of bone and brain in children. When their cow was found to be infected with tuberculosis the parents were strongly advised to get rid of it and always to sterilise their milk in future. But they had all sorts of 'alternative' medical ideas and were opposed to pasteurisation and vaccines. There was no budging them from this stance. Some time later their infant was readmitted with a recurrence of the tuberculous brain infection. This time the child did not respond to treatment and died.

Late one summer's evening a woman was brought in by her husband, who seemed to be more angry than sympathetic. He had been at the beach fishing while she picnicked nearby. In those days there were no surf-casting reels or nylon, so the line was put out beyond the breakers by whirling a heavy sinker around the head, gradually letting the line out until it had an enormous momentum, then letting it go flying away out into the ocean. Unfortunately on this occasion the fisherman misjudged and let go at the wrong moment and the large fishhook became firmly embedded in the arm of his poor wife nearby, in such a fashion that the bend completely surrounded the large artery in the flexure of her elbow. With carefully introduced local anaesthetic we were able to get to the barbed tip, cut it off and remove it backwards without damage to the artery. I was amazed at how little the husband seemed to care – he seemed much more concerned at having missed an evening's fishing and was oblivious to the risk of permanent damage to his wife's arm.

Hastings Hospital was where I had probably the saddest and most traumatic experience of my medical life. I was very close to my brother Dan and his wife Margaret, who were expecting their first baby. Margaret came into labour, was admitted to the maternity section and had a lovely wee girl. I visited them often and was almost as thrilled as they were. (The patients in the maternity section were under the care of their obstetricians or general practitioners, not the ordinary hospital staff.)

Next day the baby suddenly became ill, worsening rapidly. Senior doctors could not find a specific cause but everything pointed to it being a serious problem in the abdomen. Dr Cashmore decided to operate urgently and asked me to give the anaesthetic which I did quite uneventfully but with great care, as can be imagined. The surgeon found a congenital cyst which had twisted on itself to become strangulated and then gangrenous due to cutting off its own blood supply. This had caused a massive peritonitis. He did what he could and completed the closure, but the seriousness of the operation and the toxaemia of the peritonitis were too much for the wee mite whose pulse steadily faded until she died in my arms while still in theatre.

It was a nightmare which has remained with me, but my grief was nothing compared with the shock and sadness for my brother and his wife.

I loved hospital work and felt that the years of study and scratching for money were finally paying off. It had all been worth it.

I had a sixth year of study to do at Wellington Hospital, followed by final examinations in Dunedin, after which it would be necessary to do at least one year, and preferably two, as a house surgeon in an accredited hospital. After the few months at Hastings I was enamoured of the atmosphere of the small provincial hospital and was encouraged to commit myself to return and practise in Hastings. I seriously thought about it but Dr Whyte strongly advised against, pointing out that large metropolitan hospital experience was invaluable and almost essential. He said that whereas in Hastings I might see one case of a rare disease in a year or even none at all, in a metropolitan hospital I would see many. His advice influenced me to seek eventual employment in the largest hospital I could.

Early in 1950 I reported at Wellington Hospital. As one of the group allowed to 'live in', I had a comfortable single room furnished with desk, bed, shelves, cupboard and chest of drawers. There was a kitchen in which we could cook if we wanted to, a large bathroom and a comfortable common room.

All domestic work including bedmaking was done for us, and meals were supplied: we were treated like fully fledged doctor house surgeons. There were six men and one woman in this group: David Frankish, Bill Chisholm, Geoff Weston, Malcolm McKellar, Owen Prior, Susi Levinsohn and me. We all became friends and have remained so to this day, with several reaching high positions in the profession. There were a total of about 25 final-year students at Wellington Hospital for the year, the others living at home or boarding.

All final-year students wore short white coats to distinguish them from the proper doctors in their long white coats. There was one unauthorised exception: one final-year student wore a long white coat most of the time and tried to pass himself off as a qualified doctor to patients and others. He was a very smooth-talking gent who kept conning his way through life to a career in medical salesmanship, which was much more lucrative and less tiring than looking after the sick.

We were allocated positions on a rotating basis with various specialists and we accompanied them and their less exalted staff, such as registrars and house surgeons, around the wards as well as to operating theatres and other places. This is how we spent our days. At night we would do some study on the types of cases we had seen, and talk about them. On our rounds the specialists would point out important features or ask us questions in a helpful fashion. Sometimes they asked us to examine a patient and report our findings (always with permission from the patient). In puzzling, unusual or particularly interesting cases we would sometimes go back in our own time to talk further to the patient.

But the great advantage of living in at the hospital was our accessibility to urgent cases. As soon as a patient with something unusual or urgent turned up, the word would go out and we would go and see for ourselves. Also, when house surgeons went on holiday or were off ill, one of us would be asked to fill in. This was a great honour (not to mention a boost to our finances as we were paid for that relieving work) but mainly this work was sought after for its inherent interest and the direct contact with patients.

One of the jobs we liked best was usually at night when an urgent operation was required and the surgeon on duty was not available – perhaps because he was operating elsewhere at the time. In these circumstances the senior surgical registrar would usually be asked to do the job and he nearly always asked a live-in final-year student to assist him. We would learn a lot on such occasions.

Another place to learn new skills in rapid diagnosis and treatment was the Casualty Department – now known as Accident and Emergency. When time allowed we would go down there and hang around watching, assisting and asking questions of doctors and senior nursing staff. The latter were great in those days in shepherding junior near-doctors along the correct path.

I found it interesting that when we settled in to our first full-time hospital positions, after so many years of hard work and study, it was obvious that we had been starved of light reading. We all found ourselves compulsively reading non-medical literature! What intrigued me was that most of us were reading sometimes the most rubbishy sort of books imaginable: thrillers and Wild West adventures seemed to be the favourites. Almost no one could be found to be reading more serious books – except for medical literature when necessary for our current case work.

We held some pretty boisterous parties occasionally. At one an air rifle was produced by someone imitating William Tell who proceeded to shoot matchboxes off the heads or out of the lips of volunteers – in the common room if you please. I shudder to think of it nowadays.

And so the final year of formal training went by. It seemed to me that each year of my medical course was more exciting and enjoyable than the last – I was in my element. I could not believe that it could get any better, but it continued to do so for many many years.

Came the end of the year and we had to go to Dunedin to sit our final examinations in medicine, surgery, obstetrics and gynaecology, with written, practical and oral exams in each. About a month or two before we were due down there I was horrified to find that I did not have enough funds to pay for the trip – my savings had finally run out, despite my extra earnings and thrift. I had a matched set of golf clubs in a fancy leather bag that I had picked up cheaply, so I sold these to a registrar for a fair sum, and this enabled me to finish without asking for help from anyone.

I do not remember final exams being a problem, although I do recall incurring the ire of one Mr James Jenkins, a senior surgeon and associate professor noted for a degree of crustiness and low patience, when I accidentally dropped a bandage while demonstrating some complicated dressing. Such an offence was almost a capital one, but I got away with it.

Results were announced within an hour or two of the last person having their oral examination, in one of the most bizarre, potentially traumatic, cruel and almost sadistic rituals I have ever seen. Instead of posting the results on a noticeboard for candidates to read quietly, it was traditional that at an appointed time (I think it was 6pm) the results would be read out by the Dean of Medical School's secretary or registrar from the first landing on the stairs of the old medical school. We mostly had waited some hours – in the pub or somewhere on our own. At the allotted time 120 students gathered to await their fate. Some were garrulous, others quiet, some pale and drawn, a few near fainting. I found it quite weird.

It went something like this. The secretary came from upstairs to the first landing and announced: 'The following have passed in the subject of medicine …' Names were then read out in alphabetical order and you could have heard a pin drop. Then it was: 'The following have passed in surgery …', then similarly for obstetrics, then gynaecology.

One could see those whose names were not in the first group growing paler and paler as the other lists followed, with others, successful and unsuccessful walking out. If you failed only one subject you could sit a special exam a month or two later, but if you failed more than one subject you had to repeat the whole year.

I cannot imagine who dreamed up this ritual but it was quite inhumane, since it brought the emotions of winners and losers into direct conflict. We were all pretty close friends and it was stressful to be so proud, happy and relieved while one's friends alongside were trying to hide their own bitter disappointment while valiantly endeavouring to be pleased and supportive for the successful ones.

I managed to pass all subjects. A lifelong ambition was fulfilled and I had gained degrees of Bachelor of Medicine and Bachelor of Surgery and the right to be addressed as 'Doctor'! Further I had been accepted as a house surgeon at Wellington Hospital, from 1 January 1951.

I headed off in haste to Hastings where, a week or so later, on 16 December, Jillian and I were to be married. We very happy and flat broke.

At Hastings Jillian was flat out preparing for the wedding, with family flying in all directions. Her parents planned a large gathering for the first marriage of one of their offspring: they had many relations in the district and were very active socially so they felt they had many obligations to return hospitality. And so it was that 426 guests attended the reception at an old homestead in the grounds of the local A & P showgrounds.

In those days weddings were arranged and financed solely by the parents of the bride, who were also responsible for the invitation list. The bridegroom's parents were asked to submit a list of their guests, but this list was required to be much shorter and the bride and groom could have only a few of their closest friends at their wedding. The construction of a wedding invitation list was fraught with difficulty and danger of giving offence, and took countless hours of discussion, consultation and argument.

The day was a wonderful one for me, with perfect weather, a perfect bride and a lovely service at a packed St Matthew's Church with full choir and flowers. The formal reception passed all too quickly and we were off on our honeymoon, leaving in the same 1919 Buick tourer in which Jill's parents had left after their wedding. It was driven – unbelievably – by the same driver, and towed along behind were a couple of dead rabbits.

This old car, a six-cylinder tourer, had been used as a farm vehicle for years. It had never been restored but still ran well, although driving across paddocks in it was an experience: the chassis was quite flexible because the rivets and bolts that held it together had loosened and on rolling hillsides one could feel the whole car flexing as it followed the contours like an earwig. It had not been registered for many years and there was absolutely no possibility of its being classed as roadworthy, so the problem was how to get it along the 30 public road miles into Hastings. A sympathetic traffic department agreed to turn a blind eye on condition it was used only for this occasion.

We had hidden our old Morris 8 soft-top tourer, acquired the previous year, some miles away at a friend's home and transferred to it from the Buick. At last we were on our own in our own wee car, on our way to a house in Taupo for a week. Looking back I am amazed that we ever got there as the roads were notoriously steep and difficult and our car was very 'basic', with no front wheel brakes and almost non-existent handbrake activity. The cooling system found the hills beyond its capabilities, which meant frequent stops to top up with the water we had carried in cans in anticipation. There was no speedometer but the generator apparently had no voltage regulation so that the ammeter and battery-charging rate increased with speed. The engine ran without fault but needed a top-up of oil – not unusual in those days. It took us about seven hours to reach Taupo from Napier – a distance of 98 miles.

## VINTAGE DOCTOR

Our wonderful holiday was over all too soon as Wellington Hospital did not make any allowances for newly marrieds. So we headed back to Hastings to Jill's former home, where we spent a day or two sorting things out. We had an enormous quantity of wedding presents, seemingly enough to furnish a mansion, but because we were going to a small flat as a temporary home we arranged for a minimum of gear to be sent and headed off in our 'Morrie'.

The poor little car trundled us to Wellington without trouble. We took turns at driving, changing over each hour for the nine hours it took us to travel the 200-odd miles. At one stage, when Jill was driving, I noticed that her speed had crept up to 30mph and I had to warn her to curb her speedy habits and drop back to our touring speed of 28mph! We have often laughed about that incident over the last 50 years.

We settled into our flat in Central Terrace, Kelburn, and I immediately started work at Wellington Hospital.

# 10

*IT IS HARD TO CONVEY JUST HOW MUCH* these next two years meant to me. I had never been so happy. Wellington Hospital was the largest single hospital in New Zealand at that time, with about 50 house surgeons. This may sound a lot but we worked hard and long – my goodness we did. There was no additional finanancial provision for married house surgeons, who were rare in those days, so my salary for the first year was £5 *less* than the rent we had to pay for our flat. This meant Jill had to try to find a job, which was by no means easy. She tried desperately to obtain work using her music degree but no one was interested in taking her on short term. But there was a big demand for typists so she took a course in typing and landed a job in an accountant's office, where she worked for about 18 months. But finances were a struggle.

At the hospital we were allocated 'runs'. Each senior specialist was allotted a house surgeon for a three-month period, during which we had to look after all new admissions under his care, arrange all investigations, do daily checks on every patient, ward rounds with the specialist and his team and report any urgent changes or occurrences. As well, one had to take turns at emergency night duty, weekend duty and the Casualty Department, and also relieve for house surgeons who were away.

Hutt Hospital was then under the care and administration of Wellington Hospital so we also worked there. If I remember rightly there were two medical, two or three surgical, one paediatric (children's) and one casualty run there. There were also much-detested runs at Silverstream Hospital and the tuberculosis hospital adjacent to Wellington Hospital.

Allocation of positions was interesting. We drew lots to determine our position on the 'choosing' list and selected from what was left when it was our turn. Senior house surgeons, in their second year, had the first pickings. It soon became clear who were the best teachers – they were always the first to be chosen. The lazy or those who were poor teachers or, dare I say it, less intelligent and competent, were always at the bottom of the barrel – along with Silverstream and tuberculosis jobs.

For the record, 'top billing' while I was there was the medical run of the late Sir Charles Burns, a meticulous, clever, outstanding teacher who also drove his house surgeons ruthlessly. I shall not say who was always bottom, but I had my share of him when I struck the bottom of the choose list!

I did some heavy thinking about my future to develop a strategy for my two-year training period. The drama of surgery often steals the limelight among lay people but it seemed to me then, and still does, that it is more of a craftsman technique than a diagnostic technique. Sure, surgeons have to make diagnoses, but in general these are more straightforward than those sometimes faced by physicians. (Although at this stage I must mention that Jill would not be alive had it not been for a very clever diagnosis by a Nelson surgeon when others had failed and she was nigh unto death. That story later.)

So, given that I had eight runs ahead in the two years of hospital work, my thinking was that because I contemplated a future of general practice with maybe some minor surgery and perhaps a hospital position as an anaesthetist, I should seek some medical work, children's work, and some time in casualty and anaesthetics, with less work in surgery. That is the way it worked out. Of course when relieving one saw a lot of every type of work, and I saw an enormous amount of surgery as an anaesthetist.

It was a tiring life with long hours and night duty every few days. One might be called out of bed several times during the night, often for quite long periods and with no allowance made for a sleep or time off the next day. It was also hard on the wives of those of us who were married as we were at the hospital from 8am until often quite late in the day, living at the hospital for at least two nights a week as well. At least meals were free to us in the cafeteria, so this was a saving.

After prolonged spells of hard work for low pay, with little time off, we would grumble and attempt to have our conditions improved – as house surgeons do to this day. But never was striking contemplated. The idea of withholding medical services was completely abhorrent to us in those days. We did consider withholding our clerical services, except for writing what was necessary for diagnosis and treatment of the patients. We discussed refusing to sign death or cremation certificates, or to write discharge letters to outside doctors (whom we would phone instead), or complete patients' notes after discharge. However, these measures were never implemented in our time: we were too busy and too interested in our work to do much 'stirring'. We were a happy team – but we could not help realise how much we still had to learn.

Casualty work gave a window into every possible form of injury, illness and human behaviour and it was an excellent training ground for general practice. It was not a popular run on the whole as it was very pressured at times and one did not get to know the 'whole patient' the way one did with in-patients. There was also very little time off, day or night. I did a three-month stint of this in Hutt Hospital as well as a lot of relieving work in Casualty at Wellington Hospital.

We all found it difficult dealing with drunks who had bashed themselves up in some way, and also detested the early stages of the rugby season when we used to see a lot of serious knee injuries from lack of fitness and hard ground. It really upset us to see a young man come in with badly torn knee ligaments since we knew that his knee would never be the same again and would probably give him serious trouble from middle age onwards.

A good Casualty Department depended upon having good staff, in particular the sister or senior nurse in charge, who could make things run smoothly or allow chaos. A very close working relationship developed between casualty officers and a good sister in charge, especially when one was new to doctoring.

One night, after a big day's work dealing with injuries, minor illnesses and the usual drunks, I was called out several times, with little or no sleep between calls, to attend to the results of fights and accidents. This went on until at about 3am, when I had just fallen off to sleep, the night sister called me to do a major suture repair to a drunk who had cut his head. I lay there for a few moments, thoroughly exhausted, gathering the energy to throw on some clothes and go down to Casualty. To my shame and embarrassment I next woke at about 6am. I wondered why the sister had not called me again, quickly dressed and went down, fearing the worst. The smiling sister told me she thought I had had enough for one night and decided it would do the drunk no harm to wait for a few hours – which it didn't.

One inevitably saw awful injuries, horrible deaths and unbelievable misery. Hutt Hospital in particular drained a large area and was very busy. We once saw more than 100 patients in one morning, which kept one literally on the run.

I think the saddest case was that of a small boy, about seven, who had a gunshot wound to the head. His younger brother had picked up dad's .22 rifle from behind the hall door, pointed it and pulled the trigger. There was nothing we could do and he died on our examination couch. His family was waiting in the waiting room for us to perform some miracle, and we were all very upset. I went to give them the news while the nursing staff cleaned and bandaged him, rushed out to the garden, got a few flowers and laid them on him so that he looked at peace when they came in. One does not forget these incidents.

On another occasion we heard a siren come shrieking into the grounds and rushed to the door to see a police car followed by an old heap of a car packed with people. The patient was a wee boy of about 18 months who was blue with suffocation and barely conscious. His folk said he had choked on a piece of coal so we grabbed him, held him up by his ankles, smacked him hard on the back once and the lump of coal fell out! Whew, it was a close call.

The medical superintendent of Hutt Hospital was Dr Fogg, and a wise old bird he was. He was profane, sarcastic, intolerant of error and smoked incessantly, even in the wards and in Casualty. Most of us liked him a lot but a few could not tolerate him. He was a good surgeon and taught me a lot about simple procedures as well as a great deal about general surgery.

At that time the railway tunnel through the Rimutaka Range was being engineered and we saw a regular stream of minor casualties from the mainly Italian workforce. One day word came that there had been a major rockfall with a number of men injured. They were all rescued quickly, except for one man who was buried from the waist down by masses of rock debris. The rescue services and the man's mates worked frantically to free him but it took a long time – I think from memory about 16 hours. He was conscious the whole time, with a doctor at his head.

He was a fine and handsome man in about his late thirties, still conscious and quite rational on arrival. From the waist up there were no injuries, but his lower body and limbs were like sculpted marble with the indentations from the rocks beneath which he had been buried, and were cold and lifeless as stone. There was no sign of pulses in these limbs, while his blood pressure and vital signs indicated severe, life-threatening shock. Prolonged injuries of this nature are liable to cause a serious condition known as 'crush syndrome', which brings on kidney failure, among other things. We immediately took blood samples and set up an intravenous drip, ready for transfusion when his blood group was identified. During this, his blood pressure became dangerously low, making any surgical procedure quite impossible.

Dr Fogg, who was duty surgeon, appeared with the usual cigarette hanging from his mouth and in his laconic way asked me for all relevant details. After an examination and some thought he announced that we would have to do a bilateral amputation at the level of the pelvis, but he was not sure whether even this would save him. He instructed me to get blood and serum into him rapidly and try to get his blood pressure up. In the meantime we were not to try to warm his legs, as this would promote the flow of damaging chemicals from the crushed tissue into his system.

We then found that he had an unusual blood type, which we did not hold at Hutt Hospital, although some was available at Wellington Hospital. One of our registrars, Dr Bruce Cook, had a sports car, an Allard K3 he had imported, so it was decided he would drive to Wellington to get the blood. He shot off while we rang the police to ask for an escort and clearway. They never caught up with him and he was back in a flash. While waiting we transfused with serum and his pressure started to rise slowly, which it continued to do with the whole blood when it arrived.

We all watched, waited and prayed for the poor fellow while the blood ran in. He was still quite conscious. It was awful to think of the mutilation this man was going to suffer when and if we managed to rescue him. I often wonder if this is why Dr Fogg, who was watching with us as the hours went by, allowed me to continue the transfusion at a rate that I later realised may have been too fast for him. Or did he realise that the poor man was doomed by the onset of crush syndrome and could not survive the massive operation anyway? I'll never know.

After some hours of our attempted resuscitation attempts the patient quietly closed his eyes and died. We were all upset. 'Foggy', as we called him, quietly and gently said, 'Well done, all of you. It's better for him this way, – he didn't have a show.' And he walked away.

We liked our tours of duty at Hutt since it was a modern building with good accommodation and facilities. There was no provision for recreation or music but off duty on standby we used to have all sorts of fun.

One day an argument developed as to the inflammability of a chemical called ethyl chloride, used as a powerful agent to start an anaesthetic. Its glass container had a lever at the top which, when pressed down, allowed a stream of the substance to come out of the bottle with some force – a sort of elderly equivalent to a modern aerosol.

Those who were convinced that it was inflammable were violently opposed to any attempt to resolve this argument indoors so a long broomstick was 'found' and the bottle of ethyl chloride was taped with sticking plaster to one end. Then the lever was pressed down and taped to the stick to keep it open. The whole thing was thrust out of the sitting-room window and a match lit to settle the argument.

My goodness, it was certainly inflammable: a yellow smoking flame shot out about three metres from the head of the broom. Then heat melted the tape holding the bottle to the stick and it fell to the ground, still burning furiously, shattered and burst with a mighty yellow conflagration and masses of smoke.

Unfortunately the sitting room was almost directly above the main hospital entrance, and it was a Sunday evening when there were lots of visitors. In no time the sound of sirens heralded the arrival of the fire service, who never did find the cause of this mystery fire. We all, naturally, were peacefully sitting reading in the sitting room when they entered. But I bet wise old Dr Fogg knew all that went on.

I was on duty one day when a middle-aged man was admitted with a severe cerebral haemorrhage. I was staggered to find he was the husband of my cousin Mary Thompson, née Hursthouse. He died while I was with him and I had to tell Mary, who was at home. I was godfather to their only child Christopher, aged about three at the time.

Unknown to all, including himself, Lisle had increasing blood pressure. On this Sunday afternoon he had been visiting relations at York Bay and had been asked to replace a fuse up a high pole. The effort of climbing the ladder had caused him to rupture a blood vessel in his brain. It was an immensely sad time for all of us.

One Sunday afternoon I walked past a trolley, complete with covered patient, on its way to an apparent emergency operation. I had not heard of this on the grapevine so peered at the patient in passing. I was more than a little astonished to see the head of a large dog with tubes coming from its mouth. I followed the procession to watch and learn. It turned out that one of the specialist surgeons had a friend with a very valuable and very large pedigree dog. This dog had one leg a little longer than the others and was thus quite useless as a show dog. The mission was to shorten the leg, so the dog was hooked up by the anaesthetist, who had to use an endotracheal tube down the windpipe since there was no mask to fit a dog's face. When it was all screwed together and sewn up the leg was plastered and the dog taken away on the trolley. The face of one passing nurse in the corridor was a picture. The operation was an outstanding success, I am glad to say.

There was one surgeon at Hutt who had a courteous, pleasant manner to all his patients even when pushed for time. This courtesy saved him from a serious professional error one day. It was customary, and I think still is, that a few minor operations are placed at the end of a surgeon's operating list. On this occasion there was a patient put down for a sigmoidoscopy. This is an examination of the lower bowel by the use of a long tube-like instrument, about 2cm diameter and about 40cm length, which is inserted into the rectum and gradually pushed up into the bowel.

For the patient it is neither a dignified nor a pleasant procedure, as I can testify from personal experience.

Patients for these 'minor' procedures were ushered into an anteroom, where they waited until called, after being garbed in suitable sterile clothing. Came the end of the great man's operation list and an attractive young woman was brought in and laid on the table on her side with her gown drawn up at the back. The gentlemanly surgeon, sigmoidoscope in hand, poised at 'the brink', so to speak, and made small talk. 'Good morning miss, and how are you?' Then, 'Having a little trouble down below, are you?' His quiet voice was further muffled by his mask.

She muttered something back and this inaudible question and answer conversation went on for a few more moments until the surgeon raised his voice and asked loudly, 'Are you having a bit of bowel trouble?' 'Not at all,' said she. 'Why are you here, then?' asked he. 'I am a new blood donor,' said she. Pandemonium. I dread to think of the consequences had he proceeded without his courteous small talk!

At Hutt I did a paediatric run with a Dr Watt. He was a fine doctor and a good teacher, very good with children. Managing these usually unhappy, homesick children, some with a lot of pain and all feeling unwell, was an enormous learning curve. In those days some of the senior nursing sisters felt that strong discipline was necessary and the effects of this were pretty upsetting. Also, unbelievably, visits by parents and relatives were strictly limited. Since a lot of the parents were working, many visited only in the weekend and when the bell rang and the parents and family left there was absolute bedlam, with distraught children weeping, sobbing and often screaming. One could hear it from a long distance along the corridor.

In the warped thinking of the time this upset to the quiet routine of the ward was blamed on the fact that visitors were allowed in at all and some of the 'battle-axe brigade' campaigned for further restrictions, saying that the visitors only upset the children. I am glad to have lived through the changes that not only allowed but actively encouraged the presence of family with sick people of all ages in hospital.

An unforgettably dismal period in the Hutt area was during the infamous 1951 waterfront strike, which lasted for many months, with the army being brought in to keep the wharves and ships running. This caused massive unemployment, serious social divisions, shortage of food for families and finally violence, the results of which came our way. We saw numerous injuries from beatings given to those with opposing views, as well as to those who continued to work in desperation to feed their families. I was shocked at how rapidly humans could become ugly in their behaviour, even to those whom they had regarded as friends.

One high point at Hutt Hospital was that when we were on weekend duty, from Friday night until Monday morning, those of us who were married and had no children had our wives come and stay in the house surgeons' quarters. This was actually not permitted but those in command turned a blind eye. One night Jill and I were in my single bed when the night sister came in to get me for some emergency. There was a sharp intake of breath when she turned on the light and it was probably the most unusual introduction either she or Jill had ever experienced when I said, 'Sister Williams, I would like to introduce my wife, Jillian.'

All house surgeons employed by the Wellington Hospital Board had to do a stint at Silverstream Hospital. This complex consisted of one or two houses, accommodation for nursing and other staff and a series of large open wards arranged as a quadrangle. It had been built by the armed forces but after the war it was taken over by Wellington Hospital and used for long-stay patients. Many of these were orthopaedic cases with the not uncommon bony tuberculosis, which occurs when the germ causing tuberculosis gets into bones or joints, quite often from drinking infected non-pasteurised milk. There were also many serious bone injuries such as fractured femurs, which required months of immobilisation in all sorts of plasters or frames. Most of these patients were youngish adults and used to get into all sorts of bother due to their exuberance. There was also a children's ward that housed mostly young children with bone infections, cerebral palsy (called spastic back then) and congenital dislocated hips, for which they had to be immobilised in 'frog plaster' with their legs splayed out like a frog, following operations.

This tour of duty was unpopular since there was virtually no tuition and mostly we simply had to ensure that the patients did not get complications or other illnesses. We did daily ward rounds to chat to and check up on each patient but there was little else to do, so in the weekends two of the three house surgeons were allowed leave. I went there with two mates, Bill Chisholm and Owen Prior, and we got on famously, playing bridge and reading a lot. Alcohol was strictly forbidden on the premises but a few times when patients had birthdays we had to ignore the rather increased size of their beds and irregular shapes therein.

The medical superintendent for many years was a Dr Mclagan, an elderly lady who was reputed to be related to the famous actor Victor Mclagan. She was universally know as 'Aunty', and a nice person, but she had her hands full trying to control somewhat high-spirited young doctors. She retired during the course of our stay there, being replaced by a middle-aged English doctor who was determined to correct certain irregularities. Little did this poor chap, totally lacking in experience or understanding of the Kiwi character, realise what he was up against, especially with a goodly proportion of the doctors being returned servicemen.

All sorts of pin-pricking notices were put up around the place but we just ignored these if we deemed them stupid or impractical. His Waterloo came when he tried to enforce the rule prohibiting wives from staying on the premises during the weekend. With two of the three doctors off for the weekend the sole remaining doctor was suddenly not allowed to have his wife to stay in the ample doctors' quarters.

The new broom called us to his office and laid it down in person. We listened courteously, did not argue and thereafter went back to our duties, totally ignoring his instructions and continuing to entertain our wives. The new man was livid, having apparently not yet learned that Kiwis never obeyed stupid rules. I understand he made complaint to the Superintendent in Chief in Wellington but was advised to handle it himself. He called us into his office and told us that if any of us dared have his wife stay again he would call the police and have her evicted.

I decided this stupidity had gone on long enough and told him that if he did so we would have the press, complete with photographer, waiting to record the occasion and would make a statement to the effect that the doctor in sole charge of a hospital of about 100 patients was not allowed to have his wife on the premises for the weekend although the caretaker/boiler man in the other half of the building had his wife live there permanently. The poor man gibbered for a while but no more was heard of that stupid rule.

When we completed our tour of duty and were officially signing off from Silverstream, he said words to the effect that 'You New Zealanders are a very difficult race. When you are given orders, you not only dare to argue and question them, but if you don't like or agree with them you just disobey.' I told him that was the way it was and this was why Kiwi troops could not stick being in British units during the war, and why they did so well when finally put under the control of a Kiwi general who knew, understood and was one of them.

Back at the main Wellington Hospital life was as busy, tiring and interesting as ever, with excellent teachers pouring information and advice into us day and night. We all made mistakes, but mostly we recognised these. Now it seems to me that I can always remember my serious errors, whereas my memory dims on other matters.

One day when I was a house surgeon for physician and great teacher Dr Adams, a middle-aged man was admitted with an apparent stroke. He was semi-conscious and partly paralysed from the neck down. His blood pressure was high and it seemed to me a clear case of a cerebral haemorrhage. After a full examination, and before calling in Dr Adams, I decided to do a lumbar (spinal) puncture to get a sample of cerebrospinal fluid to be checked for blood cells and other ingredients to help determine the extent of the damage. After putting in the local anaesthetic and inserting the long spinal puncture needle I was horrified to find that the spinal fluid came out under quite high pressure. I had heard about this phenomenon but never seen it, and I knew it was dangerous for the patient.

I immediately removed the needle and reported it to the ward sister and senior doctor. The patient died later that day, and although I was of course upset I was also relieved when an autopsy showed that he did not have a cerebral haemorrhage but an inoperable brain tumour. I subsequently performed countless lumbar punctures, but never forgot that particular one.

I learnt so much from some of the wise medical people at Wellington Hospital and much of it remains with me. One physician for whom I worked, Dr Tim Williams, had a patient admitted with severe backache. He was ordered nothing but complete bed rest and mild pain-relief. Each time we saw him, on our twice-weekly rounds, I expected to be asked to obtain a surgical opinion with a view to surgical intervention, but week after week went by with instructions to continue with bed-rest only.

Eventually I ventured to the great man, 'Don't you think he could be seen with a view to surgery?' He replied, 'You will find that almost every backache eventually disappears with bed rest and no specific treatment. I have seen many backs operated on for laminectomy and a large number of them not cured, with some made permanently worse. Don't be in a hurry to send people with backache to see a surgeon.' He was quite right.

I once said to Sir Charles Burns, commenting on an unusual case, 'I thought this never occurred in this age group.' His reply: 'Hursthouse, in medicine it is never "never" and never "always".'

In the operating theatre I was giving an anaesthetic to a seriously ill patient when I became concerned by his condition and unsure whether I could safely give him any more. My teacher was that great pioneer of modern anaesthetic techniques, Dr Alf Slater. He was in the adjacent theatre, so I slipped through and asked his advice. He came and looked over the state of affairs and said, 'If you want to know how a patient is, look at the patient's dial, not the dials of the instruments.' How right he was, bringing the focus back to the individual and not the mass of surrounding gadgetry.

I had become increasingly interested in anaesthetics, which were evolving rapidly to become much safer and more complex. Up until about that time most anaesthetics were administered by pouring ether onto a gauze mask placed over the face of the patient, sometimes after he or she had been put to sleep with an injection of pentothal.

Ether had many disadvantages. The first was that it was highly inflammable so that no type of electrical diathermy or electrical cutting apparatus could be used, nor any apparatus that might produce a spark. It was also difficult to control the depth of the anaesthesia accurately as there was a time lag between its application and its effect. This was often a cause of great embarrassment to the anaesthetist and irritation to the surgeon, since if the depth of anaesthesia lessened significantly there might be involuntary movements of the patient, which made life difficult for the surgeon. (On one famous occasion in Dunedin Hospital the professor of surgery, Dr Gordon Bell, apparently erupted after enduring all sorts of moves and twitches by the patient, and noting, that the anaesthetist was apparently paying little attention said, 'Dr O'C, if the patient can stay awake surely you can too!')

Ether also made for a slow recovery and the patient was frequently sick. An even greater disadvantage was that operations requiring significant muscular relaxation required a fairly deep state of anaesthesia, and high doses of ether could be toxic and dangerous for patients who were seriously ill. The advent of muscle relaxants changed the face of anaesthesia, since they allowed separation of the individual aspects involved: depth of unconsciousness, pain suppression, muscle relaxation and involuntary movement during unconsciousness. An entirely new set of skills and equipment was also required. By administering intravenous anaesthetic agents that wore off quickly, muscle relaxants to give the surgeon good access where needed, intravenous anti-pain drugs, and quick-acting light gas and oxygen mixtures direct to the windpipe, a whole new field of possible operations was opened up. One example was open chest surgery to remove lungs or parts thereof, and another was surgery on seriously shocked, sick or elderly people who would never previously have survived or indeed been considered for operation.

It was exciting to be witness to this major development in medical science. I did quite a lot of relieving anaesthestic work at Wellington Hospital under the tutelage of Dr Slater and Dr Dick Climie, registrar at that time and a man of renowned skill, as well as many others who helped me towards a stint as anaesthetic registrar towards the end of my stay in Wellington.

If a next of kin or close relative wanted to have a talk about a patient there was a daily session for this immediately after lunch. The relative would go to the main reception desk and give the name of the patient, whereupon the house surgeon assigned would be paged by flashing his code number on illuminated signs scattered throughout the hospital. One would then proceed to the large outpatient waiting room where all the relatives were gathered, and call out the name of the patient to get the appropriate relative. There were no privacy regulations then and the whole business makes me shudder now. One spoke fully and freely, answering all the queries as to condition, progress and outlook, with no authorisation from the patient.

During my term one house surgeon had a rough time because of this system. A man came to see him and asked how his wife was. The house surgeon said she was getting on well following her minor operation, a dilatation and curettage after an incomplete miscarriage. The man asked if she had definitely been pregnant and the house surgeon reassured him and said the curettings had been examined and proved to be the remains of a pregnancy.

Subsequent events showed that the man had been legally separated from his wife and paying her maintenance, which was to be terminated if she ever became pregnant by another man! The poor house surgeon had to appear in court and give evidence and got a roasting for divulging information without patient permission. He would never, from that day, ever give any information to anyone without signed permission. I don't blame him and we all learnt a lesson.

I had one nasty personal fright in Wellington when I cut my hand quite badly on a piece of broken headlight glass that had horse manure on it. I went along to Casualty to get it sewn up and for an anti-tetanus injection. I convinced them that I did not need a test dose of the latter as I had never had any allergy to it and so, against regulations, they gave me the full injection. Some days later I came out in a terrible rash, followed by swollen joints and a high temperature, and felt quite ill.

This reaction is known as serum sickness and is easily controlled nowadays with cortisone-type drugs. But at that time we had only antihistamine drugs and injections of adrenalin. The hospital sent up a registrar who gave me some adrenalin, which made a rapid improvement. He left me a syringe and supply of adrenalin with instructions to inject myself with a small dose every four hours, saying that he would be back in a few days. But one day when I had the needle in place, I made the mistake of not drawing back the plunger to check that it was not in a vein before injecting the lot at once. When I felt it go in so easily without any tissue swelling I knew at once it had gone intravenously, so I lay back and warned Jill that I was in trouble.

My heart started beating like a steam hammer and my head pounded as my blood pressure rose, probably to extreme limits. Jill saw my face drain of blood and could actually hear my heart pounding – the bed was shaking with the force of it. I lay there and hoped I did not have any weak-walled arteries anywhere. It passed after a few minutes and I had no more bother with my allergy, which cleared completely. This was another lesson for general practice which I never forgot, namely always to check that a needle is not in a vein when giving a subcutaneous or intramuscular injection.

One day a seriously ill patient had to be transferred to the neurosurgical unit at Dunedin Hospital by air, requiring a doctor to accompany her in case of emergency. I volunteered for this trip, which served to drip-feed, a little further, my passion for flying. We left the old Rongotai aerodrome in a low-wing Percival Proctor aircraft, powered by a six-cylinder Gipsy Queen engine and fitted out to take a stretcher fore and aft on one side, with a passenger sitting behind the pilot alongside the patient.

On the return trip we were north of Christchurch flying in lovely conditions when the pilot, who could sense my interest and who patiently answered my endless questions, asked if I had ever flown an aircraft. I said no, and was somewhat astonished when he told me to have a go, because the aircraft did not have dual controls fitted – the stretcher occupied the space where a co-pilot would normally sit. He trimmed it to fly straight and level, climbed out of his seat and told me to jump in, belt up and take over. After carrying on straight and level for a while he got me to do some gentle turns, watching me closely from the seat behind, by which time we were at the northern end of the South Island where he said we had to circle the Cape Campbell lighthouse to let air traffic control know we were there and about to cross Cook Strait since we had no radio communication. I duly circled the lighthouse, in quite steep turns, until the keeper saw and acknowledged. The pilot took a photo of me flying the aircraft and will always have my gratitude for according me that rare privilege.

Dr Dick Stone, a senior house surgeon, did aeroclub flying in Wellington and offered to take me up. We had a short and pleasant flight which so whetted my appetite that I asked him if he was able to do aerobatics, which he could. He took me up again one fine afternoon and went to an authorised area over Palliser Bay, this time in a de Havilland Chipmunk aircraft, a lovely small monoplane with a de Havilland Gipsy Major engine. He did some loops, stall turns and a couple of spins, which I initially found almost heart-stopping but thoroughly enjoyed once the spin was established. Many years later I was able to repeat these manoeuvres myself.

# 11

*JILL'S AND MY DOMESTIC LIFE WAS FUN*, even though I was away from home several nights a week. Our flat in Kelburn, kindly let to us by my cousin Bill Hursthouse, was comfortable with a grand view over the harbour. Mostly I walked down to Lambton Quay and caught a tram to the hospital but when a bit tired or feeling lazy I took the cable car down. Our finances were perilous, with Jill topping them up by getting occasional jobs, but we managed.

Our wee Morris took us around the beaches and city when we had time off but it was pretty rummy and not particularly safe on Wellington's hills. One day we saw a beautiful red MG with a 'for sale' notice on it. We fell in love with it, took some cash out of the bank, sold the Morris and became the proud owners of an immaculate 1932 MG PA with knock-on wire wheels, a small canvas hood, sidescreens, and a windscreen that folded flat in the ultimate sports car manner of the time. It gave us great pleasure and I also joined the Wellington Car Club, competing in hill climbs, sprints and trials.

I had only one 'incident' in this car. The front suspension and steering spindles were a little worn so I took it into the agent, Dominion Motors, to have the front axle removed and kingpins and so on refurbished. Shortly after this I competed in a hill climb competition at the Paekakariki Hill. On the way home Jill and I were belting along the motorway near Ngauranga Gorge when I heard a clang and saw in the rear-vision mirror something bouncing along the road. I stopped and to my horror found that one of the central wheel nuts had come off a front wheel, this being the only thing holding the wheel on. If I had not heard it bounce along the tar seal the wheel would have fallen off with who knows what disastrous results?

I simply could not understand this. The threads on these centre-lock wheels are so arranged that the direction of rotation tends to tighten them. I replaced it, doing it up tightly and then noticed that this wheel nut was going on to the left-hand side despite being labelled 'Right'. Dominion Motors had made the dreadful and dangerous mistake of reassembling the wheel hubs and wheels on the wrong side of the axle so that rotation of the wheels tended to *undo* the centre-locking wheel nuts. We had been unbelievably lucky.

Towards the end of 1951 we found with great pleasure that Jill was pregnant. We gradually came to realise that we would soon face massive changes to our lifestyle. The pregnancy proceeded normally but it became apparent after a few months that our wee MG was in no way suitable for a well pregnant mum-to-be and would be totally impossible when there were three of us. And so we kept our eyes and ears open for a replacement. We were in Hastings for a few days seeing our families when we spotted an elegant and rare car in Tourist Motors. It was an AC two-litre convertible that had been imported and owned by Maurice Chambers. He had just got the latest model so this 'old' one was on the market with a meticulously applied repaint. It was too expensive but we fell in love with it and borrowed the money.

For the technically minded, it was a four-seat drop-head saloon with air cushion leather upholstery, wooden trim, aluminium body and mudguards, twin side-mounted spare wheels, centre-lock wire wheels, built-in jacks, built-in starting handle, two-litre six-cylinder aluminium overhead camshaft motor with triple SU carburettors, telecontrol shock absorbers adjustable from inside the car with pressure gauges to show the settings, and automatic chassis lubrication to all suspension and steering points. It was immaculate and is still – now in the hands of vintage enthusiasts. It ran so smoothly one could place a coin the size of a 20 cent piece on edge on top of the engine when it was running and the coin would not fall over. This was always an impressive 'show-off' stunt for enthusiasts.

We sold the MG to fellow house surgeon David Frankish. He had fun with it but bust a hole in the sump and it was a job to fix as it proved to be made of magnesium and promptly burst into flames during welding.

Our baby was due in June 1952, but June proceeded in July with no activity, despite trying a long drive on very rough roads in the Akatarawas, which caused nothing but discomfort to poor Jill, as did the almost daily well-meaning concerns of close relations. Medical intervention for overdue pregnancies that were proceeding normally was rare at that time. Eventually on 4 July our daughter Linda was delivered, with difficulty for Jill, by a much-loved obstetrician, Dr Gordon Finlay. In the manner of those days I was not allowed anywhere near the place, not even in the ward, so I spent the evening with my friends David and Jennifer Wright at their flat, eventually receiving a telephone call to tell me the news.

Next morning I was finally allowed to visit them in hospital. My first sight was of a grinning mum with a wee wrinkle-faced, somewhat bruised baby who was feeding contentedly. I was quite overcome and temporarily speechless. Real married life began from that day.

My experiences at this time made me determined not to exclude husbands from their wives during their confinements when I had my own maternity practice some day, and this I achieved, pioneering it in Nelson against considerable opposition from entrenched senior nursing and medical personnel.

During my years of medical training my father became increasingly difficult, suffering delusions of persecution largely directed at my mother. He did not physically touch her but was very rough verbally and would not allow her any money for herself. He was also very difficult with relatives, including his own brothers and sisters, some of whom he fell out with over minor, imagined insults and to whom he never spoke again. I tried to reason with him about his treatment of my mother but was virtually told to mind my own business. He never ever forgave me for my criticism of him. He eventually left his wife of about 38 years and lived by himself in a small bach on some land he owned at Havelock North, and later in a house he bought there. He finally divorced my mother some years later. My brother and I made sure that Mother got good legal advice so she retained the house at Te Awanga, near Hastings, but she had insufficient to live on so Dan and I added to her support from then on.

Dad became reclusive, always in fear of someone opening his mail, entering his property or stealing things. He fought with everyone, especially local authorities, and had virtually no friends. Even those of his grandchildren who used to call on him were gradually driven away. I was always able to manage him because I would not be bullied, and used to go to Hawke's Bay regularly to see him and take our children with me. He loved Jill, who was wonderful to him, but he was very difficult with Dan and Margaret, who bore the brunt of his behaviour despite doing more for him, since they lived nearby.

During this family upset we had my mother come and live with us for some months. She was absolutely no bother, always good fun and she liked living with us, but she always insisted that she must go and live in her own home when things settled down. This she did, living happily at Te Awanga, which was always a haven for family and friends, of whom she had a multitude.

As my time at Wellington Hospital drew to an end Jill and I decided we should make some plans. There were many openings around New Zealand – as well as in Australia and the rest of the world – but one item of valuable advice my father had given me many years previously was to choose where I wanted to live and then 'go for it'.

We made lists of our requirements and thought hard. I decided against setting up general practice in Hastings. Our family connections there were very socially inclined people, which we were not. We liked occasional parties or celebrations but did not care for frequent and apparently endless rounds of social gatherings.

I wanted to be in a community with a medium-sized hospital so that I could do anaesthetic work, which might not be available to a GP in a metropolitan area. Our other requirements were for a good climate, good schools, hills to explore and climb, navigable water – and nothing south of Kaikoura! There were few places in New Zealand with these attributes, but Nelson had them all. We decided to go there to make our lives, and we have never once regretted this decision. The area has treated us handsomely and kept us fit, well and happy.

I wrote to the senior Nelson doctor, J.P.S. Jamieson, to ask him if he thought there was an opening for me to set up in general practice there. His reply was typical of the man: analytical, conservative and very helpful. He neither encouraged nor discouraged me, but just laid out the present situation and the future economic position of Nelson as he saw it. There were seven GPs in Nelson at that time and word must have spread quickly because I soon had a phone call from a Dr Kurt Meyer, with a country practice in Wakefield, about 25 miles south of Nelson, asking me to take over his practice. This was pretty exciting stuff so I booked flights to go to see him.

I shall never forget that flight for a number of reasons, one of them being already outlined in the prologue to this autobiography. Another was that we left Wellington in an awful southerly storm, with the cold wind and driving rain so well known to all of us who have lived there for any length of time. About an hour later in our DC3 we arrived in Nelson to clear blue skies, not a breath of wind, and the mountains clear and beautiful with a heavy coating of snow. It was a sight for sore eyes all right, a foretaste of our future.

Dr Meyer was a slightly elderly gentleman of German extraction. He took me to his home where I met his wife, a charming woman who gave us lunch. It was my first taste of sauerkraut and very good it was indeed. I liked his style of practice, which was from his big old home in large grounds serving a widespread country district, and I loved the area. He was prepared virtually to make me a gift of the practice and it was very tempting, but after much discussion Jill and I turned it down. The road to Wakefield was unsealed part of the way and pretty rough. I could see that this would make access slow to Nelson Hospital in the case of any emergencies – and I had my heart set on being a part-time anaesthetist there.

Then I had a call from a Dr Francis Stenhouse, who offered me a partnership in his general practice right in Nelson. I flew to Nelson again to discuss it but did not find the proposition at all attractive, either financially or in some other features. I thanked him for the offer but declined, saying I thought I would start up on my own. I always remember his comment: 'Do you realise that you will probably starve?'

From then on we regularly got newspapers from Nelson and scanned the market for somewhere to live. This was difficult because houses were in short supply for a few years after the war. Then my cousin John Oliver and his wife Gwynneth came to the rescue. Gwynneth's brother, Noel Jones, was a real estate agent with a large family business and they took on the job of finding somewhere for to me to practise and for us to live. Eventually I flew over to Nelson once more to approve a very suitable set of rooms from which to practise, and a nice home to rent, both at fair rates from businessmen sympathetic to a new chum with no money.

During this visit I made a point of visiting every doctor in Nelson, specialists as well as GPs, to introduce myself and tell them my plans. This was a very interesting exercise. About half were courteous (without enthusiasm or warmth), one or two were a bit critical, one was vehemently opposed and the three newest ones welcomed me warmly. I will always remember Dr Ken Galloway's reaction. He said, 'Well, I've got my 30 patients a day and you are very welcome to come and make your own way.' Dr Keith Emanuel, a returned serviceman medico, was equally welcoming, and Dr Humphrey Belton, who had been there a year or two only, turned up at our house the night we arrived to welcome us, assuring us there would be plenty of room for us in the town. I was also warmly supported by eye specialist Dr Gordon Campbell and ear, nose and throat specialist Dr Dick Lucas.

Came the end of the year and the termination of my two-year hospital appointment. We packed up and I headed off in a car full of heavy luggage onto the ferry, which then used to run to Nelson, while Jill followed by air with Linda. It was all very exciting and very strange. We settled into the house and I set about getting my new rooms painted, carpeted and furnished using a government loan given to ex-servicemen. In a few weeks we were in business.

Things were very quiet for some months, except that, as the 'new man' in the town I had visits from all the well-known problem patients. This happens everywhere. The town's worriers, many of whom may not have any real physical or nervous illness except a preoccupation with their own state of health, decide to seek a new opinion and the newly arrived doctor is a sitting duck. Not knowing them previously sometimes helps, as one tackles each of these people with a fresh mind. Occasionally – and I emphasise *occasionally* – one picks up something that has been missed by the regular doctor. This of course does no harm to one's reputation as a newcomer. However, almost all of these unfortunate people are chronic neurotics who simply refuse to believe that they have no significant illness. Several of them seem to be suffering only from boredom, which I think is inexcusable as there is so much to do in every way, including helping other people who are really ill.

One such lady, who was well into her seventies, used to come to see me week after week with new symptoms each time, none of these showing any sign of being caused by illness. Many of her troubles stemmed from refusing to acknowledge her age and trying to live like a 50-year-old. She took a lot of trouble over her appearance and admittedly did not look her age. One day she came when I was busy and described some aches and pains for which I could not find any cause except those usual for elderly folk. However, she insisted on an explanation – so she got one. I said, 'Mrs G, you look and act like a 50-year-old, but your body is that of a woman of 70-plus. You are just like a well-restored and preserved vintage car. It may look as good as new, but the parts are still old and you simply cannot drive that car as if it were a new one.' She was furious, and said, 'Dr Hursthouse, if you compare your patients to vintage cars you will not be getting much of a practice.' And she stormed out, never to be seen again.

I set some standards as the basis for my practice. I suppose this would now be called a 'Strategic Plan' in the jargon of the corporates that so many try to emulate, although some of my ideas were rubbished by some of my colleagues at the time.

I charged a flat fee that was slightly higher than the usual Nelson fee but based on fees elsewhere in New Zealand. This fee was regardless of whether the patient had been visited at home or seen at the surgery. Patients got 75 per cent of the fee refunded by the Health Department.

I gave patients three months to pay their bill, after which they received a polite notice, followed by a sterner one at five months. If there was still no payment or explanation by six months then these accounts were sent to a debt collecting agency.

I gave all my patients an appointment time. This was not common practice amongst most of the others, who simply told everyone to come, say between 2 and 4.30pm. I had been on the receiving end of this system in my younger days and thought it arrogant and unacceptable. I found that my system worked well. Some follow-ups were brief, allowing longer than the allotted time to be given to other patients. New patients were always given a double appointment at their first attendance. We soon learnt those who were always late and my nurse and I had a code so that these patients were given a time 10-15 minutes ahead of when we needed them.

I put up a notice in the waiting room to the effect that patients with appointments had priority over those who may have arrived late and missed their time. These latter would have to wait for a gap to occur so that I could fit them in, or else make a new appointment. I also stated that emergencies would always take priority over other cases. This system worked well and patients did appreciate being taken on time.

I also made a decision to try to treat my own patients at nights and weekends if I could, rather than ask them to call the emergency doctor.

I resolved never to go away from the telephone when I had a patient due to have a baby. My wife and my receptionist were trained never to refuse for me to attend a home call or see someone urgently. (I must say this particular resolution tended to backfire at times.)

I made a point of always going to visit the patients I had admitted to hospital, realising of course that these were not now in my care. I insisted that every patient I had treated for anything was seen or telephoned for a follow-up, for which I often made no charge. In common with most doctors, I did not charge other doctors, practising nurses, dentists, clergymen or any of their families, nor most of the chemists or any close friends.

These were the guidelines I hoped to follow for future general practice and over the years they worked out pretty well.

I had my own portable anaesthetic machine, which would allow the use of modern anaesthetics in dental surgeries and in private general and maternity hospitals, all of which existed in Nelson. I gradually got work of this type until I was giving anaesthetics several mornings a week for an hour or two. In particular I did a lot of children's work with tonsil, eye and other such operations that required endotracheal techniques and good apparatus. I eventually became regular anaesthetist at Nelson Hospital for Dr Dick Lucas for his tonsil and throat sessions, continuing to work with him for about 14 years.

Until the advent of modern anaesthesia for dental surgeons in Nelson, most anaesthetics for this work were administered by the patient's GP, using a shot of intravenously injected pentothal as the sole agent. This was a dangerous technique as it could sometimes induce a spasm in the breathing and muscles, with the patient becoming short of oxygen, and there was no way to administer the latter without a proper machine. These short, sharp dental anaesthetics were regarded by doctors as a quick way to get a fee, so there was some irritation at my giving anaesthetics to the patients of other doctors.

This was aired at a doctors' meeting one night, and I came under pressure. But the opposition soon subsided when it was realised that the dentists were demanding a safer and higher standard of anaesthesia. It was agreed that if a dentist wanted to do some work under general anaesthetic he would ring that patient's doctor and ask him to arrange an endotracheal one. This settled the whole matter, and quite amicably.

The Nelson doctors had an excellent scheme for helping each other. We took turns at weekend duty so that those who wanted to could get time off. We also relieved each other on holidays or in case of illness. When one saw a patient for another doctor one sent the other doctor a note stating the patient's name, address and brief statement of the reason for the visit.

The doctor who 'owned' the patient, as it were, would then send the emergency doctor an appropriate fee. This worked well and was unique at the time, I believe. If the patient wished to transfer to the doctor who had seen him for the emergency, this was done quite formally, but it was discouraged.

A more testing relationship was with the Nelson Hospital hierarchy, which was famous (or infamous) for its autocracy. The 150-bed hospital was run by medical superintendent Dr P.C. Brunette with an iron fist. The elected Hospital Board employed at that time one surgical registrar, three or four house surgeons, visiting medical specialists, two or three visiting surgeons and two visiting anaesthetists. Nothing was done – no treatment given, no patient admitted or discharged – without authority from 'Percy' Brunette. If he did not approve of a treatment (and he had some very unorthodox ideas) he would sometimes intervene and change what the physician in charge had prescribed – without even letting the physician know! This could and did cause considerable resentment, especially as Percy was a surgeon and had no training as a specialist physician.

However, he did institute some ideas at Nelson Hospital that were somewhat radical but positive. He encouraged all the private doctors in the area to have morning tea in the doctors' common room at the hospital where the full-time medical staff also foregathered at that time, thus enabling all doctors to inquire about patients they had sent in. He also encouraged all the doctors in private practice to visit their patients in hospital at any time. These measures were great for morale and for the community – but Percy could not bear to be crossed.

Shortly after arriving in Nelson I went to see the feared Dr Brunette to introduce myself. I made it known that I had some specialist training in anaesthetics and would like to get some work in that speciality if possible. He made it quite clear that he had two perfectly capable such doctors, Eric Peat and Keith Emanuel, doing this work, and there was no vacancy for me. Thankfully this soon changed as demand increased.

I had a few serious differences of opinion with Dr Brunette but refused to be bullied, which was apparently quite a new experience for him. The first concerned one of the first patients I saw in general practice, a youngish man living across the road from us. His wife came to our house as her doctor was away. She was very distressed and said he had a terrible headache and high temperature with aching muscles. After examination it was only too evident to me from my experience in Wellington that this man had developed a fulminating and severe infection of poliomyelitis.

I knew he would rapidly become paralytic and might well need artificial respiration. I did not tell his wife all this, but did tell her I was almost positive he had polio. At that time the polio epidemic that was raging in the rest of New Zealand had not reached Nelson. When I rang Dr Brunette at the hospital and asked for him to be admitted, he argued, saying I was a very new GP to be so sure of myself and he would not admit the patient without a second opinion.

I made it quite plain that I had seen hundreds of polio cases quite recently and that I was sending the man up in an ambulance forthwith, which I did. The diagnosis was confirmed, but sadly the man did not survive. I hasten to point out that this was through no fault of the hospital – it was the severity of his infection.

This was my introduction to the sadness that all GPs meet from time to time – and of which there was a lot more to come in the years ahead.

I gradually built up a practice but in those days it was almost unknown for a patient to pay cash for any attendance. This meant sending out accounts each month and this by no means saw the money paid immediately. No way. In fact it was sometimes months before bills were paid – sometimes they were not paid at all. Jill and I found it very difficult for those first few months and had problems in paying our grocer's account and for other home supplies.

After about six months my parents-in-law came to stay. One afternoon my father-in-law, Noel Beamish, came to the surgery; he looked around and asked me how things were going. I told him the practice was going well, with patients and work building up and a good income on paper, but that people were slow to pay. He pulled out his cheque book. 'Would a hundred pounds help?' This was a large sum of money and I was absolutely staggered. I started to protest but he interrupted: 'No, don't misunderstand me. I am not giving you this: I am making it a loan. I want you to take out an endowment insurance policy for Linda, my first grandchild, to mature when she is 21, and I want you to repay this money by paying the annual premium, which I will subsidise, pound for pound.' Thus he got us out of our financial difficulties and allowed me to keep my pride at the same time. Such is the wisdom of Solomon.

During this time Jill became pregnant again, proceeding quite normally under the care of Dr Frank Hudson, and in February 1954 she produced our first son, Tim. We were delighted of course and he soon had us knocked into shape – and still keeps us there!

Most of the GPs in Nelson followed the same general procedure. The mornings were used in visiting patients in their homes. Most of these were in response to calls that started coming in from 7am, predominantly for sick children, with a number of follow-ups of acute cases seen a day or two before, as well as a sprinkling of chronic, usually elderly, patients whom we visited once a month to check on them. A typical sort of morning entailed visiting about 10 homes, but in times of epidemics this could be greatly increased and one had to plan one's route efficiently to save back-tracking. I always left a list of my planned visits with my receptionist so that I could be tracked down if an emergency should arise. (Home visiting would be a piece of cake nowadays with radios and cellphones.) I usually started my home calls from about 7.45am, as did one or two of the others whom I usually saw somewhere en route.

We usually tried to arrange being close to the hospital by about mid-morning. This meant we could pop in for a cup of tea and inquire about or visit any of our hospitalised patients. After this we continued our calls until about noon, when we got back to the surgery and saw appointment patients until 1pm. Then we would go home for lunch. In the afternoon I had appointments from 2pm to 5pm, after which I would visit any urgent cases who had rung from their home that afternoon, finally reaching my own home about 6pm.

Night calls were never popular but were a necessary part of the occupation. In Nelson we GPs had a good relationship with our patients, who were mostly very considerate to us and we had few unnecessary or trivial night calls. But they could still be tiring. I learnt never to accept the offered cup of tea on such visits as it prevented me from getting to sleep again when I got back home.

One night I had finally got back to bed after a call out when the phone rang beside the bed. When I answered, it kept ringing, despite my continued 'Hello'. Then Jill dug me in the ribs and said, 'Pick up the receiver!' I was so tired I was stupid! On another occasion when I was also exhausted, a nurse at a private maternity hospital rang me in the middle of the night to tell me that Mrs J was in labour and ready for delivery. Would I come down? I said, 'I am sorry, I am at Torrent Bay, would you get someone else to come.' (Torrent Bay in the Abel Tasman National Park was a haven we ducked to whenever we could. There were no phones or other forms of communication to that area.) I dropped straight off to sleep again but the phone soon rang again. When I answered this time, the sister in charge of the hospital was on the line saying, 'Is there some sort of problem, doctor?' Then I awoke fully, remembered what I had said and felt a right idiot. 'No,' I said and went straight down, delivered the baby and explained myself to the poor bewildered nurse and the sister.

One of the most frustrating night calls I had was when I was awoken by a request from a long-standing patient to visit someone in the house next door to him – a name I did not recognise. I asked him if they could not get the patient's regular doctor but he said, 'There are some unusual and special features to this case, doctor, and I think you should see him.' So down I went to find a teenage lad with minor chest pains – no cold, no temperature and no abnormalities to be found. There was nothing I could do except reassure all and sundry, but I asked the neighbour, 'What are the "peculiar features" you mentioned to me?' He said, 'Oh, it was just that his own doctor refused to come and see him.' This was one of the few occasions I felt cross with a patient, but I said nothing.

Looking back, I think about my mistakes. Fatigue or shortage of time was the cause of some, while for others I could make no excuse. The worst of these could have ended my medical career, almost before it began.

A middle-aged lady came in one day and said she would like a complete checkup.

After a full interrogation I asked her to go into the examination room next door, remove her clothes and cover up with the sheet on the bed. I then proceeded to examine her, finding nothing wrong in any department except for a black superficial mole (a benign seborrhoeic wart) on her right temple inside the hair line. I asked her if she would like the mole removed by the simple method of touching it with an 'electric needle', which she said she would.

Now, you should understand that I had only just started my practice and had a lot of lovely new shiny equipment that I had never used, so here was my chance. I prepared a shiny stainless steel tray with forceps, swabs, local anaesthetic and sterilising solutions and got my receptionist to take it into the examination room where the patient lay, still with no clothes, underneath her sheet. I injected a little local anaesthetic, swabbed the area, took hold of my brand new diathermy machine, put the business end of it onto the mole, pressed the foot switch … and the patient burst into flames about the head. Truly, I had committed the unforgivable: I had swabbed her with spirit instead of some non-inflammable sterilising solution. The spark from the diathermy set it alight in dramatic fashion, hair and all.

I beat her about the face and head to put out the flames, burning my own hands in the process, and stood there appalled, absolutely devastated. Then a new impression came to my senses and I smelt a strange smell. I looked around and my morale sank even further, if that were possible. Her pile of clothes on the adjacent chair was merrily smouldering, set alight when the spirit swab I had flung away landed on them. I still shudder when I remember that little fire with a pink full-body corset lying on top with large black holes, their edges smouldering, and a small thread of smoke drifting up to the ceiling.

After dousing all the burning components I could only apologise: I had never felt so ashamed or humiliated. I sent her home in a taxi, rang my friend Dr Humphrey Belton who helped me treat her thankfully superficial burns. We visited her daily until she was completely healed. I also rang a local clothing shop and told them to replace her clothes at my expense.

Well, that lady, who I now realise held my future in her hands, stayed with me as a patient, as did her family, and never did I receive any complaints about the incident from her or any of her family. Bless her.

There is a sequel to this story. Some years later a gentleman from England, who represented the accident insurance company that covered doctors for these sorts of things, came to New Zealand and gave lectures about the mistakes doctors were prone to make and which might lay us open to a claim from the patient. At the end of his lecture to nearly all the doctors in the district, he asked if anyone had experienced any other hazards which might be useful to him to tell other doctors about. I took a deep breath and told them all of this incident. It seems to have acted as a cautionary tale since it has come back to me on many occasions – and it happened 45 years ago.

# 12

MATERNITY WORK GRADUALLY BUILT UP. I really enjoyed this as I was dealing with normality rather than illness, and I never got over the miracle of seeing a baby born and the dazzling pleasure of the mother after the trials and tribulations of the labour and the long nine months preceding.

We had no specialist obstetrician in Nelson and some of us did more maternity work than others. At the nearby town of Richmond Dr John Shearer had a high reputation among his colleagues as well as the public, while in Nelson Dr Frank Hudson was similarly regarded. When Dr Hudson retired a few of us took on more and more of this work with Dr Ken Galloway, who had done a post-graduate obstetrics course, being probably the busiest. I also became steadily busier, with the help of those more skilled, until I was eventually attending about 120 deliveries a year.

I was also asked by the hospital to give lectures to the trainee nurses and at the end of one of these courses the leader of the group, a girl called Evelyn, presented me, on behalf of her class, with an LP record of Mozart's *Marriage of Figaro*. This record soon became a favourite, and still is. Shortly before writing this memoir, I met a lovely young woman at a conference who turned out to be Evelyn's daughter, whom I had delivered. I told her about this old LP and a month or so later, in the post there came a parcel with a CD of *Marriage of Figaro* featuring Kiri te Kanawa, along with a note that read: 'I thought that after 40 years you needed a new copy of this. Lots of love and happy memories, Evelyn.' What a lovely reward.

After the first full consultation and general checkup we saw patients monthly for the first six months of the pregnancy, then fortnightly for the next two months, then weekly until delivery. At each consultation we weighed the mother, tested her urine and blood pressure, checked the baby and gave any needed advice. Then we looked after them during the confinement and postnatal period, with a major checkup three months later. This was all at no cost to the patient, and poor remuneration from the government, but it was lovely work and part of family medical practice.

I loved obstetric work but the broken nights were tiring. One night I got up and delivered one baby, went home and was barely off to sleep when they rang again to say that another one of my 'mums' was in labour, so I went down and did that delivery. While I was there, another of my patients was admitted in full labour, so instead of going home I decided to bed down at the hospital in one of the empty single rooms until I was woken to do this next delivery. The nursing staff were a great bunch and full of fun, but I was a little frightened when they said they would come in and 'prep' me if I wasn't careful!

I made my share of mistakes too. I attended a young woman whose family head was a politically important figure. She had a quite normal pregnancy with an apparently large baby. After delivery of a normal infant, we were all shattered to find that there was another baby still present and this one was also normally produced. I still don't know how I missed it, but never forgot the lesson. Thereafter I always hunted around for extra limbs and foetal heartbeats. I must say, the parents were very forgiving about my error! What can one do except apologise?

Multiple births were always a great excitement (I never missed another). The first one I managed caused me concern as the pregnancy went well past the due date, whereas multiple pregnancies tend to start labour earlier. The mother was in robust good health and the twins' foetal hearts and movements were all quite normal but I sought advice from the more experienced, who were unanimous that it was better to wait than attempt to induce early labour, as it would allow the babies to grow to a good size. We eventually delivered two hefty beautiful boys, Rex and Neil. The parents gave me a beautiful gold top Parker fountain pen with my name engraved on it which I still have.

Difficult births were a terrible strain and I would seek a second opinion in many cases, especially if it appeared that a caesarean section was needed. Forceps deliveries were also difficult, requiring skill, experience and patience from everyone involved, but thank goodness I did not lose a baby from this type of delivery.

When I'd been in practice for some years a new method of assisted delivery known as 'vacuum extraction' was written up in the journals. The apparatus consisted of a large suction cap to fit on top of the infant's head, with a tube to a reservoir attached to a hand pump. The idea was that if one could gently pull on the head of the infant, this was better than using forceps around its head, since they took up a fair bit of space in the birth canal that was badly needed for the baby. This apparatus was highly recommended for assisting in the late stages of delivery where delay was occurring due, possibly, to maternal fatigue with perhaps a slightly narrowed birth canal.

Dr Ken Galloway and I were by this time probably doing the majority of the deliveries at Nelson Hospital. He agreed that it would be worthwhile asking the hospital to purchase the equipment, which it did. I used it with great success on a number of occasions and found it wonderful.

Stillbirths were a terrible blow, but thankfully they were rare and nearly always able to be foreseen. But it was bad practice to try to remove the dead foetus artificially, so the poor parents, and the mother in particular, had this awful time waiting for and going through labour, knowing that her baby was dead. Other stressful events were the birth of mentally or physically handicapped infants. We did not have ultrasound investigations in those days, and did not routinely x-ray foetuses unless we had strong reason to suspect serious trouble. Nor did we have amniocentesis to check on the foetus. Abnormalities were nearly always as much of a shock to the doctor as to the parents.

Some strange things could happen in this work. I was called urgently to the hospital one evening to see a middle-aged woman who had been admitted with severe abdominal pain. She said she had no doctor and had just arrived on the doorstep. She had a very large abdomen and on examination appeared to be pregnant, probably full term, and coming into labour. But she vehemently denied this: said she had several children and knew all about that. The house surgeon in charge was baffled and was advised to call the obstetric duty doctor who happened to be me. I was also sure she was in labour but she denied this, shouting loudly. In the meantime her pains became much worse and closer together …

We called the duty x-ray technician out and took a quick shot of her abdomen, which showed quite plainly a full term foetus in normal position. I tried to show her but she would not look or listen. At this point we rushed her trolley at high speed to the nearby maternity ward where I delivered a healthy baby girl. Even as I was delivering it the poor mother was still in denial. She did not look at or handle her baby, but signed it for adoption and left the hospital in a few days, refusing further attention or follow-ups. She was not a local resident.

Another sad case involved an attractive local young woman who came to see me in the early stages of pregnancy. She was unmarried and living at home with her parents, who were well known in the community. She asked for total confidentiality, which I confirmed as a matter of course. At no time did she hint as to who the father of her baby might be, but said quite firmly that she was not going to keep the baby, or stop work during her pregnancy, which was normal throughout.

I saw her regularly but was perturbed by the fact that she concealed the pregnancy with tight clothing in quite an amazing fashion right up to the end, despite living at home. At the first signs of labour she 'went for a short holiday' – at least that is what she told her parents – and I admitted her to a private maternity hospital, where she had a bonny wee babe without any complications, but which she never saw at all. She discharged herself after three days and went home again, and back to work.

Adoption laws were quite different in those days, and adoptions were mostly arranged by the doctors in collaboration with the Social Welfare Department. Almost no unmarried mothers kept their babies as significant social stigma attached to both mother and child. We used to see a number of pregnant single women, many of them from other districts and often under pseudonyms. They had come to our town to live anonymously, occasionally with a relative, until the baby was delivered, after which they would disappear again. Mostly they would never see their baby.

The new baby was thoroughly checked physically and blood samples taken, as were the background and health of the parents, if they could be traced. The doctor would have chosen the next one on his list of adoption applicants whom he would have advised of the approximate due date. If all went well, the new baby was taken to the new parents by the doctor, a nurse or a welfare officer in some secrecy. No one ever divulged the origin of the infants or identity of the new parents. The system worked well, even though no doubt it would be subject to criticism nowadays.

I have many happy memories of these adoptions, although they are tinged with sadness for the mothers who abandoned their babies under the pressure of public opinion. There was one couple, Mr and Mrs T, whom I had known and attended for many years. They were unable to conceive and eventually asked if they could adopt, so their names were put on the list. It so happened that a nice woman from 'out of town', somewhat older than usual, came along at this time for help. As the pregnancy proceeded it became apparent that she was going to have twins and although she was excited about this she was adamant she could not keep them. I told Mr and Mrs T that these twins were coming along and they decided with great excitement to adopt them, so this was arranged with the Social Welfare Department.

Two beautiful boys were eventually delivered and I decided that I would like to help take them out to the new parents. It was a memorable day with my wife and a nurse sitting in the back seat of my car holding these two boys while I drove ever so carefully to their new home, where we were met by the ecstatic new parents. Experiences such as these gave one a glow and made maternity work just so rewarding.

About 30 years later I had a telephone call from one of these now grown-up businessmen asking if I remembered him, which, I assured him I certainly did. He went on to say he and his brother wanted to trace their birth mother and wondered whether I could help. Of course ethically I was not able to do so, but I was able to tell him what a nice person she was. I often wonder whether he found her.

One of the difficult aspects of general practice is having to keep secrets from one's wife. I would quite freely discuss cases in a general way with Jill – never with or in the hearing of the children – but I did not tell her the names of the patients. She sometimes found this difficult since her friends, who had been to me for some ailment, would sometimes seem to expect her to know about their troubles and almost be a little aggrieved that I had not told her. Once a close friend came to me in the early stages of pregnancy. She met Jill in the street a week or two later and was quite upset that Jill didn't know about it. But a doctor, especially a general practitioner, is trusted with a multitude of secrets which always must stay as such.

Rhesus (Rh) factor incompatibility was a terrible worry in those days. If a father's blood type was Rh positive and the mother Rh negative, the infant was almost certain to be Rh positive, which then caused antibodies to form in the mother, attacking and destroying the infant's blood while in the womb. It virtually never affected a first pregnancy, rarely the second, but almost always any subsequent pregnancies were affected, with the probable loss of the baby. To make matters worse, any miscarriages, even very early ones, counted as pregnancies, with the likelihood of antibodies having been formed. At this time there was no cure and when this set of conditions was found couples were advised of the dangers.

Well, my best friend married my receptionist and they had a lovely baby boy. Tests had shown that they had Rhesus incompatibility but I was not concerned for early pregnancies. But when she became pregnant again, tests showed antibodies rising gradually and then to such a dangerous level that I was in despair.

At that time Dr John Hiddlestone had come back to Nelson Hospital as resident physician and assistant superintendent, and had studied and learnt the new technique of exchange transfusion. As soon as the baby was born and tests showed that he was in real danger, Dr Hiddlestone undertook to carry out the procedure. We would otherwise have had to send the baby to a main-centre hospital.

I think this may have been the first such case treated in Nelson. It was a long and painstaking job and I seem to remember we had to have two or three such exchanges until the baby was out of the woods and the destruction of his blood had stopped. I was honoured to be his godfather and we remain the closest of friends to this day, 40 years on, enjoying innumerable outings together on motorbikes, fishing in lakes and rivers, and on back-country mountain trails.

The busiest day I had with obstetrics was when I delivered three human babies and six pups in 24 hours. Our lawyer, Jim Glasgow, had a lovely pedigree dachshund named Trudi. Somebody accidentally let her loose when she was on heat and she obviously met up with a largish fox terrier, as far as could be made out later on. But it was feared that a larger dog may have been involved and the family was concerned that she might produce oversized pups, with difficulty in giving birth. So they asked if I would come and attend the event.

Trudi had six lovely pups without any difficulty, except for one, which was not only a bit larger than the others but which was born inside the amniotic sac. The poor wee pup was gasping futilely for air when born and I snipped the membranes with a pair of scissors, after which he never looked back.

I asked if I could have him, as they did not want to keep any of these non-pedigree offspring. And so we acquired Jasper, who was a real character, loving and loved all his 17 years with us. He had the black and tan colouring of his mother, but was about the size of a large fox terrier. He was a possum killer, loved boating and fishing and was absolutely devoted to all our family. He fell off the back of our uncle's launch one day as we sat scanning the ocean. When he was finally noted to be missing we went back and found him still swimming gamely along after us.

After a number of years a fully trained specialist obstetrician and gynaecologist come to Nelson to set up practice. This, we all realised, was a great step forward for Nelson, even though it would mean less maternity work for us. Dr Brian Neill helped us with all with our problems and difficult cases thereafter, and also brought us up to date with the latest ideas and techniques.

Shortly after Dr Neill arrived I had a very difficult case that could have ended disastrously all round. A young married woman patient of mine, whom we shall call 'Betty', became pregnant. All went well until confinement, when she became obstructed. With specialist advice from Dr Neill, the decision was made for her to have a caesarean section. I gave the anaesthetic and Dr Neill performed the operation and delivered a healthy baby. However, post-operatively Betty developed a raging high temperature and became gravely ill to the point that we thought we might lose her. Investigations and bacterial culture showed a serious and dangerous type of infection of the uterus similar to a gangrene. Then, to add to the severity of her condition, she developed renal failure, with total loss of function of her kidneys. This needed immediate treatment at Dunedin Hospital, the only place available with a so-called 'artificial kidney'. So an ambulance plane was arranged for the next morning.

The air ambulance service in Nelson at that time used a de Havilland Dragon aircraft, a large cabin biplane with two four-cylinder Gipsy motors, giving a cruising speed of about 100mph. To add to our problems that morning the ambulance driver was late and this was to have serious results. By the time Betty arrived, on a stretcher with an intravenous drip, she was virtually unconscious. We bolted the stretcher to the floor of the aircraft and got aboard. The pilot was the chief flying instructor of the Nelson Aero Club, Derek Erskine, an experienced pilot and ex-topdressing man. Betty's husband came with us and also the Nelson Aero Club captain, Ray Sigley. (I was also a qualified pilot at this stage.)

I had been advised that because of her condition Betty should on no account be flown at any greater altitude than 5000 feet. This meant that we could not fly directly south from Nelson but had to go a little way north, get through to the East Coast around the northern end of the Kaikoura Ranges and thus proceed via Christchurch.

The weather was fine but there was an easterly air stream coming over from Marlborough and all pilots familiar with Nelson well know that this can cause vicious turbulence. After going north up the coast to a point where the pilot could cut through to the east while keeping below 5000 feet, he made his turn into the hills and all hell broke loose. Violent turbulence caused the stretcher to break loose, complete with patient and intravenous apparatus.

Ray, Betty's husband and I undid our belts and grappled with the problem while Derek did a steep turn back out to sea where we flew in calm conditions while making our repairs and getting the stretcher bolted back securely. We then flew almost right to the northern tip of the South Island to keep clear of the hill-generated turbulence. After a calm trip we landed briefly at Christchurch for fuel.

The patient was by now deeply unconscious and started having epileptic-type fits, which I could only control with small doses of intravenous pentothal. But the weather was good to us, and Derek pushed the old Dragon as hard as he dared and as low as he could. Nevertheless Betty's condition was by now so low that I seriously thought she might die before we got to Dunedin.

We arrived at Taieri Airport in the early afternoon, skimming the last bunch of hills, to be met by a full medical and nursing team of specialists who thankfully took charge immediately.

Our pilot was determined to get back that day, despite its being almost midwinter with short days. The Dragon was not equipped with night-flying instruments, had no lights and was not licensed for night flying – and I also found out later that there were no aeronautical charts aboard. But he insisted we go so we left Betty's husband with her and took off for the return to Nelson.

We went up the snowy centre of the South Island, but as the day drew on it got darker and darker, finally became fully dark when we were over exceedingly mountainous country north of Christchurch and still a long way from Nelson. It was bright moonlight, thank goodness, and this saved us in the end. None of the three of us had the faintest idea exactly where we were and I can still vividly recollect the moonlit midwinter scene of these enormous craggy snow-covered mountains all around us.

Eventually Derek consulted Ray and me, saying fuel was beginning to get down and there were no lights or signs of Nelson or the sea in any direction. I said I thought he should look for a flat area in some valley and do an emergency landing while we had fuel. After discussion Derek decided he would climb as high as he was able, to see if we were near the northern end of the mountain chain. Suddenly, we saw the lights of Nelson and the large powerful sweeping beacon of Nelson Airport about 50 miles north of us. At least now we knew where we were, but Derek did not wish to continue to Nelson as he knew there would be trouble about his illegal night flying if he did so – and fuel was low. He decided to land in a grass paddock near Lake Rotoiti, where we used to land light aircraft at times for medical emergencies.

To get into this field in the Dragon at night with either non-existent or very poor brakes was quite a flying feat and I was glad of Derek's top-dressing background. He asked Ray and me to climb right into the back of the fuselage as far as we could so that he could drag her in low over the fence with her tail well down. This he did and we landed in bitter cold with a heavy frost – the paddock was at 2000 feet.

We walked to the nearby house of Alex McConochie, whom I knew from previous professional incidents, and rang my wife Jill, who by now was quite worried. She got straight into our car and drove the 70-odd miles to collect us. I was very thankful to get home: we were all exceedingly lucky.

The poor old Dragon stayed out in that icy night and was hard to get going again next day when they went to fly her home. But she is still flying in restored condition in Auckland and is quite a famous vintage aircraft. I wonder whether the present owners know of this episode in her life?

The sequel to this trip occurred many weeks later when Betty flew back to Nelson, fully recovered after her stormy illness. I went to greet her off the DC3 and she eventually tottered out and over to me, giving me a big hug and crying tears of happiness.

But not all cases ended in victory. As I gradually cut down my maternity work, recommending to patients that they consult Dr Neill instead, some stayed on. These were mostly those whose previous babies I had delivered and they specifically wanted me to look after them.

One such was an older woman whose family I knew and liked. She had had several previous babies and this pregnancy was proceeding well until suddenly, in late labour, the foetal heartbeat speeded up and then foetal heart sounds disappeared completely. The baby was stillborn with the umbilical cord wound tightly twice around its neck, having been tightened as the baby descended. It was heartbreaking for all of us but especially for the mother of course. Nowadays sophisticated electronic surveillance can monitor foetal behaviour during labour so that the earliest signs of distress can be detected.

That was the last baby I delivered.

# 13

THERE WAS A FARMING FAMILY living on D'Urville Island near the northern end of the Marlborough Sounds, about 50 miles by sea from Nelson. At this time there was no road access from Nelson to French Pass, which is close to D'Urville Island, so that those living there had to come by boat.

Brian, head of the family, rang one day to say he had had a bad fall from his horse and injured his knee. He had crawled several miles back to the farmhouse for help. It sounded pretty nasty and he said he would come up. Unbelievably, this man managed to get aboard his large elderly launch and drive it the 50 miles to Nelson where he was met by friends and brought to my surgery. He must have had the most awful pain doing this, especially the long trip in open sea. He was admitted to hospital and made a full recovery from his serious injury.

Our families became close friends over the years, having lots of fun together and many a medical adventure as well. Brian was a Spitfire fighter pilot in World War 2, qualifying as an ace. His photo graces the walls of the Alpine Fighter Museum at Wanaka.

One day his wife rang me to say that he was quite ill – nauseated, vomiting and with a lot of abdominal pain. Next day he seemed worse and I decided I had to fly down to see him. The local aero club landed me on the beach across the bay from their farm. I took one look at Brian and saw that he was jaundiced. A urine test confirmed this and when I found he had a tender, somewhat enlarged liver I made a diagnosis of infective hepatitis. Since there was no specific treatment available for him, we decided he could stay put and we would monitor the situation by daily phone calls.

He became suddenly worse one evening, with evidence of early liver failure. I consulted with local specialist physician, Dr Leo Hannah, who said I should go down, start Brian on an intravenous drip, and get him back to Nelson Hospital as fast as possible. With only boat access, I rang a few of Brian's friends who had boats and Ted Biddle, a local pharmacist, agreed at once to take me down. I swung into action, with help from Jill, who got thermoses and some food. The hospital quickly got ready all the gear I needed to take.

We left Monaco boat ramp at about 11pm on a calm night in an 18-foot Karl Augustin runabout with a small Penta inboard engine of about 20hp. We went straight up the coast from Nelson for the first 20–25 miles, then made a straight line across open sea to Greville Harbour, arriving about 1.30am.

It has to be the most dangerous boat trip I have ever made. It was pitch dark and we had no means of navigation, with only a torch to spot logs or other obstructions in the sea. Good old Ted. The patient, his family and I never forgot his willingness to undertake such a trip.

I attended to the patient, set up a drip, hanging it from the wardrobe door, and sat up with him until daylight, when the Nelson Aero Club sent an aircraft to take him to hospital. Brian subsequently made a full recovery.

This family were noted farmers and residents of 'The Island', as it was called. So much so, that when the then Governor-General was making a goodwill tour of the Sounds area the vice-regal party arranged to have a luncheon stop at their farm, landing by helicopters in the paddock next to the homestead. The event was made much of in the local newspaper, who publicised that their reporter and photographer were taking carrier pigeons with them to take their film and copy back to the *Nelson Evening Mail* office.

The evening of this event I rang my friend Brian, and in a somewhat affected voice spoke to him as follows. 'My name is Hamilton. I am one of the Governor-General's security staff. Lady Fergusson has lost a diamond brooch and we think it may have occurred during her visit there at lunchtime today, possibly in the cow paddock.'

'Goodness me,' he said. 'We'll institute a search at once.'

Then I spoilt it by saying, 'If you find it, could you send it back by one of the carrier pigeons?'

There was a significant pause and then he said, 'Is that you, Hursthouse?'

He swore he would get his own back, and this he did by making a rowdy entrance into my waiting room one day in front of several patients. He went up to the receptionist's desk, waved a farming tool used to castrate animals, and in a loud voice said, 'Where is he? I'll fix him.' It caused quite a stir.

Sadly, this great friend came to see me professionally some years later, saying that he had discomfort in his abdominal area. When I examined him I found a large tumour, which proved malignant and he died some time later, to our great sadness.

Jill and I were gradually making headway financially, but still could not afford a home of our own. We rented houses for a year or two and then a well-known local doctor, Frank Hudson, decided to visit Europe with his wife for about a year. He offered us his house to rent and also asked me to look after his practice while he was away. We moved in and I saw his patients in the small consulting rooms at his home a few times a week as well as having regular sessions at my own rooms.

His house was immaculate, as the Hudsons were a childless elderly couple, but by this time we had two young children and it was not so easy for Jill to maintain this standard. We did try, but our cat scratched the cover on a sitting-room chair and Linda pulled at an irresistible edge of the very expensive wallpaper by her cot, tearing a great hunk off it. I managed to get an identical replacement, thank goodness, but it was a close call.

Then, we shall never forget (and neither will the friends and acquaintances of the late Dr Hudson) our worst crime. He and his wife had emphasised to us their fear of fire and we were very cautious about this. In fact we were quite proud of the place when we left it, having had a real cleanup with professional help inside and out. Their friends who saw the place said they would be very pleased. In the cleanup, Jill took ashes out of the kitchen stove and dumped them on the compost heap. We locked up, left the keys as directed and moved to our new premises.

When the Hudsons arrived home the compost heap and its wooden bin were alight and smouldering happily. We were never allowed to forget this, even though we, naturally, made good the damage. Even our mutual lawyer got sick of hearing about it and told them to either make a claim or stop talking about it!

While we were living there another of my worst practice tragedies occurred. My two best friends in Nelson burst into our bedroom late one night (no doors were locked in houses in Nelson in those days) and said, 'Hank,' (which they used to call me), 'Can you come up to the hospital now – we think B is dying.'

This young woman was the wife of one of them, and sister-in-law of the other. She was in hospital for a minor gynaecological procedure, admitted off the waiting list, and had been operated on a few days previously by the senior visiting surgeon. I was shattered to hear their news and hurried to the hospital with my two friends.

She was almost unconscious, with a very high temperature, rapid shallow breathing and signs of a lot of pain. A brief examination showed that she had an infection of the abdominal cavity – peritonitis. I had no right to be there at all, and certainly no right to fling my weight round which I immediately started to do, insisting that the house surgeon and night nursing supervisor come at once.

It turned out that B had complained of abdominal pain and showed a rising temperature not long after her operation. The ward sister had said it was only a minor post-operative reaction, but when it worsened she called the house surgeon, who had diagnosed a tummy bug. He said it wasn't serious and gave no treatment or orders for special attention.

Well, I did my bun: told them to get an intravenous drip going, with antibiotics as well as serum, and said they should call the senior surgeon who had done the operation. When he arrived he arranged an urgent exploratory operation which confirmed the diagnosis of peritonitis, later found caused by a streptococcal germ.

We could do no more than sit with poor B and hope that the treatment had been started in time. But it had not, and even at this stage of my life it pains me to recall it. She died in the early hours of the morning.

I simply could not go straight home. I went to our Nelson cathedral (Christ Church Cathedral), which was always open, and sat there in the quiet tranquillity for some time, as devastated as I have ever been before or since.

This was a quite unnecessary death. She should never have got a virulent infection into her abdominal cavity in the first place, but this could happen on rare occasions. However, once it had, there was absolutely no excuse for the neglect by the senior nursing sister in charge of the ward or for the house surgeon's wrong diagnosis and failure to follow up. As well, the senior surgeon was very callous and offhand in his manner when finally notified.

This was not the end of the matter. The patient's husband, an intelligent man, wanted to know exactly what had gone wrong, and why. He tried to find out from the medical superintendent, Dr Percy Brunette, but was fobbed off. He then made complaints to the Minister of Health with little satisfaction until he got backing from some fairly powerful local people. Finally the minister decided there should be an inquiry by a committee comprising a senior medical superintendent from elsewhere and a solicitor unassociated with Nelson Hospital Board, with an independent Nelson doctor permitted to be present.

The local division of the Medical Association had a meeting at which the case was discussed, and it was obvious that some wished to 'close ranks'. They all knew I was heavily involved, both as the family doctor and as a friend, and were highly critical of my backing and my approval for the inquiry. I made few friends among my colleagues at that time. The inquiry was held in an impartial and orderly manner and the findings are summarised as follows:

- The original surgical treatment was satisfactory. The source of the infection could not be determined, and there was no evidence that it was due to neglect.
- Medical treatment was inadequate – a more vigorous course of investigation of the symptoms that developed was warranted.
- A special nurse should have been provided after the second operation, and in this respect the nursing care was inadequate; but failure to do this did not contribute to the death of the patient.
- The inadequacies mentioned might have been minimised by having standing orders covering such situations.
- There should be detailed records in critical cases so that incoming personnel can be briefed when there is staff change-over, and thus given the opportunity to anticipate adverse developments.

The patient's husband received a copy of these findings, which he showed me. I then waited, expecting to hear the findings being discussed and acted on from the medical superintendent's office, and perhaps distributed to the local Medical Association. I looked forward to seeing some standing orders drawn up.

But I never heard another word, and nor did any of my close colleagues.

As well as the poor patient, the other principal players are all dead now, and that is why I can tell this sad and sorry story in detail. I have permission from my friend to include it in my memoirs.

I still find it difficult to cope with emotionally. My anger has subsided but the misery of the occasion has not.

As a footnote, after a long period of personal devastation, my friend remarried and they have three lovely children. We are all close friends.

It was difficult to get ahead financially while we were paying rent and moving house frequently, but we just did not have enough cash to put down as deposit for a house. In those days mortgages seemed to be granted as a sort of favour to the bank's client rather than anything else, and the maximum one could get was about two-thirds of the valuation.

One day we saw a house we liked enough to want to buy, but no way could we raise the money so we abandoned the idea. Then I had a telephone call from the owner, Mr Lloyd Cole, who asked why I had not bought it when I had seemed so keen. I told him I could not afford it as I could not raise the full price. He rang me back a few days later and said he had made inquiries and would lend me the balance of the funds required. When I asked him the interest rate he said there would be no interest. When I asked him the term, he said there was no fixed term – it was to be repaid as and when I could afford it, in dribs and drabs.

This sort of thing makes a young man realise the goodness that can be found in a community. I accepted his very generous offer, bought the property and repaid him over a few years, taking around to his office every spare bit of money I accumulated. He has remained a lifelong respected friend and I have used his example as a role model from time to time.

And so we moved into our house at 24 Allan Street, Nelson. It was there, in 1956, that with great delight we had our third child and second son, Mark. Like the others he has been a constant source of amusement and pleasure to us. We had many happy years in that home, with primary school and colleges nearby, and good neighbours with plenty of other children. But we did have one bad fright.

The garage opened straight on to the road below the house and I developed a bad habit when coming home at lunchtime, always in a hurry. I would back into the open garage, leaving the car in gear but with the handbrake off. I left the key in the ignition, which was quite safe in those days. By this time we had a Morris Minor convertible that nearly always had the hood down, and Linda, then aged about four, used to love coming with me on my morning visits to patients, as well as being fond of motoring generally.

After lunch one day I went off to my afternoon surgery in my other car but soon had an urgent call from Jill. Linda had somehow driven the Morris out of the garage, across the road and down the bank, where she had hit a tree and partially overturned the car. I went home at high speed to find Linda battered but conscious, with no cuts or apparent serious injury. She had got into the car and turned the key; since the car was in gear it had taken off. The small tree had stopped it halfway down the slope and prevented it rolling over completely. The steering wheel was badly bent where Linda had hit it and there was severe damage to the front and side of the car.

There was a sequel to this. Linda spent the afternoon in bed but developed severe abdominal pain as the afternoon wore on. I feared she might have ruptured her bladder or bowel when she hit the steering wheel, so called in a surgeon friend who quickly diagnosed nothing more than fear and an over-full bladder!

Now we were in our own home at last the kids were able to have pets and animals in the way of chooks, pet sheep, a lovely dog, a cat, a small pony kept in the city council land next door and sundry other animals such as baby rabbits or hares. I am afraid these latter did not last long – Jasper was rather good at digging into their pens.

*117*

Mark, like the others became very fond of animals, accumulating pets when he could, although most if not all of them suffered from the depredations of Jasper.

Jasper became a well-known character in the district. He was able to turn on a toothy grin and used to tour the homes of sympathetic neighbours, using his wiles to beg a scrap of food. He did the rounds of a number of houses every day. His greatest moment of glory came about when Linda, then at primary school, made a morning appearance on the local radio station for a brief interview. The announcer asked her a number of questions, including about pets. Linda said we had a dog called Jasper and then added, 'He isn't allowed out at present.' 'Why is that?' 'Because his girl friend who lives near us isn't well,' replied Linda. End of interview.

Linda was given a pet lamb by one of my farmer patients. She absolutely worshipped this pet, which bonded to her immediately, following her wherever it could, even to school if it was not tied up. One of the sights of Allan Street was of Jill riding our small BSA Bantam motorcycle up the hill from school with Linda on the back and the pet lamb running frantically after them, maaing loudly until it could catch up with its surrogate mum.

We also had a series of cats, which all the kids loved, as we did. We tended to take them on holidays. This was not always without incident since they often seemed to disappear just when we were about to depart for home again. Our favourite was a Siamese whom we named Ming and who lived with us for 18 years. He was a lovely puss of great character, as this breed can be. Despite being only a kitten he soon sorted Jasper out when he got aggressive on first acquaintance, and they lived in a state of armed neutrality thereafter.

Ming used to demand to sleep in our bed when he was cold, especially in the winter. He would jump up on the bed, pulling at an exposed nose, thankfully usually my wife's, until allowed under the bedclothes. Everyone knows how you can hear your heartbeat in your ear when you lie on your side? One night I came half awake in the middle of the night to hear my heart pounding along at a frightening speed. Coronary, I thought, this being the fear of most over-busy doctors with Type A personality (which apparently I have). I felt for my wrist pulse and found it thudding along happily at its usual rate, so I lay down again to ponder the matter. Immediately there was this rapid pulse in my ears again. In my bemused state from a deep sleep it took me a short time to find that Ming was asleep on the pillow between us and my ear was close to his chest.

Life seemed to be a series of laughs – most of them, in retrospect, at my expense. We had steps down to the street below which had become distorted by a very large tree root growing underneath. It so happened that our neighbour had a pepper tree adjacent to this invasion and I asked him if we could perhaps sever this root. He was not only unwilling but was somewhat put out at my request. But it bothered me that our place was crumbling under our very eyes, so one day I drilled a hole in the exposed root and filled it with plant poison 2-4-5T. The result was dramatic: a large part of our boundary hedge promptly died, while the pepper tree continued to thrive!

Our house was on a hillside of the Grampians. We had made reasonable tracks to the top and we used to go for walks up there. One weekend I glanced up from my gardening to see a couple of young lads doing something odd about halfway up. I got my binoculars and was horrified to see them pushing and heaving with their feet at a large boulder embedded in the hillside directly above us. There would be few boys who have not done something similar, but if this large mass had been released it could have gone clean through a wall or roof. I yelled out to them and shot through the fence and up the hill at top speed. But I ran out of puff a bit before getting to their altitude, finally stopping in distress. I shall never forget – and nor would Jill who was watching – that these two scallywags, instead of taking to their scrapers, came down to meet me.

It was hard to tell them off after that, but I did describe the horrific possibilities had they been successful in their excavation of the rock. I also asked their names, which they freely gave, and found I knew their parents. It went no further and I watched the progress of these two into successful professional men of good standing in our community.

Jillian had an uncle, Ivan Mackersey, whose wife had inherited a large private hotel in lovely grounds quite close to town. Wainui House was the upmarket venue at that time for most of the visiting gentry, including vice-regal parties. Uncle Ivan had an accountancy practice in Wellington and used to commute to and from Nelson in the weekends, helping to run the hotel when he was here. He had always been a keen amateur fisherman and much taken with the sea fishing in and around Nelson. He bought a launch, which he used to take out every weekend, coming back with enough fish to last the hotel for the following week.

Uncle Ivan was a very generous man and loved our kids. He had one son, who was away at university doing architecture at this time, so he lavished a lot of attention on our family. He was also a man of fixed ideas, some of them absolutely cranky. For example he told the story, in all seriousness, of a friend of his who had suffered a severe electric shock that nearly killed him, and said that ever since then he never needed matches as he only had to hold his finger near a gas burner to ignite it. There were many such stories and the children loved them.

The launch was quite famous locally. It was 30 feet in length, with only an eight-foot beam, double ended and planked with kauri on closely spaced ribs. It had an enormous uncovered hand-started twin-cylinder Lister diesel engine. She had an unusual name, *E1*. It was said that she was built for an ex-navy crew member of one of the famous WW1 Commander Campbell's Q ships, which were used to decoy and destroy German submarines, and named after one of them.

This boat was quite fast for her time and won quite a few races in the annual regatta on Nelson Harbour. On race day it was incredible to watch Uncle Ivan unload all his junk including ropes, anchors and life-jackets, and then wind back the engine governor to allow the poor old Lister to over-rev, then put any passengers right up forward on the deck to keep her nose down. This sort of treatment did the engine no good at all and many failures occurred in subsequent years, including a broken crankshaft.

He was an incredible fisherman and a canny weather forecaster, and a weekend trip away with him was an unforgettable experience – I went along many times. We would leave Nelson late afternoon, troll for a barracuda or kahawai to use as bait, and stop to catch some cod for the evening meal at a good spot about 12 miles up the coast. Then we'd proceed further to lay some nets at Walker's Bay near Cape Soucis, the entrance to Croisilles Harbour. We would motor into Whangarae Bay in the Croisilles to anchor for the night.

In the morning, getting up at dawn, we would go out to deep water off Cape Soucis, where we would fish for snapper and cod, always with wonderful results. Eventually we would head for home, about three hours away, cleaning fish as we rolled along in the inevitable sea breeze. There was not a moment's rest in the whole trip. Even cooking and eating were done at high speed.

Uncle Ivan was the only man I have ever seen who worked a double fishing line as a matter of routine. Never using a rod, which is far too slow apparently, he would put sinker and hooks on each end of a hemp fishing line, then bait up one set of hooks and hurl it into the sea. As soon as he got a bite he would jerk his line to set the hook and toss the other end in before pulling in his inevitable fish, removing it, rebaiting and waiting for the next bite. On a good day when the fish were really on their feed, it was a sight to behold this small man working this one line like a whirlwind.

He generously allowed us to use *E1* whenever we wished and boating became a great family pleasure – all of our kids have followed it ever since. I did routine maintenance as well as making quite a lot of improvements, and kept her fuelled and in good condition for use at any time. We had some grand holidays, taking her away for two weeks at a time to the Abel Tasman National Park with the family.

Age and time caught up with Uncle Ivan and he had to sell the launch. By this time lighter and more easily managed and maintained craft were common, but he had certainly made an impact on the local boating community, as had *E1*, which is still afloat and in the area. His wife predeceased Uncle Ivan and he retired to Nelson, where he converted Wainui House into flats. He died in his late eighties and I have been left the job of looking after the 11 flats at Wainui House, which now has a city council heritage classification. Some of the lovely old trees are also protected.

During our explorations of the Nelson region we came across a cottage at Boundary Bay, a small bay near the entrance to Torrent Bay in the Abel Tasman National Park, 25 miles north-west of Nelson. There is no road access. This cottage was owned by Ted Biddle, the pharmacist mentioned earlier. We rented it several times and ultimately bought it from him.

I had no title to the land, which was owned by the late Miss Ralphine Richardson, whom I went to see to ask if I could have some security of tenure. She had never been to see the area, despite having extensive holdings in the region, at Torrent Bay as well as Tonga Bay. I persuaded her to come for a trip and chartered a launch from Kaiteriteri, taking her to see it all. Because of my family connections with the area and because, she said, her two adopted sons were showing no interest in the property (totalling 34 acres) she granted me a lease in perpetuity at a peppercorn rental.

When she died some years later her beneficiaries were understandably not happy to find that they owned valuable property to which they had no legal access because of my registered lease. After some negotiation I bought the land around the cottage, 4.13 hectares in all, at valuation.

We have a plentiful water supply from a spring in the adjacent hill, lots of lovely bush, a cottage only about 20 metres from the sea and a haven for the family. Access is by boat. Using our runabout, which we tow to and launch at Kaiteriteri, it takes us about one hour 40 minutes from home to the cottage.

It is now held by a family trust for the use and pleasure of Jill's and my descendants, but may not be subdivided or exploited commercially. About two years ago I declined an offer from the Department of Conservation to buy part of it.

My practice was still expanding and full of interest. Most doctors have strange experiences and one such for me was close to my home where two elderly sisters lived. Both were single, and I used to see them from time to time professionally in their equally elderly home. One of them had high blood pressure for which we had little or no drug control in those days. The other was a diabetic who gradually became blind, being guided and cared for by her sister.

One day I received a call from this blind sister, who had managed to reach the phone and get the telephone exchange to call me, asking me to come at once as her sister was ill. When I got there I found this blind lady attempting to crawl back through the house to her sister, who was on the floor of another room and who was dead from a massive stroke. It was a moving and pathetic situation.

Well, this lovely woman lived on for quite some time and we arranged for home help. I called often and became close to her. She then had a series of strokes herself and became bedridden, eventually having a massive one which I realised, having been called by her live-in help, would end her life quite soon. I sat with her for the next few hours since she was alone. She was without religious beliefs but not antagonistic in the matter, which we had discussed several times. After some hours at her bedside I rang my close friend Francis Hulme Moir, Bishop of Nelson, and explained the situation. He offered to come and keep me company for a while. We sat there chatting about this and that for some time, after which he said a short prayer and departed.

Not long afterwards it was apparent that the old lady was about to die. Her heart stopped, whereupon, to my astonishment she sat straight up in bed, opened her eyes and gave an ecstatic smile while looking straight ahead. She then fell back quite dead.

Then there was another apparently tragic situation that finished in a strange fashion. One Sunday we had all been away boating for the weekend and arrived home to hear the phone ringing. It was my efficient receptionist ringing from the local Baptist church to say that one of my patients, an elderly Mr B, had died during the service. Could I come down at once? So I shot down in my rough clothes to find the minister and his congregation with a distraught elderly wife all waiting for me on the footpath outside. I apologised for my appearance, feeling very heathen on this tranquil Sunday evening, and went into the church with the minister, wife and receptionist to find Mr B lying sideways on the pew where he had fallen from a sitting position. I opened one of his eyes to check for vital signs, whereupon he woke up, sat up, and said, 'Hello, doctor, what are you doing here?'

I made no friends by muttering that it was not much of a tribute to the sermon. The congregation all came back and they all lived happily ever after – sort of.

Then there are the extraordinarily macabre situations that can occur. My consulting rooms were almost directly above a picture theatre. One afternoon one of the theatre staff came up and asked if I could come urgently as they thought one of the audience had been taken ill. Down I went into the darkened theatre, where the usher took me down the aisle, pointed to someone in the middle of the row of seats and said he seemed to have gone to sleep.

Having just come from the outside into a darkened theatre I found it hard to see, and even harder to scramble along a row of occupied seats in front of viewers who were totally engrossed with the film. 'Excuse me, excuse me,' I said as I went, and each ignored me while trying to peer around me at the screen.

Eventually I got to the fellow and found no sign of life, but we had to get him out into the aisle where I could get a better look at him. It was decided that they would continue the movie and keep the theatre dark. We cleared out the viewers who were between victim and aisle, and I managed to pull him out by the shoulders and eventually confirmed my suspicions. He was dead.

I did not know the poor man so I advised the manager to ring the police and returned to my busy surgery.

Euthanasia is a subject that surfaces from time to time for doctors, and our perspective in this matter probably differs somewhat from that of lay people. Strangely enough, it is not a subject I have heard debated among doctors, so I can only offer my own observations.

I have never had a patient ask me to terminate their life – for any reason whatsoever. I must have had tens of thousands of consultations with patients in general practice, with hundreds of people dying of old age and other conditions. But no matter how miserable some of them have been, not one has raised the subject of euthanasia. Yet it has been brought up a number of times by relatives of the sick and by other people who are themselves in good health.

I have had long discussions with some patients in normal health who strongly advocate euthanasia, but later, when they are living what they would formerly have described as 'a useless life', they never mention it again. My impression is that it is mainly advocated by people in good health – for others.

When I am asked for my opinion I ask, 'Who is going to do the killing?' Certainly I would not take on that task. Making the path easier for the disabled and dying is very advanced nowadays.

# 14

NELSON HAD AN ACTIVE CAR CLUB which ran all sorts of activities – rallies, hill climbs and gymkhanas as well as an annual two-day beach race meeting. I had retained my interest in cars and motorsport so joined up and became involved locally as well as doing marshalling work at major international events held around the country.

The annual two-day race meeting was held on the dry clay/sand at the Tahunanui back beach. An informal sort of a show, it was a great social event as well as a popular outing for locals and summer visitors, with competitors arriving from all over New Zealand with hotted-up saloon cars, genuine racing cars, high-performance sports cars and home-made 'specials'.

I did most of my competing in a Morris Minor convertible, which I modified by putting in a high-compression cylinder block fitted with an MG cylinder head, twin carburettors and a modified rear suspension. It required aviation fuel to run properly, but I also fitted a water-injection device, which allowed it be used for town running on standard fuel. It went well and I had a lot of fun.

Ever on the search for greater performance, I experimented with oxygen injection for a while. I made up a fitting to allow oxygen to be injected into the inlet manifold, connecting this to one of my cylinders of anaesthetic oxygen on the floor beside my seat. The idea was that when I wanted the extra burst of power I would turn on the oxygen slowly and also increase the fuel intake by pulling out the choke lever.

Alas, the idea was good (I still think) but the experiment failed with accompanying slight drama.

There was a steep street in Nelson, with little traffic, which was useful to test the performance of one's car. I did a test to see what speed my car would go up it in normal fashion, and then did a run to test it with oxygen. Halfway up at full revs I turned on the oxygen and pulled out the choke control. There was a loud bang followed by total silence. Inspection showed I had blown the carburettor partly off the inlet manifold. Ah well, it was just an idea.

I became active enough in motorsport to be involved in some of the major racing events around the country and made regular trips to the New Zealand Grand Prix at Ardmore, the Lady Wigram Trophy Race at Wigram airfield and several other smaller events. At these race meetings I often did flag marshalling work and had really close-up views of the masters who came to New Zealand in those days with their cars. I saw Stirling Moss, Jack Brabham, Ken Wharton, Archie Scott Brown, Peter Whitehead and countless others. We saw Bruce Mclaren and others start their racing careers.

The cars were many and varied, with a few home-built specials, including the

*123*

famous Maybach Special in the early stages. There were many famous factory-built racing cars, with names such as Alfa Romeo, Maserati, Ferrari, Jaguar, Lister, Cooper, BRM and even a demonstration by a purely jet-driven vehicle.

The most awesome was the BRM, a 16-cylinder 1500cc car with centrifugal supercharger, running on pure alcohol and developing about 600 horsepower. It had the most incredible, unforgettable shriek as it wound up its revs. Few drivers could handle it as the power came in with a surge so strong that it would often just spin around in a circle: we saw this several times at Ardmore when Ken Wharton was racing it. It was a tricky and unreliable vehicle and only three remain in existence, one of which runs from time to time at demonstrations in England.

Ken Wharton was a flamboyant driver from the UK. One year he was competing in the sportscar race in a lovely Ferrari two-seater – an extremely high-speed vehicle which is now in the Southward Museum at Paraparaumu. His only significant opposition was from a D-type Jaguar driven by Kiwi Bob Gibbons, but this could not hold the Ferrari, which Wharton drove in a very exuberant fashion, despite being in the lead. As he came past the stands in the middle of the finishing straight he slid a little – which was not surprising given the way he was driving – and clipped a straw bale on the inside of the track. With a sound like a deep explosion he and the car hurtled into the air, turned upside down and crashed back onto the track, still at high speed. Wharton died shortly afterwards.

Stirling Moss was an incredible driver, especially when he got himself worked up with his adrenaline really running. But to us marshals he seemed bad-tempered and arrogant. It was the marshal's duty if one saw a faster car trying to overtake a slower one to wave a blue flag at the slower driver to advise him to allow the faster one to pass. If Stirling Moss thought that the marshal had failed in this he waved his fist angrily at us. But it was quite a sight to see him really set out to win when he had been delayed for some small engine or chassis hitch. He would almost go berserk, flinging the car around at enormous speed in controlled slides and four-wheel drifts. He was at his best in the rain.

Jack Brabham, world champion, was quite different. He was an unspectacular driver of great courtesy and charm who turned out very high-speed laps with little apparent effort.

Our Nelson New Year two-day beach racing event went from strength to strength, with more and better cars each year. But the surface of the compacted clay/sand track was not up to modern safety standards, and neither were the cars in those days, as there were no requirements for open cars to have roll bars or any other modern safety protection. Eventually there were two fatal accidents.

In one case the driver suffered from a disability in one hand and wrist. He had consulted me professionally some time before the race meeting to obtain his competition licence, which all drivers had to have before entering any speed events. I was a friend of this chap, but was not convinced of his ability to control a car in these races (which I knew well, having competed in them myself). I told him that I could not give him a licence, and outlined the reasons. He was not happy and went to see another doctor who had no knowledge of motor racing, and to my horror he was given a competition licence. In one of the races, while driving his Chrysler Valiant saloon at highish speed, he skidded badly on one of the bends, lost control, started to roll over and his door opened. He partly fell out as it rolled over and the door slammed shut onto him, decapitating him.

The other accident occurred at the same bend to a fit, young man who had built his own vehicle from mainly Vauxhall components. It was a single-seater racing car, quite fast and very well built. But in the style of those days, when he sat in the cockpit, his head and shoulders were well outside the vehicle with no protection apart from his crash helmet.

At the western bend, which had been badly cut up in the racing, he capsized and the car landed upside down while he was still in the cockpit. We had him into an ambulance in moments and tried resuscitation measures en route to hospital but he died within a few minutes. I had the harrowing job of visiting his young wife at her parents' home to tell her this awful news.

In those days in the case of a major accident it was usually the doctor who was telephoned, not the ambulance service. If the doctor deemed it necessary he would order the ambulance (there were no helicopters then). Ministry of Transport staff gave us doctors great co-operation if we were driving to an accident at high speed. The receptionist would ring them and a patrol car would travel ahead, clearing the way for us. At one time I had a beautiful Mini Cooper which I imported new from England and it went like the clappers. One day there was a serious accident on the Whangamoa Saddle road about 15 miles from Nelson and I did not see the traffic officer until I had been on the accident site several minutes.

I think the worst drive I ever had was one night when someone rang from French Pass to say their baby daughter was very ill, describing symptoms of meningitis which made me fear for her life. I told them to wrap her up, drive towards Nelson and I would set out with an ambulance and meet them en route.

The road to French Pass is, even nowadays, very winding with a pot-holed gravel surface. Forty years ago it was even worse. But I had a good driver in the ambulance and we eventually met the couple in their car with the baby. One of the parents came with me while I took the baby in the back of the ambulance.

A brief examination confirmed my worst fears – she had meningitis and was seriously ill, almost moribund in fact. I informed the driver, who went as fast as he safely could. A journey in the back of an ambulance on a winding gravel road at night in a state of severe anxiety is not an experience I would recommend and I was quite ill myself.

However, we got there and the diagnosis was confirmed: a rare form of meningitis. The hospital medical staff did a magnificent job, injecting a special form of antibiotic directly into the spinal spaces and she recovered fully. It gives me great pleasure to see this lovely young woman and her parents from time to time at church.

## VINTAGE DOCTOR

My interest in motorsport continued and in 1955 my friend Des Hay, who was in dental practice at nearby Motueka, persuaded me to enter, with him, the Southland Centennial Trial, an international car rally to celebrate Invercargill's centennial in 1956.

The course, we found, was to be from Invercargill to Nelson and back to Invercargill, virtually circumnavigating the South Island, mostly on back-country roads. The distance was 2500 miles in five stages, to be travelled at varying speeds. These speeds, distances and routes were not advised until immediately before that stage began. The whole trip would take five days and timing was to be to the second, with a point lost for each second that one was ahead of or behind time at each secret checkpoint, of which there were several for each section. No navigating calculators were permitted, nor was there any time allowed for rest, refuelling, repairs, maintenance, food or toilet requirements.

The problem was that neither of us had a car suitable for what we knew would be a tough test. I approached Phil Vining, head of the large family motor business Vining & Scott, which had the Morris car franchise (among others), and asked if his firm might be interested in sponsoring us with some sort of vehicle. As well as being a shrewd businessman Phil was also a motoring enthusiast. He consulted with the New Zealand Morris agent, Dominion Motors in Wellington, after which he rang me with the most unbelievable offer. They would make available a brand new Morris Oxford and any spares we required. The car would be handed over to us several weeks before the event so that we could run it in, a condition being that this was done carefully and properly, and we were to allow the agents any advertising rights available.

As more information came in, Des and I gradually realised that the venture was too big for us to handle without more help, so we set about persuading our mutual friend George Topliss to join us. George is a precision engineer of renown as well as another motoring enthusiast. He took a lot of persuasion but eventually agreed to join in the fun – and thank goodness he did.

It was decided that Des would do most of the driving, except when he needed a break, I would do most of the navigating, and George would be our assistant, as well as being in charge of the mechanical side of things. I got the job of getting all the gear together for repairs, maintenance and emergencies and also took charge of the car to get it well run in and prepared.

We gathered together a mass of spares and a comprehensive kit of tools, including a portable gas welding plant and tyre chains. There were no electronic calculators then and we had to rely on the use of slide rules, logarithms and pure maths calculation, so we took plenty of paper, pens and pencils. Portable adding machines were permitted but I reasoned that any slight error in the original input figures would be greatly magnified by multiplication in these gadgets, and this proved the case in the experiences of some other competitors. Every detail was important when seconds counted.

The other main concern was our timing gear. I consulted a local watch and clock expert, the late Henry Rogers, who was most helpful. He tracked down a small chronometer type of wristwatch with a stopwatch on it, and offered to lend it to us for the duration of the trial. He also recommended a good old-fashioned alarm clock for coarse timing and as a backup in case of accident to the smaller unit, and also a normal sporting type of stopwatch for timing of short sections. The chronometer and clock were checked for accuracy and we learnt to set them by the time signals on our car radio.

I put together an emergency medical kit and added something I never had done before (or since): caffeine capsules. I had a chemist friend make them up to be used only in a dire emergency to help us stay awake.

We bought detailed road maps for the whole of the South Island, prepared formulae for the time to travel one mile, five miles etc, at all sorts of speed fractions. George made a small wheel on a handle which when run along a road line on a map measured the distance fairly accurately and we made boards for our equipment. We took plenty of torches as well as a good spotlight.

Des made the observation that fatigue was going to be an important factor, pointing out that it would be worsened by sleeping in a tent and doing our own cooking at the end of each day. He emphasised the importance of getting a good rest before trying to clean and service the car each day. Since we knew where we were going to stop after each stage, we wrote to friends in each of these towns and asked if we could have a bed for the night (or day if we had travelled at night).

With no time allowance for refuelling, accidents or incidents we needed to develop routines for these, and practise them, which we did with a stopwatch. We learnt to change a wheel in less than two minutes and our refuelling stops were magic: one put in the fuel, another checked tyre pressures, oil and water and the third paid.

On our way to Invercargill to start the trial we took time to reconnoitre some of the bad roads we thought they would put us over, which proved valuable. The car ran well and we practised navigation at all sorts of speeds for the whole way.

At Invercargill we had nice comfortable digs in a private home and duly reported to HQ. There were 70 entrants with a moderate number of experienced overseas folk and their vehicles. We had a lot of fun together, including a rabbit-skinning competition with a bunch of rabbits I had shot from the car in some of the back country. I did not tell the other competitors I had been a professional rabbiter so managed to clean up that little test and got my laundry done free of charge as a result.

The local Morris agent checked our car for us and advised us how to waterproof the ignition distributor, which he said was a bit of weakness in heavy rain. Neighbours were intrigued to see us turn the hose on the engine when it was running but it was 100 per cent effective and saved us at more than one creek crossing where others got stuck. We also painted advertising signs for our sponsors on the car.

The big day came and off we went to Dunedin, via weird and rough roads. There were frequent speed changes and many had required average speeds with decimal points in them, which made for difficult calculations. We tried to check each mile, and separately each five miles, to work out whether we were ahead of or behind time but we did not do well on this first section, partly due to an error of mine, fatigue-induced. After 12 hours or more we were all pretty stressed out and glad to be picked up by our kind hosts and taken to a home for a shower, cleanup, meal and a good sleep. We washed our clothes each night and in the morning, with a further shower, a good breakfast and clean clothes, we checked and cleaned our vehicle and awaited the next start time.

Thus went our daily routine, with other stops at Christchurch, Nelson and Timaru. We had an enormous amount of fun and made only two further serious errors, either of which could have put us out of the running. The first was when we took a wrong turn at night on one of those awful flat, featureless roads in North Canterbury and got wildly off track. We drove fast back to the main road where we knew the cars had to pass, waited until a numbered car came up and calculated our time from his time, allowing for the extra distance we had covered. We must have done our sums correctly.

The other incident was also at night when we were on a winding, dusty road, again in North Canterbury, with a much too high average speed requirement. Des was driving but occasionally ran into heavy dust hanging around from the car in front. Suddenly we came to a sharp-right hand bend where the road went around the head of a small gully. But this bend was obscured by a dust cloud and the car went straight ahead and crashed into the gully. We were travelling quite fast and nearly turned over but Des held it beautifully and bounced it straight ahead and back onto the road, with George shouting, 'Ride it, Des, ride it!'

It was over in a flash but we had a flat tyre, so went into our routine (in the dark) and managed to get the spare on before the next car arrived upon us two minutes later. We went on but there was an unpleasant rattling noise from the other back wheel and George held me out of the window as we travelled so I could look at it with a torch. I was most unhappy and we decided to make up a bit of time and stop for a thorough inspection at Cheviot. We found that we had pulled three of the four wheel nuts right off and completely pulled the tyre off the wheel, which went flat. It had grass in the well of the rim.

Our night trip to Nelson took about 14 hours and we had a good rest at our home base.

We got more and more expert at our calculations and routine and by the time we got to the second-to-last stage we felt we were doing pretty well. The points showed we were lying in third place. We walked around the carpark at Timaru and noted that our opponents were all looking pretty jaded. In fact some looked awful, especially after camping for the night. So we sent a telegram to our main sponsor, Phil Vining: 'Lying third and closing the gap.'

Our car was in good nick, George having previously welded up a cracked air filter bracket, but we were concerned at a few discrepancies in our mileage readings. We worked out that our tyre wear was significant enough to be affecting the speedometer and odometer, so measured the diameter difference and made the appropriate correction to all our calculations from then on.

We left Timaru on our final leg at about 4pm and drove for a total of 16 hours, 23 minutes and 15 seconds to the final checkpoint at Invercargill in the early morning. We were just about done so swallowed a caffeine capsule each and this helped us stay sharp. On arrival we went to our digs and fell into bed.

An hour or two later I was woken by Des shouting, 'Wake up, Hank, we've won!' And we had. We rang our sponsor and families and interviews for radio, newspapers, and films for newsreel followed. We cleaned up the car and ourselves for the parade and prizegiving at the showgrounds that night which was followed by a massive party.

First prize was £1000, and lots of other goodies thrown in by sponsoring firms. It may not sound like much money nowadays, but in 1956, to give some indication of values, that was the cost of a brand new Mark 7 Jaguar saloon in New Zealand. An equivalent new Jaguar would nowadays cost about $140,000.

We headed triumphantly for Nelson once more, this time on tarsealed roads! We were met by family and friends about 10 miles out of Nelson and drove in to a grand reception outside the Post Office where the mayor, families, friends, news people, Nelson Car Club officials and sponsors were waiting. It was pretty emotional stuff, especially as we were absolutely done in.

We went up to my home for a beer and I was immediately brought back into the real world. The telephone rang and a distraught neighbour said, 'Doctor, please come quickly, D is dying from a bee sting.' I ran flat out with my bag to an unconscious youth. His heart was still beating weakly, but I managed to inject some Adrenalin into a vein and he rapidly recovered. His acute allergic reaction to the bee sting is known as anaphylaxis and can be lethal. I often see this now middle-aged fit-looking man at our cathedral and it brings back many memories.

Looking back on the event I realise that it was far too dangerous – such driving hours with lack of rest and no refreshment would not be permitted these days. The roads were all open to all traffic and some of the average speeds were far too high for safety. Many cars were battered and damaged in the five days, some seriously. There was one death, on a section of the road in the Buller Gorge, where we had decided it was not possible to adhere safely to the average speed set.

But we made many friends and welded a lifelong tremendous bond between the three of us, Des, George and me, which is just as strong 43 years later. And the Mido chronometric watch still goes as well now as it did when it took us to victory.

We divided the spoils evenly and I spent my share on a good second-hand Jaguar, which gave me great service as well as a lifelong love and respect for that make. In fact Des, George and I all own a Jaguar today.

Our Morris Oxford ran without murmur the whole distance of the competition, as well as on the trip there and back. It wore out a set of tyres, needed a new windscreen due to pitting from driving in the wake of other cars, and also had to be completely repainted because of stone marks. But mechanically it was absolutely sound, a great tribute to a family saloon. The sponsors got good advertising.

## VINTAGE DOCTOR

A patient and a friend of mine, Ray Sharland, became interested in radio-controlled model aircraft in the early days of this hobby, and after seeing him flying his models I decided to have a go. With Ray's help I built up a balsa model with a six-foot wingspan and a small diesel model motor. These models had a one-channel radio and this controlled the rudders, which were so arranged that when held in a turn the aircraft also dived, giving some height control.

Before a flight the small fuel tank was filled with a mixture of castor oil, kerosene and ether (fairly easy to acquire in my profession). The engine was started and radio control tested and then the operator galloped across the field and hurled the model into the air. You would then dash back to the radio transmitter, grab the small cord-mounted switch and take control. This was usually successful but not always, in which case there would be a mad dash for a car with someone directing the driver where to go to keep track until the model landed after running out of fuel.

We became skilled at flying these machines, especially at spot landing them, and it was quite normal to have them come to a halt only a few paces away. We flew them at the Nelson aerodrome in the weekends and they became quite an attraction, buzzing around. But we had many unusual incidents – some excruciatingly funny, others not.

These days were always an occasion for a family picnic, with the kids usually roaring around after tennis balls and playing with Jasper, who somehow also always came. One day I was bringing my machine in for a spot landing in front of us. It was travelling quite fast when our small son Mark, aged about three, stepped out into its path. I jumped out in front of him, put my hand out into the path of the model and just managed to stop it before it hit him.

My machine weighed over 6 pounds and it split my hand right open. I had to go to hospital and finished up in the main theatre getting it sewn up. The theatre staff, whom I knew well, were most amused when they heard I had been hit by my own model plane.

My good friend George Topliss was also interested in flying so he decided to join the fun and make a model similar to ours. However, George never was conventional in any of his ideas (he later invented, patented and marketed the first unit shower control in New Zealand and this still dominates the market) and he decided to make his machine of metal, using an aluminium alloy. It was a very elegant and beautifully made affair, even having small windows along the fuselage with nylon curtains. George also made his own radio components. In finished form it was about double the weight of our balsa models and obviously needed more power, so he put on a much larger motor.

The day arrived for its trial flight and he started it up, ran madly across the field and hurled it into the air, whereupon it happily landed a little in front of him with the motor still going. After several tries and many adjustments to wing angle and so on we all realised that George's own sprint speed was inadequate to give enough flying speed for his new model.

It so happened that I had my Morris Minor convertible there and we had a great idea. I drove it across the field, straight into the wind while George stood up in the passenger seat holding the model with engine running. When he judged it was going fast enough to fly he gave it a shove and let go. Eureka! It flew all right, and flew well – for a while, but it developed some cranky characteristics.

It occasionally had radio trouble, with consequent loss of control. The first time this happened it ran into and damaged the main power lines for the airport, thus throwing the control tower into chaos. Somehow George talked his way out of that and was allowed to continue flying at the airport. But a week or two later suddenly it started climbing steeply until it stalled, pitched nose down, dived a short distance, reared up again, stalled, and so on, with each climb and dive becoming more severe and longer. The large concrete apron in front of an ex-RNZAF hangar was often used by skaters and on this fine sunny day it was crowded with young people happily swinging around, doing no one any harm. To our horror, George's heavy metal model was now doing vertical dives just above these people, unbeknown to them. It did its final kamikaze and disappeared. We waited for the screams of the injured, but to our happy surprise there were none. So we drove over to find the offending machine buried nose deep into the turf beside the concrete, with a small crowd of surprised folk staring at it.

We were banished from the airport after that, but found another suitable field between Stoke and Richmond, which has now been developed into a full sports complex. The following weekend George's plane was the centre of interest as he reckoned he had ironed out all the bugs – and he had. It flew beautifully and handled like a dream. When it ran out of fuel, George started to bring it in towards us on the glide, but, with little experience of successfully landing it under control, and the model perilously close to some power lines, George thrust the control knob at me and said, 'You bring it in.'

Too late – there was no way to avoid the power lines and the plane flew straight into them.

This set of lines was not just any old power line but was a main line to the local substation and carried, I think, 30,000 volts. There was a blinding flash, a loud boom, and the plane fell to the ground in flames (George's curtains). Then we saw a series of flashes between pylons as the cables swung together as a result of the short circuit, and finally a deep boom from the Stoke substation. We stood there in sickened silence with our hearts racing, appalled at the carnage. The only sound was the wailing of a small child on whom I had trodden as I reared back at the first strike.

Next we saw a farmer in the distance bounding down the hills from his cowshed where his afternoon milking had been brought to an abrupt halt. George with his customary diplomatic ability apologised to the farmer, then drove to the nearest phone and rang the Waimea Power Board emergency number. A model plane had flown into some power lines and interrupted the afternoon milking of a nearby farmer, he told them. The chap who answered the phone said, 'That's a funny thing: the same thing happened a weekend or two ago somewhere else.' No more was heard. That model never flew again but hangs on a wall in George's home.

Ray Sharland and I talked about making our models into flying-boats as we would then have limitless unobstructed surfaces from which to fly and land. Ray made a beautiful conversion of his fuselage to a hull and we headed off to try it. I got out Uncle Ivan's launch and, towing the dinghy, headed up the harbour where we anchored far from all obstructions.

Nelson's harbour has tides of up to 4.5 metres, and this gives a goodly flow of current. Ray stoked up his flying-boat, cranked it up, and when it was running smoothly he placed it in the water, head to wind, and let it go. It promptly and gracefully turned its tail to the wind and headed off up harbour, planing beautifully but not taking off because of the tail wind. Ray tried to turn it by radio but it would not respond.

There was no alternative but to follow and retrieve it when it finally ran out of fuel. We had to use the dinghy as the upper harbour was too shallow for the launch. Ray is no boatie but he put oars to rowlocks and set off in the heavy old clinker-built dinghy in manful style, aided by a strong inflowing tide. He finally picked it up and then spent ages rowing back against the tide to the anchored launch.

I guessed what would happen and it surely did. He reached the boat, had his back to it, shipped the oars neatly, picked up his precious plane and turned around to find the launch by now about 50 metres away – the current had carried him upstream again. How we laughed.

Ray was an absolute wonder to watch, performing with and low flying his plane, and he entered the South Island championships. His exquisitely built machine was accidentally smashed shortly before the competition so I offered my cranky out-of-line affair and he took it, winning the championship.

Our time spent with these radio-controlled models, especially the ability to spot land them when the engines ran out of fuel, was an enormous help to us when we both took up gliding a few years later.

# 15

IN ABOUT THE EARLY 1960s there was an epidemic of Asian flu. As usual, Nelson was hit later than most other areas but we still had a pretty bad time, with several deaths. We GPs worked night and day seeing hundreds of people but were able to offer little except for good nursing care and treatment for complications such as pneumonia.

At Nelson College, which had a large boarding establishment, several hundred were affected and one whole hostel had to be converted to a temporary hospital with the beds so closely packed that there was barely room between them to stand. The sister in charge of the college first aid centre, Isobel Hay, was absolutely wonderful at caring for all her patients. With her good care and some luck, none of the boys succumbed, although we certainly had our worries. All the GPs seemed to stay unaffected until late in the epidemic when we went down one by one, with the workload for the others increasing as a result. It was a tough time for patients, nurses and doctors.

Eventually I also succumbed, but thankfully the epidemic was nearly over by then. I felt awful for a week or two, and my friend Des Hay came to see me when I was convalescent. I told him how annoying it was not to be able to smoke a cigarette without coughing, whereupon he said, 'What a good opportunity to give it away,' which I did – for the first time.

In those days most doctors were smokers: In Nelson I knew of only two who were not. Quite suddenly, from research overseas, the penny dropped as to the causal relationship with lung cancer and later with heart disease and other conditions. Every doctor in Nelson managed to stop smoking and for many years if a new doctor planned to come to the district we told him or her that a smoker would not be welcome. Nowadays very few doctors smoke: they know the dangers only too well.

One day a middle-aged lady came to see me. She had no specific health concerns but was without doubt the largest woman I had ever seen before – or since. She wanted a full checkup and general health advice. I put her on the scales, which I had difficulty reading as she was so large and was astonished to find that the needle went past the end of the scale (at 21 stone) and hard up against the emergency stop.

I asked her to undress and lie on the couch for a full examination. It was very difficult to hear her heart or chest sounds at all, but from what I could hear they seemed all right. But when I took her blood pressure I was astonished to find it also at the top of the scale. I was checking this again when suddenly I noticed that she was going red in the face. When I asked if she was feeling all right she did not answer but quite quickly her red face turned blue, her eyes protruded and she became unconscious.

She had developed pulmonary oedema (congestion of the lungs) due to acute left ventricular failure of the heart. I was in an awful pickle (and she was in a worse one). The required emergency treatment was an intravenous injection and it was almost impossible to find a vein due to her size. And here she was totally naked in an upstairs office in the main street of Nelson, needing emergency admission to hospital.

We rang the hospital, asked for an ambulance and told them to back right across the footpath with the back of the vehicle open against the street door. In the meantime we managed to prop her up, get some oxygen in and give her an injection, some of which went into a vein. She recovered consciousness but was in a dangerous state, still 'poised on the brink'. The ambulance arrived with driver and assistant and between the four of us we managed to get her down the stairs and into it without incident.

She eventually recovered from this attack and came back to see me to discuss a weight-reduction programme with professional help from the Nelson Hospital dietician. She was very good at sticking to the programme and came to see me to be weighed, encouraged and checked over every week for several years.

Her weight and blood pressure gradually reduced until she was about 13 stone, and she was looking and feeling great. We were both so pleased. However, after she left Nelson to live in Motueka she slipped back into her old eating habits, eventually falling dead in the street one day, still quite young.

This woman had the most extraordinary family history I came across in my practice. She had been married, with a daughter. Her husband left and divorced her, then married her sister, producing another family before leaving that wife too. The sisters then set up house together, both with the same name of Mrs .... and both with children of the same name, who were not only cousins but also half-sisters. Very strange.

Another lady patient of mine who was also very much overweight met a new man and decided to reduce. She did so very effectively – so much so that she was left with a large, so-called abdominal apron of loose skin that had once been occupied with fat. It was arranged for a surgeon to excise this. He had not done the operation before but it looked as though it would be a relatively simple procedure. He duly removed the 'apron' and stitched her up, but across her tummy she had a suture line at each end of which was a sort of dog ear sticking up, almost like an adolescent emerging breast. She was most unimpressed with this and I must say it looked a bit bizarre.

It so happened that this woman was employed as a cleaner at the hospital and worked there at night. Among her duties was cleaning the library and the doctors' offices. In the medical library she found a book on plastic surgical work that not only outlined the operation she had just had, but also specified the complications that could ensue if it was not properly performed, including the very cosmetic 'disability' that had resulted in her case. She confronted the surgeon with these facts, claiming negligence, and he had to correct it.

Unfortunately her prying habits brought this woman to a sticky end. She could not resist having a quick look at any medical records she found on a doctor's desk and after she saw some private details of someone she knew she was stupid enough to gossip about it. It got back to the patient who made an official complaint and the woman was sacked and lucky not to be prosecuted.

I mentioned earlier that I (along with many of my colleagues) had had a falling-out with Dr Percy Brunette, Medical Superintendent of Nelson Hospital. One day I sent in a young patient with severe asthma and bronchitis who was placed in the care of resident physician, Dr John Hiddlestone, whom we all respected. He made excellent progress and upon discharge Dr Brunette told his mother it would be far wiser to bring him to Dr Hiddlestone's asthma clinic than to return to me for follow-up and treatment. The mother was furious because I had been their GP for several years. Dr Hiddlestone's asthma clinic was very good but it was not up to Dr Brunette to advise patients to leave their GPs.

This was the last straw for me, after a series of obnoxious, arrogant actions by this man and I decided to make a formal complaint to the Ethical Committee of the New Zealand Medical Association. I never did hear a formal result of the investigation but I was informed that he had been found to be in error, and I have no doubt that he was reprimanded.

A week or two later he saw me at the hospital, asked me into his office and said, 'Hursthouse, you put me up to the ethics committee?' I said I had, and he actually had the temerity to ask me why. I explained in detail and gained the impression that this man was so sealed in his little cocoon and had been the great dictator for so long that he really had no idea of how he behaved to junior doctors.

He was in no doubt after our chat, and we seemed to have a better understanding from then on. Certainly he never ever attempted to 'ride' me again. But it was a welcome day for many of us when he retired and Dr Hiddlestone was appointed in his place.

A new technique had been developed for cardiac resuscitation, called external cardiac massage, this now being part of the standard CPR method. I was appointed by Nelson Hospital to attend a demonstration course and was delegated to teach appropriate groups of doctors and nurses the technique.

One day a 13-year-old girl came to my surgery for her weekly desensitising injection as recommended by a specialist for her allergic hay fever/asthma. Shortly after she left to go home I had a frantic phone call from her mother. 'Come quickly, doctor, Madeleine is dying!' she said. I leapt into my car and drove like the wind to her home to find her indeed clinically dead, with no sign of heart activity. I applied my first cardiac massage to her, and blew into her lungs. To my astonishment and gratification her pulse returned and she started breathing. In the meantime I had told an aunt who was present to phone the hospital, order an ambulance with doctor and equipment for a case of cardiac arrest. Before it arrived she had another heart arrest, then two or three more in hospital, before she finally stabilised under the care of Dr John Hiddlestone, and made a complete recovery.

I had always wanted to speak to someone whom I knew had been clinically dead, so I asked Madeleine what she had experienced. To my regret she had no memories of anything except 'going to sleep and waking up'. No dreams, tunnels, lights, nothing …

However, one did not always win and the losses always lingered as a shadow in one's mind. If you thought a mistake on your part had caused a tragedy, the mental stress could last for ever.

An elderly man, for whom I had a high regard as well as great personal liking, came to me one day feeling poorly. He had had a dental extraction a week or so previously, apparently quite uncomplicated. He had no specific symptoms, just loss of appetite and energy, which was most unusual for him. A full examination and full blood count revealed no apparent abnormality in any system. It just seemed like a prolonged influenzal bout, or post-influenzal debility.

I sent him home to bed and visited him often to judge progress. He steadily became weaker, found himself unable to eat but still showed no specific symptoms to help me with a diagnosis. A specialist physician, whom I asked for a second opinion, confirmed the lack of specific medical signs except pallor and weakness, so we admitted him to hospital for closer monitoring and arranged a battery of further blood tests.

While we were awaiting the results he died. I was quite shattered and his family were naturally devastated. An autopsy revealed infection of a heart valve with low-grade bacteria, a condition known as subacute bacterial endocarditis. I had seen only one case of this fairly rare condition (in Wellington Hospital) which responds to heavy doses of penicillin. It not uncommonly occurs after extraction of an infected or abscessed tooth, when the walled-off infection is allowed to get into the bloodstream, and sometimes settles onto a damaged or roughened heart valve.

In my anaesthetic work I was interested to observe the surgeons and their differing techniques and personalities. Some were technicians, with little apparent regard for the patient as a person; some were slow and meticulous; others were quick and meticulous; and there were a few who really were not good at handling tools.

I believe a surgeon should be skilled in handling tools of any nature, should have a strong compassion and interest in the patient's whole state, should be deft and quick, and should have a wide view of medical diagnosis in order to avoid unnecessary operations, which I have seen happen.

One man became ill, developed abdominal pain and then jaundice. His surgeon friend decided he had a gallstone and operated on him in a private hospital. During the operation it was found he had nothing wrong with his gall bladder, but had infective hepatitis. With his liver seriously disordered, his system was unable to detoxify the drugs he had been given and he died. Had he been properly investigated, the correct diagnosis would have been obvious.

On the whole, we were lucky in Nelson to be well served with a good team of surgeons and other specialists. However, I can tell of one surgeon at Nelson Hospital who was a charismatic man but who began to drink so heavily that it gradually became evident to his colleagues that it was affecting his work. It got to the point where several anaesthetists decided they would no longer give anaesthetics for him.

One night there was an emergency admission of the offspring of a well-known citizen with an acute appendicitis. This surgeon was on emergency call but was too drunk to operate, and another surgeon did the job for him. All three involved were upset and it was decided to bring up the matter at a meeting of the local branch of the Medical Association.

I was president of the local division at the time. The surgeon in question did not attend, but there was long and frank discussion about him. It was acknowledged that this man had considerable skill in medical insurance matters, arbitration and especially with industrial injuries and claims, but none present had any faith in the safety of his operating. We decided that if he would give up operating his colleagues would refer to him as much work as they could of the specialist consulting type, much of which would probably finish up in court where he performed well.

As president I was given the unenviable task of talking to him about this. I had always got on well with him and bided my time until I met him in the hospital corridor a few days later, whereupon I asked him if we could have a brief chat on Medical Association matters. He listened to me quietly and attentively and then said, 'Thank you, Miles. It is good of you to tell me this,' and smiling quietly he went on his way.

He did not modify his drinking or cease operating in any way but thank goodness we had a Medical Superintendent who realised the real danger and promptly relieved him of his duties. The man eventually finished up being prosecuted and found guilty in an overseas court for gross negligence following a patient's death.

One small bother for GPs is when a patient goes straight to a specialist rather than being checked by a GP first. I know that patients think this can be a waste of money but it is not. For instance, a pain in the back could have a number of causes. A patient could waste a lot of time and money by going to the wrong sort of specialist. Far better to be seen by a GP, who has an open mind and can do some initial investigations before referring the patient to the appropriate specialist.

All doctors have skills which they have been taught at medical school and during their hospital training years. In an emergency they can use these. We were gathered for a meeting one evening at Nelson Hospital but were delayed by the absence of one of our senior physicians. We later found that when he was on his way to the meeting a nursing sister had rushed out into the corridor from the maternity ward to say that a patient had suddenly died. She had been suffering from increasingly severe headaches and was full-term pregnant. The physician did not hesitate but grabbed a scalpel and did a post-mortem Caesarean section to try to save the baby. Unfortunately it was too late and this was unsuccessful. The mother's death was caused by a cerebral haemorrhage from a congenitally weak artery in the brain.

A new doctor decided to set up in town. He was given every encouragement, as we had known him to be an industrious, intelligent, hard-working house surgeon at the hospital. He arranged to buy out the practice of the then most senior doctor, who was keen to retire, and he began work. At Christmas time I asked if he would look after any emergencies for me while I took my family to Hastings for a holiday and he agreed, making similar arrangements with one or two other doctors.

A few days after arriving in Hastings I had a frantic call from a Nelson colleague to say that this new doctor had disappeared, leaving all his own as well as our patients in the lurch. Would I come back at once to help out with the chaos?

I drove back to Nelson at once and it was bedlam. The absent doctor had failed to turn up at his consulting rooms for his afternoon appointments. His receptionist rang his home and spoke to his wife, to find that he had long since left, apparently heading for his surgery. When he could not be traced the police were notified, and they quite rapidly found that he had departed Nelson by air, connected with an international flight and ended up in Western Australia. We never heard from him again but I gather he had female company joining him there.

# 16

*FROM THE TIME I WAS A NIPPER* I was madly interested in aeroplanes and flying and I have retained this interest right through my life. But active participation was quite out of the question when I was young – one had to be wealthy, or to have joined the air force, as a favoured few were able to do. And so my childhood friends and I used to spend a lot of our time hanging around airfields, reading about aircraft, going to airshows, flying models – usually powered by rubber bands – and just dreaming.

One day a friend came to see me at my surgery and asked if I would be interested in the formation of a gliding club in Nelson. To help gather support for the idea, Nelson enthusiasts invited the Blenheim club to come over and have a field day. They agreed, and one lovely day, with almost no wind and clear skies they towed their glider over with a Tiger Moth plane and gave flights from Nelson Airport for quite reasonable fees. My trip that day in their Australian-built Kookaburra two-seat glider, towed off the ground by the Tiger Moth, was the beginning of a long involvement in the sport.

In those days the tow rope was made of nylon and when the tug moved off and the rope became taut, there was no movement of the glider for a time because the rope stretched quite a lot. But then we zipped forward and seemed to leap off the ground, flying at low level for a while until the tug became airborne. After a short while we released the rope and were in free flight. I was hooked! Apart from a slight hiss it was dead quiet, with a beautiful sensation of floating around in space. All too soon we had to return to the airfield, where the pilot did his circuit to a smooth landing on the grass. This short flight was to lead me into a new world, with its culmination some 35 years later when I was allowed to fly one of the world's fastest propeller-driven aircraft.

The enthusiasm generated by this visit of the Blenheim glider led to the formation of the Nelson Gliding Club and the purchase of a new German-built Rhonlerche glider – with pledged, borrowed and donated funds. We were given permission to operate from an area of the Nelson aerodrome and soon had considerable interest from pilot members of the Nelson Aero Club. Especially keen were pilots who were heading towards obtaining their commercial licence, as they could top up their flying hours by acting as tow pilots. Other pilots were interested in gliding itself, finding a new challenge especially in soaring, using rising air and the wind to stay airborne. One pilot, Ivan Evans, became one of the top glider pilots in New Zealand and indeed the world.

We had no bother getting instructors for our operations. As well as the aeroclub-rated instructors, some former World War 2 air force pilots of vast experience enjoyed getting back into flying. One such was Lloyd Parry, who taught many of us and also became hooked on gliding and skilled at soaring our dual machine. He taught me a great deal on and off the field, but I regret to say that his time with the club was brief. He paid a visit to the gliding club at Wigram in Christchurch and was given permission to go off in one of their gliders. This he proceeded to rig, as it was in the usual dismantled state of gliders that are stored away. Special attention was always needed to ensure correct hooking up of the control wires and levers to the various rudder, elevator and aileron bits and pieces. After rigging, a final complete inspection by an independent person was mandatory. Apparently this inspection was not done and when Lloyd was towed off, the glider reared up and then plunged back into the ground, killing him outright. It was found that the elevator control cable had not been correctly connected to the tail unit.

Arthur Jordan, already a pilot, was a prime mover in getting the club off the ground so the various instructors who were helping the club concentrated on training him up to instructor level. As soon as he achieved this he was able to train other club members. Arthur is a stalwart adviser and engineer for the club still, and his conservative approach gave the club an enviable safety record in its early days – and ever since.

The instructor who probably had the most influence on the club in its early stages was Arthur Bradshaw. He certainly had more influence on my flying than any other person. President of the Nelson Aero Club, he had vast experience, having helped pioneer early flying along the lower South Island west coast, landing on beaches in southern Westland. He later became a pilot overseas, rising to be senior captain in Belgium's Sabena Airline. Brad's extensive flying and ferrying of multi-engined bombers during World War 2 saw him clock up about 12,000 hours flying time in 100 different types of aircraft.

When he decided to return to New Zealand after the war, he planned to fly out with his wife and small child, purchasing a Percival Proctor single-engined light aircraft for this purpose. However, on his arrival in Australia the authorities would not allow him to take off to New Zealand since very few single-engined planes had made this trip, and none with wife and baby aboard. Little did they know our Brad. He fought them and when they eventually agreed to let him fly solo if his wife and child travelled by TEAL flying-boat, he demanded that the authorities pay the fares, which they did! Brad kept his plane, *Kiwi Wanderer*, in Nelson and used it regularly. It is now stored at Hunua near Auckland.

Brad and I became close friends and he not only taught me how to fly, (along with other instructors) but gave me lots of hints regarding safety and efficiency gleaned over his lifetime of flying in countless different situations. He also let me take the controls of his Proctor on several occasions. I probably owe my safe flying life to 'Brad' and some ex-topdressing pilot instructors.

He had one nasty accident, however, when he failed to follow one safety precaution. He had bought a de Havilland twin-engined Dragon Rapide, which he restored immaculately. On a trip back from the North Island, with his son aboard, he stopped at Paraparaumu Airport. While there, he wanted to test the magnetoes on one of the engines since it was proving difficult to start. He slowly turned the engine over by hand, pulling the propeller around and listening for the tell-tale click of the impulse. Unbeknown to him the engine ignition switch was on when he pulled it over, but it did not initially start. Hearing no click Brad decided to remove the engine cowl to tap the sticky impulse (a not uncommon thing to do), whereupon the impulse suddenly freed and the engine started. The propeller came around and hit his hand, causing a severe injury. I saw him when he got back to Nelson, with his hand all dressed and plastered up. Typically, he played it down and was instructing again soon afterwards.

Brad sent me to do my first solo after 15 flights, mainly with him and Arthur Jordan, totalling two hours and 28 minutes' flying.

As all pilots know, the first solo is a never-to-be-forgotten occasion. I can remember every detail, including the stage when I suddenly took stock that I was alone in an aircraft at 1200 feet and had a moment's alarm. But all went well.

Flying light aircraft and gliders was cheap in those days, particularly in our club, and those of us who were keen on gliding spent a lot of time on the airfield each weekend. Occasionally we would strike some lift (rising air currents) in our Rhonlerche and get a longish flight, but mostly we had air tow to about 3000 feet and practised simple manoeuvres while gliding back to base. Instructors would also test us for more advanced flying, but our machine was not rated for aerobatics.

One beautiful winter's day, with a crystal clear sky and heavy frost, our tow pilot, ex-Battle of Britain pilot Ross Craig, said he wanted to see how high our Auster aircraft tow plane could take us. He offered me a free ride for this, with Jillian as passenger. Our glider had only a cloth covering over the steel tube frame and of course no heating of any sort. It got colder and colder as we climbed into the mid-winter air, with the poor old Auster huffing and puffing its way up. Eventually at about 8000 feet, I got the signal from Ross to cast off the tow.

After trimming out and checking around we started to drift along when suddenly there was an awful drumming sound, with marked vibration. I did not want to scare Jill but cautiously looked to see what was wrong, wondering if some component(s) had been affected by the cold. I could see nothing wrong and the controls were acting quite normally and moving freely. Suddenly it came again and I was quite concerned. Jill saw me looking around and asked me why, but I said that it was just routine. How was she? I asked. 'I'm fine, but my feet are frozen so I have been drumming them on the floor to try to get them warm.'

I flew the glider nearly every weekend and was eventually rated as a safety pilot, which allowed me to fly with pilots who had only recently gone solo. The next step up after a lot more flying was to be rated as an instructor, which I found an interesting job, but occasionally stressful. We had one pupil who was keen but heavy handed on the controls. He simply would not let go when told to do so, which was sometimes necessary when he was making a serious error. It was no pleasure to teach him and the club had to tell him to abandon it – he would have been a danger to himself as well to others and our machine.

Our Rhonlerche was not suitable for landing away from its base as it was not easily dismantled and we had no trailer to transport it. This was well illustrated one day when Ray got into a bit of strife on tow in rough conditions, causing him to cast off from the tow aircraft and make an emergency landing on the adjacent Tahunanui Beach. Then we were faced with the problem of how to get it back to the field. Thank goodness for living in a smallish town with sympathetic authorities: we were given permission to tow it back on the road. Now this machine had a 26-foot wingspan so it took up quite a bit of road, and the wing tips were too low in places to clear obstructions, but we managed with police escort, lifting the aircraft over any obstructions or parked vehicles by brute force.

Our club was going from strength to strength, particularly after we obtained the lease of a large hangar at Nelson Airport, which we sublet to owners of private aircraft and caravans, to commercial firms for storage, and to an aircraft engineering firm. This revenue saw the club finances becoming very healthy, so that we were able to consider expansion.

It became apparent that while our machine was an excellent trainer (and is still giving faithful service 35 years later), it could not be used for soaring flights except on rare occasions. As well, any pilot disappearing for lengthy periods interrupted the training of booked pupils. After a lot of thought and research we decided to buy a second glider: capable of soaring but still with the two-seat configuration to enable advanced instruction. We had been well pleased with our Rhonlerche so we ordered the next grade up from the same firm, a Rhonadler. This aircraft gave a lot of pleasure and was used extensively for cross-country work. We also decided to buy our own tow plane and located a Tiger Moth in a barn in the North Island with a whole lot of spares. We bought it for a song and restored it to towing condition.

Mecca for the gliding fraternity was Omarama at the southern end of the Mackenzie Basin. It was world famous for world records being set by Dick Georgeson and other Kiwis, both in height gain and long-distance flights, using the strong wind currents and waves generated by the Southern Alps. Brad suggested we go down in his Proctor and have a look. He and his son and I took off, enjoyed a lovely trip south and landed at Omarama where we stayed for a few days. There were plenty of machines there and we had chances to fly a few, soaring on the adjacent hills. I even flew a single-seat Skylark 2 machine, which was regarded as a 'hot ship' at that time. I was amazed at its performance compared with our Rhonlerche. Also present was another beautiful single-seater, an Olympia 2. Brad flew this but when he landed he told me there was something wrong with it. Apparently the controls were not moving freely, nor would the aircraft fly straight and level 'hands off'.

On another trip to Omarama Ray, who was knowledgeable about aircraft, especially wooden ones, was taken with the Olympia that Brad had said had control problems. It was up for sale and Ray reckoned it was sound but needed a massive overhaul. So we formed a syndicate and bought it. It was easily dismantled and had a good trailer in which Ray brought it back to Nelson some weeks later. He had a large shed in which we could fit the fuselage, while the wings and tail assembly were kept in the trailer.

The machine had been manufactured in England and was a famous and successful Olympic-class competition type which had been imported to New Zealand in kitset form and assembled at Timaru, from where it was flown for many years. Alas, upon investigation we found serious faults.

The first thing we found was that the wire cable from the cockpit to the release for the tow hook was hanging on by one strand. We gave it a tug and it broke. Had this happened in flight, the pilot would not have been able to release from the tow plane. Had the plane's pilot released, the glider would have had 100 feet of nylon rope hanging down from its nose. It was a disgrace that this had not been picked up in airworthiness inspections.

Then we noticed that the joystick movements were accompanied by a grating noise. We eventually tracked this down, with great difficulty, to the control wires from the joystick being crossed and recrossed in complex fashion in their path back inside the fuselage. No wonder Brad had found it had peculiar flying characteristics! We carefully mapped all the faults, then asked the local aero engineer to check it for us before we did any work. It was just as well we did, as we had a threat of defamation action from the engineers responsible when I wrote to the chap who had sold it to us to let him know. But our engineer soon backed us up and that was the end of that.

We overhauled the aircraft in detail, supervised by the engineer, finally painting it with great care. When she was finished she was beautiful and much admired. For those who may be interested in aircraft she is now hanging from the ceiling of an aircraft museum in Ashburton. We did a lot of flying in the Olly, as we called her. She was very quiet, with good visibility, and would drift around at slow speed in the slightest lift of rising air.

As a family we used to go to Hawke's Bay to spend Christmas with our families. I found that there was a gliding club which flew from a strip at Havelock North beside the Tuki Tuki River. This club launched its glider by means of a winch, using about 800 yards of No. 8 fencing wire which, when it broke, was tied together with an ordinary reef knot. The cable was pulled out, the glider attached and on a given signal the wire was winched onto a large drum by a V8 motor. It was quite exciting to try this form of launch, the acceleration being 0 to 60mph in three seconds. The slopes of the hills leading to Te Mata Peak were close by the strip and the sea breeze would commonly provide steady lift on fine days for soaring along these hills.

One of the targets for most glider pilots was an international award known as the Silver C. This required a solo flight of five hours or more, a cross-country flight of 32 miles and a flight with a height gain of 1000 metres, all properly certified.

I asked the Hawke's Bay Gliding Club members if they would allow me to have a go at my five-hour flight for the Silver C award. They kindly agreed, even though it would tie up their training glider for the day. So, when the breeze came up, off I went from a winch launch, onto the hill, where I found lift, and along which I flew up and down to the summit of Te Mata Peak for the next five hours and 17 minutes.

There was quite marginal lift at times and it was very tiring. I'd taken a sandwich and an apple with me, as well as a few sweets to keep my blood sugar at a reasonable level, and the usual bottle that solo pilots need to have on long flights, but it was hard work. I was close to the hill all this time in order to stay airborne and became an object of interest for sightseers who lined the hill road and summit. They prevented any thought of using the bottle as they had a clear view into the cockpit.

By this time we were getting quite a bit of experience in our lovely Olympia, with long soaring flights. She was rated as an aerobatic aircraft and I simply had to have a go. So a few of us went over to Blenheim, having arranged for an instructor to take us through some simple manoeuvres. After this I took the Olly for its first loop in Nelson, which I thoroughly enjoyed. I then gradually started to fling it around a bit, with stall turns, spins and wingovers.

I loved this type of flying, but decided that since the Olly was wooden with rather elderly glued joints I would be wise to have a parachute. These were almost unknown in private ownership at that time so I imported one from RAF surplus stock in England and had it checked and repacked here by the RNZAF in Blenheim. I wore that on all future aerobatic flights.

One parachute incident which we thought utterly hilarious stands out. Perhaps we had warped minds. An aircraft agent arrived in Nelson with a new glider which he wanted to sell to our club. It was a beautiful low-wing sleek single-seat machine known as a Sagitta, and was stressed for severe aerobatic manoeuvres as well as inverted flight. Ray and I were asked to help evaluate it.

I had first flight, getting towed to a good height, from where I did some fairly hefty loops, spins and other moves – wearing my parachute, of course. Then it was Ray's turn. I helped him into the parachute, which he assured me he knew how to work, and off he went, really pulling the Sagitta around the sky.

After he landed and climbed out of the aircraft, he could not work out how to get out of the parachute harness, so I turned the quick-release round knob on the front of his chest, gave it a bang and it fell off. 'My gosh,' said Ray, 'I thought that was how you opened it if you needed it in flight!' We all had visions of Ray pulling a wing off and banging the quick release on his chute, only to see the parachute pack fall quietly to the floor alongside him.

As it happens, we did not buy that aircraft, and just as well. It went to Australia where it did lose a wing, killing the pilot.

A group of us also went over to Blenheim to have a ride in a Skylark 4 based there, noted for its speed and soaring ability. We found it very exhilarating and were all amazed at the rapid speed build-up in a dive. Unfortunately, shortly after our visit, another pilot put it into a steep dive, then tried to pull it out too quickly, with the resultant loss of both wings and his life.

Our Olympia was flown regularly by the syndicate. Ray took it to a national meeting in Otago and flew it to about 12,000 feet to give him a Gold C award, which he did without oxygen or radio. He already had his five-hour flight, and a distance flight for his Silver C.

We decided we would allow experienced non-syndicate pilots fly it too. At that

*ABOVE:* In 1955 my friends Des Hay (left), George Topliss and I competed in the Southland Centennial Trial, an international car rally to celebrate Invercargill's centennial in 1956. We won!

Racing my 1956 Morris Minor at the Tahunanui back beach, Nelson, about 1958.

My next Morris Minor – down a bank after Linda's first attempt to drive. I never left the keys in the ignition again!

My friend Ray Sharland (right) introduced me to flying radio-controlled model aircraft in the early days of this hobby. Our experience with these was an enormous help when we both took up gliding a few years later.

OPPOSITE

*CENTRE LEFT:* Just before takeoff in Nelson Gliding Club's first aircraft, a Rhonlerche, which is still flying regularly.

*CENTRE RIGHT:* Proud owners of the Olympia: Me, Ron McKnight, Gerry Stewart, Ray Sharland, Doug Guthrie.

*BELOW:* Soaring high above the Waimea Plains in our Olympia glider.
(*photo courtesy C.S. Collier*).

*TOP:* Coming in to land at Okuri Point, near French Pass, with a smoky fire lit to indicate the wind direction.

*CENTRE:* The flying doctor (always in a suit and tie in those days) arrives to see patients at his 'consulting room' – the large Holden station wagon at right.

*LEFT:* About to leave from Okuri airstrip.

*TOP:* Setting off with my Vincent 1000cc to Christchurch for a national motorcycle rally, 1975.

*BELOW:* Pride and joy: my 1951 Vincent 1000cc Rapide and 1954 Vincent Comet 500cc with sidecar, and the designer of their engines, Phil Irving.

time there was in Nelson the first helicopter we had seen, flown by a Canadian, Dick de Blecquy. His wife was also a very experienced pilot and an instructor at the aero club. One day she went off for a flight in our Olly, being towed off by her husband in an Auster plane. This glider had very powerful air brakes, which were always tested in a preflight check to see that they would deploy properly. As they took off it was suddenly noted that Lorna had left the airbrakes out. The poor old Auster, with hubby flying, got her off the ground but at full throttle was only just able to fly and could not do a safe turn, which would have risked stalling. A private Cessna owner took off and flew alongside Lorna to try to signal to her what the trouble was but she did not cotton on and the pair struggled on, barely gaining height, with Dick flogging the poor Auster up the Nelson harbour alongside the Boulder Bank, barely able to keep flying due to the glider air brake drag.

Eventually Lorna decided that her husband's plane was in trouble, so she released the tow and landed unhurt on the Boulder Bank, where our lovely Olly was severely damaged in the wing and less so in the fuselage. A team walked across the mudflats of the upper harbour at low tide, took off wings and tail assembly and carried all of these plus the fuselage back to the trailer. Lorna and Dick were mortified and guaranteed full recompense.

After careful assessment, Ray accepted the job of repair, with supervision by the local aircraft engineer and Civil Aviation. It was a long and tedious process requiring meticulous grafting and fashioning of wooden components. Ray excelled himself to such an extent that when the inspector from Wellington came from time to time for progress checks, he said that it was the best wooden aircraft repair work that he had ever seen. And so she flew again.

I had a crazy experience one day when attempting to fly Olly from Nelson to Blenheim. I misjudged conditions, which were very turbulent, and near Blenheim I struck a strong downdraft, so made the decision to land in a paddock adjacent to the main highway before crossing the Wairau river. I landed uneventfully but the wind was so strong that I could not safely get out of the glider in case it blew over before I could secure it. So I just kept it upright facing into wind, 'flying it on the ground' to keep the wings level, with stick hard forward to stop it lifting, hoping that some passing motorist would realise my predicament and come to help so that I could get out and anchor the machine safely. I put my free hand out of a small side window and waggled it at passing traffic, but most of them just waved back in happy fashion until after about 20 minutes of this farce, a passing glider pilot saw the problem at once and ran to help.

To complete my Silver C award I had to do a cross-country flight, which I did from a field near Lake Rotoiti where we had found there were often good soaring conditions. I had to do a triangular course from the airstrip to Kikiwa Junction, then to the old Glenhope railway station and back to the strip. I managed it in one hour 50 mins, with a maximum height of 4500 feet and a low point of 1600 feet at the Glenhope Saddle where I could hear car horns tooting as I struggled for height.

I did a number of aerobatics displays in Olly, one of them being at the Nelson A &

P show where I landed after the display with the glider then on show for the day. Another display was at an airshow at Motueka but this went a bit awry. It so happened that the chief air inspector of the Civil Aviation Department was there to keep an eye on safety, which turned out to be a bit embarrassing. The man who put the tow rope onto the tow plane hook did not attach it properly and just over the aerodrome boundary the rope fell off the tow plane.

I was glad of the Olympia's powerful air brakes which, when fully open, allowed the glider to dive as steeply as one wanted without overspeeding. I immediately pulled the lever to release the rope, fully opened the brakes and dived almost vertically to the left, managing to do a normal landing in a corner of the airfield.

We towed Olly back to the start point to find the CAA inspector, standing with arms akimbo and a 'please explain' look on his face. Fair enough. It could have been serious if it had happened a moment later over a housing area, and signalled a breakdown in our usual check and double-check system.

Most of our 'incidents' on the gliding fields were funny rather than serious. We always had a vehicle at the gliding site which we used to tow the glider back to start point after it had landed. We took turns using our own vehicles for this. Somehow visitors and other people always seemed to have left things lying near or even under my car when it was my turn. I once managed to drive over the top of a brand new bike belonging to the young son of the duty airport controller, and another time drove clean over the top of the afternoon tea tray, laden with cups and saucers.

We used to tease each other mercilessly about our flying. One day I thought it looked good for a longish flight in the Olympia, but managed only to get to Brightwater, about 10 miles south of Nelson, before landing in a field. Ray gave me a terrible time about that 'long cross-country flight', but I had the last laugh as the owners of the house from where I phoned were just sitting down to a roast dinner which they asked me to share, whereas Ray spent his lunchtime coming out with the trailer.

The gliding club was going so well that we decided to run a flying scholarship. We obtained sponsorship for first prize, which was to be free training to solo stage and we had about a couple of dozen entrants, none of whom had previous flying experience.

It was decided that all candidates should be taken by the one instructor so that there would be uniformity of judging. It fell to me to do this. I gave each one the same test, which consisted of a ground briefing as to how an aircraft flew, how the controls worked and how to do turns with stick and rudder as well as alter speed with fore and aft movement of the stick. Then we towed up to about 2000 feet and released. After trimming the glider for normal glide I gave control to the pupil, whom I then asked to alter speeds and do simple turns, while judging his or her ability.

It was a fascinating exercise and those with the highest marks had quickly realised that an aircraft, when properly trimmed, will fly along happily until disturbed by pilot or weather. Those who held the controls lightly and were confident did the best, and a young woman was the outright winner, going on to solo stage and becoming a staunch member of the club.

# 17

*A MAJOR TURNING POINT* in my flying career occurred one day when the gliding club had a day at Lake Rotoiti and I went up as one of the glider instructors. After a successful day I was to return in the tow plane while the other instructor went back in a glider. The tow pilot, Ivan Stade, told me to sit in the front seat of the Piper Cub plane and after a cockpit check said, 'You do the takeoff and fly her back.' I had handled the controls of a powered aircraft in flight often enough but never taken off or manoeuvred. So, under instructions as to what to do, I did the takeoff and flew it all the way back to Nelson, where Ivan even let me land it. I realised that I wanted more of this, so started off as a pupil with the Nelson Aero Club.

I had had a few instructional flights in powered aircraft, mainly to learn the dangers and management of stalling and spinning to assist me in my glider management, but no basic training in engine management and navigation. I was sent solo after two flights with the chief flying instructor, after which I did quite a lot of solo practice and had a lot more dual instruction with low flying, precautionary landings, and cross country. Sometimes if I wanted to have a flight in a glider, I would go to the aero club, hop into a Piper Cub and go up to see if there was any lift around before going to the trouble of getting the glider out and getting towed up.

After the requisite solo time I sat my private pilot examination and passed both the written exam and the flight tests. Somehow I even got a cup for my exam results in navigation. My pilot's licence was to come in very handy in my work.

One day I had a telephone call from the district nurse at French Pass to say that she had a child she was worried about and could I get down to see him. As I have described, the road access to French Pass was terrible, so I rang the chief instructor of the aero club and asked if there was any way of flying down. He said there was a topdressing strip near French Pass and with fine weather he could fly me down.

This landing strip is an interesting one. It is at Okuri Point, at the top of a 900-foot cliff. The strip has about 100 metres of flat, then rises at a gradient of about one in four to a small flat parking area alongside the topdressing bin at the top. There is no possibility of aborting a landing here once committed. One has to come in from the sea at exactly the correct height, drop with certainty onto the short flat area, then give full throttle to taxi to the top, turn around and shut off smartly on the small area. One small complication was that the strip was used for grazing and one first had to clear any stock from it by buzzing them before coming in to land.

On this occasion the patient did not need to come to Nelson and the district nurse was able to manage after receiving advice. But this trip was a milestone as it meant the people of French Pass, D'Urville Island and a few other remote places could receive emergency medical attention and I was asked not infrequently to go to them.

Initially the instructors would take me, but soon they decided to train me to go solo into these unlicensed areas. The rated instructors chosen were all active or ex-topdressing pilots – all survivors in a profession of very high mortality. Derek Erskine, Allan Hackston, Don Brewer, Denny Atkinson and a few others were not only incredibly good instructors but also outstanding pilots. Flying with these men made me realise how professional their skills were compared with amateurs': they seemed to 'wear' the aircraft as though they had grown to be part of it. It was an inspiration to fly with them. They would teach me the only safe way to get onto a strip or paddock, then get me do it while they sat in the back seat, making me go round and round until they were happy with my performance, after which the club would authorise me to land on that area for emergencies only.

But even these outstanding pilots couldn't help themselves at times and could show incredible boyish irresponsibility. Coming back from one instructional trip to D'Urville Island, with an open carton of blue cod and snapper fillets behind the rear seat, I was flying from the front at about 1500 feet over the sea in the Piper Cub when the instructor said, 'Miles, did you know these Cubs will loop very well?' No, I hadn't known that, I said, whereupon he said, 'I have control,' pushed the nose down and brought it up and over into a perfect loop. I was shattered as I was very safety conscious and this guy had busted so many rules: the Piper Cub was not authorised to do aerobatics; there was insufficient height for safe aerobatics; we had no complete aerobatic harness; no pre-aerobatic check; and an unsecured load in the cabin. Fortunately the box of fish stayed put.

When the district nurse at French Pass found she had an emergency on her hands she would ask me to come down and would meet me at the airstrip with her patients. She always arranged for a lump of petrol-soaked rag to be lit to act as a wind indicator when they heard the plane coming, but later they rigged up a proper windsock on the most commonly used strip at Okuri. We used her large Holden station wagon as a consulting room and the tailboard when folded down made quite a good examination table. The patients gathered around would always avert their eyes and mind their own affairs while I was making any examinations.

One of the strange trips I had was to D'Urville Island where a lad was quite ill. His mother had rung me several times in the previous 24 hours and it appeared that he was brewing up an acute appendicitis. Their side of the island was no place to try to reach either by sea or air in the gale-force westerly that was blowing at the time. But he was worse next day, so I simply had to try to get him out. I approached Alan Hackston and asked if he would try to land me in the paddock next to the house. Alan said that if the wind dropped a bit he would have a go, so we asked the mother to report the moment there was any reduction in the gale.

That morning I was rostered to give anaesthetics at Nelson Hospital and we were in the middle of an operation when the phone went: the wind at D'Urville had dropped away completely. Someone took over from me, I rang Alan, met him at the airport and we took off in a Piper Cub. Alan landed skilfully in a paddock, in which the farmer had rapidly lowered a section of fence to give us a better approach and landing.

I examined the lad and confirmed the diagnosis of acute appendicitis. Alan said he could fly out with the patient on my knee, even though the aircraft was slightly overloaded. Our takeoff aided by some downhill, we flew back to Nelson in calm conditions and, would you believe it, as we landed, the westerly gale resumed. I found out later that it also returned down at the island just after we had taken off. The patient had his appendix removed and all was well. Sometimes luck is on one's side.

One day a doctor at Wakefield rang to say that one of his patients about 60 miles away thought his young son had been bitten by a katipo spider under the woolshed. The boy was very unwell and my doctor friend asked if I could go by plane, as it would be much quicker. I duly flew to Lake Rotoiti airstrip where I saw the young patient, who by then was quite recovered. I am sure he was not bitten by a katipo: he was quite small and had crawled under the shed and I wonder if he had panicked after being pricked by stinging nettle or some such. So I came home again.

The upside to this particular episode was that the farmer was most grateful and never forgot my efforts. He had a large property with lovely fishing rivers, but was a known martinet who would not allow easy access. But he made us welcome on the several occasions on which I asked, and even let us take tents and our labrador dog to camp on his land beside the river.

As every pilot knows (or should know), almost every aircraft accident is due to pilot error somewhere along the line. It may be an error of judgment, momentary inattention, flying below legal limits, showing off, failure to do proper inspections or preparations, attempting something beyond one's skills and experience or pressing on when it would be prudent not to do so. I had an experience that fitted some of these categories when our gliding club went to Lake Rotoiti for a day's flying. I had spent the day as an instructor so perhaps fatigue was a factor.

After we had finished flying, the tow pilot and I swapped roles so that I could fly the tow plane home. He told me to check the oil as it might need topping up and there was some in the luggage compartment. I did this, added a full bottle, closed up, took off and headed over the hills for Nelson. About halfway there I noticed a flicker of the oil pressure gauge but could find no other abnormality. A few minutes later it flickered again. I watched carefully and was shattered to see it fall right down to zero a few minutes later.

I pulled back the throttle to idle and found that the pressure came up again, so carefully opened up the throttle again and continued on. After a few minutes the same sequence of events recurred, but for longer, and I had to glide quite a long way looking for an emergency landing area.

By this time I was over the Waimea Plains and had found that as long as the nose of the aircraft was a little lowered, the oil pressure was up to normal, so I gradually lost height and set up to land on the racecourse at Richmond, calling the control tower to advise them. However, when I got over the racecourse I found I still had enough height to proceed with great care at slow speed to the air field a little further on. As soon as I landed the oil pressure gauge again fell to zero so I switched off and waited to be towed in.

The aero club duty instructor came out and, after being told what had happened, said, 'Hop out of the aircraft, Miles, and take a look at it.' When I did I found the engine cowlings smothered with oil, with a lot of it blown back onto the fuselage. When we lifted a cowling, there was the cap of the oil filler tube lying underneath the engine. It had fallen there after being blown off because I had not done it up adequately after I had topped up with oil. My punishment was, quite rightly, having to clean the aircraft, but my shame was a greater punishment ...

I suppose everyone has phobias, and one of mine from then on was always to check that the oil filler cap in every aircraft I flew was securely tightened, even if it had just come in from being flown by another pilot.

I had another near accident one day when landing on the beach at Greville Harbour on D'Urville Island, which I had done a number of times before. I cannot remember why I had to go down, but my friend Brian Woodman was waiting in his runabout at the beach to take me over to his house. Something went wrong as I landed: the plane's nose swung a bit, probably due to one wheel digging into the sand, or I may have touched the brakes at the wrong time. Within moments the gentle swing became violent and we spun around through more than 180 degrees, with the inside wheel lifting and the outside wing almost dragging in the sand. I felt completely helpless as it was totally out of my control and I can remember seeing Brian, an ex-World War 2 Spitfire pilot, covering his face with his hands and turning his back in mock horror.

In 1965 there was an outbreak of whooping cough, which was distressingly severe in those who had not been inoculated and quite severe still in a few of those who had. Somewhere I had read that taking people with this condition to high altitude was beneficial, so I consulted local specialist physician, Dr Leo Hannah. He found an article in *Lancet*, the prestigious English medical magazine, citing research which concluded that taking patients with whooping cough to a height of 10,000 feet for a minimum of 20 minutes had been shown to be beneficial. I decided to try it if patients were willing.

It so happened that some young patients of mine on D'Urville Island became badly affected with this bug and the parents were frantic. I don't know whether they had been properly vaccinated as infants, but they were certainly severely affected as older children. I talked to the parents about my idea and they elected to give it a try. So, with an instructor and a larger aircraft, we landed on the beach at Greville Harbour where three distressed children were waiting with their parents. They were coughing almost incessantly and occasionally vomiting at the end of a coughing spasm. We packed them into the aircraft, took off and slowly climbed to 10,000 feet, where we stooged around for about 20 minutes and then landed.

Had I not been there and seen it for myself I would never have believed it. After landing from that flight none of those three children coughed again – from that very moment. It was quite miraculous and they all felt so wonderfully improved it was quite moving. Jillian, who knew them well, had come down with us and was waiting on the beach for us to return. She was equally astounded at the almost magical change.

I did quite a number of such flights for severely affected children and each showed the same wonderful improvement, although none had been as severely affected as that D'Urville Island trio. My godson David was quite bad and I took him up for one of these trips. He was quite small so his father came and held him in his arms while we clambered up to 10,000 feet in a Piper Cub. After a few minutes I said, 'How is he?' (They were in the back seat behind me.) 'Oh,' said his dad, 'he's gone to sleep.' I thought that was a bit odd and turned around to find that David was noticeably blue in the face! I decided we had had enough so made a fairly rapid descent. But David was another almost miraculous success.

My flying for medical emergencies came to an end after a few years. A helicopter came to be stationed in the district and one day when there was a case of severe burns, again at French Pass, I was taken in it right to the settlement. Previously we had to land a few kilometres from it and that was only possible if the wind was favourable. The helicopter revolutionised flying to emergencies in areas with poor accessibility.

Looking back on that era, I feel privileged to have been involved with the people in remote areas who were stuck. People have asked what it cost the patient. The answer is: nothing. The Health Department approved payment for the aircraft if I recommended it, and I made no charge ever to any patient to whom I had to fly. When I worked out a cost after my first few flights I realised that with the time involved away from my busy surgery or anaesthetics, plus the flying, the figure would be outrageous. I decided it was better left. I never regretted this decision and allowed the patients to think the Health Department paid me.

One day I had a close insight into the exuberant nature of some World War 2 air force pilots. A close friend was a Spitfire fighter pilot, an ace, during the war. He was a member of the Brevet Club, who were a pretty playful bunch. Wellington airport was to open in the 1950s with a large airshow and lots of interesting visiting aircraft, so the local branch of the Brevet Club decided to charter a DC3 Dakota and go to this event. They had a spare seat and I was privileged to join them.

Shortly after takeoff from Nelson we were settled on course in level flight when I noticed some strange co-ordinated activity among all these chaps. They silently got out of their seats and gathered in a bunch just behind the door to the cockpit. On a signal from one man they all ran to the back of the cabin, with the result that the aircraft suddenly climbed until the pilot regained control and retrimmed, whereupon they all ran to the front of the cabin, causing further trouble for the pilot.

Thankfully the pilot and co-pilot knew their passengers only too well and soon stopped this by initiating their own exuberant dives and zooms, with the desired result. I was glad I was strapped in. While they were fooling around it was also found they had a stowaway in the baggage compartment – a young flying enthusiast from the aero club. What a day we had with this bunch of wild fellows.

The opening of the airport was not without high drama also. The first 'incident' occurred when a Sunderland flying-boat was doing a demonstration and flew low along the runway, apparently not knowing it had a slight hump. To our astonishment he scraped the bottom of his hull on the new surface and out came a stream of bilge water as he pulled this enormous machine up off the surface. It must have made a terrible din on his aluminium hull. He then shot off straight ahead and landed in Evans Bay, beaching his holed aircraft on the shore to stop it sinking.

The next drama occurred with a Royal Air Force Vulcan delta wing bomber, three of which came to the show from England. It was announced that one would do a parachute landing on this new airport. He came in low from the Cook Strait end with his wheels down, but he was a fraction too low and his undercarriage hit the banked-up end of the runway with a cloud of dust while one wing dropped almost onto the surface and may even have hit it. We thought this giant was going to swing to the left into the crowd but the pilot managed to pour on the power and get away. In front of our grandstand seats stood the RAF Comet airliner and it was quite a sight to see all the RAF bigwigs leap aboard and take off in a hurry after the damaged Vulcan as it headed off, undercarriage dangling. It flew to Ohakea air base where it did a belly landing on the grass. It was eventually repaired and sent back to England.

Another memorable trip was when Jill and I went off to Western Samoa on holiday once, travelling in a four-jet DC8. When we were well out over the Pacific I asked the air hostess if I could go up to the flight deck. Obligingly, she went to ask the captain who agreed 'as long as I didn't look like a hijacker'. Up I went and the first thing I noticed was a piece of wool or cotton stuck onto the outside of the centre of the windscreen with chewing gum. I was thunderstruck. This was the simple system used by glider pilots to check that they were not slipping sideways in the air but always keeping the aircraft dead straight. It was very accurate, but this was a DC8 travelling at about 600mph! I asked the captain about it and he said, 'That is our most accurate instrument for measuring slip. Watch.' He put a small bit of rudder on to make the aircraft slip, and the wool immediately went slightly sideways. His other instruments, meanwhile, showed no slip, except for the engine fuel flow indicators, which showed an increase due to inefficient flying with extra drag.

He asked me about my flying and when I asked him what these big birds were like to fly he said, 'Have a go.' He got out of his seat, told me to get in, turned off the auto pilot and said, 'You have control!'

I did nothing, of course, so he told me to do some turns. So I did a few turns with this big bird and found it very easy and a very interesting experience. When I returned to my seat, Jill looked at me knowingly and said with a grin, 'I know what you've been doing.'

When I went away for a while to do postgraduate work I sold my share in the Olympia. On my return I became a tow pilot on the Pawnee 235. It was a single-seater so that one had to learn everything about it on the ground since there was no dual control. With all its topdressing equipment removed it was a delight to fly, being like a powerful sports car in some ways – rigid with firm controls and instant response.

But I was so busy in my practice I found the stress of flying the tow plane sometimes too great: it is intensive work. Came a day when I flew eight tows in a brisk and turbulent easterly, all the while with a severe headache, when I thought, 'Am I enjoying this?' The answer was 'No.'

I had done somewhere between 1500 and 2000 takeoffs and landings from Nelson airport, with all my glider instruction and towing, and enough was enough. So, with no flying required for medical purposes any more I decided to give it away.

But still I retain my interest in flying and aircraft. Many years later I heard that there was a WW2 Mustang fighter aircraft at Wanaka that had been converted to a two-seater, with dual control. While on a motoring holiday through the South Island we called in at Wanaka and I saw the Mustang sitting there. I went into the office and said, 'Have you got any specials for "gerries" on Mustang flights?' Pilot Tom Middleton laughed and said, 'No, we don't, I am afraid.'

The long and short of it was that I decided to shout myself a flight for my 80th birthday, which was just around the corner. Next day we reported to the aerodrome, where Tom asked me about my flying and my health and then gave me a very interesting briefing about the Mustang. For those who are unfamiliar with it, it is an American-built World War 2 fighter, with a Rolls-Royce 12-cylinder Merlin engine of about 1650hp and a maximum flying speed of about 450mph. I climbed in, donned parachute, helmet and intercom and as we took off I could not resist a 'Yahoo!' at the incredible acceleration and lift-off.

After a few minutes, to my absolute astonishment, Tom lifted his hands in the air and said, 'You have control.' I put hands and feet onto the controls and did nothing for a few moments, revelling in the feel and the sound of the Merlin burbling away in front. Then I did some gentle turns, after which Tom made me dive at 350mph and bring her up into a 360-degree roll. We did this two or three times, as well as a loop or two. Then he had me fly it back to the airfield, with a few somewhat bolder turns along the way. Before landing Tom took control again and did an aerobatic show routine, starting with a low pass over the field at 400mph, followed by some loops, rolls and a low 'cockpit run' the length of the field with the aircraft on its side. He pulled off speed, did his circuit and landing check and taxied in.

It turned out I was well and truly the oldest person he had ever taken up in the Mustang. I shall never ever forget that flight: it was the ultimate for me in my lifelong passion for flying.

My pilot was highly regarded and very skilled, especially at flying vintage warbirds. Famed for his aerobatic show routines, he was held in affectionate esteem by colleagues all over the world. Tom Middleton was killed at Wanaka early in 2001 while doing aerobatics with a passenger in a Pitts Special aircraft.

# 18

*AS MY PRACTICE GOT BIGGER* my time with the family reduced. One lovely fine day we were about to go on a family picnic when the telephone rang. One of my patients had gone into labour, so I had to go out and tell the disappointed family that the picnic was off. Poor Linda burst into tears and said something that struck me to the core: 'I wish my dad wasn't a doctor.'

Not long after, I was in the hospital common room discussing some of my patients with house surgeons and senior specialists. The conversation is engraved on my mind because as the house surgeon outlined some of the laboratory readings of tests they had done on a patient with a suspected heart attack I was shattered and appalled to find that I did not know the meaning of some of these tests.

I was always a keen reader and subscribed to a number of medical journals, local and overseas, but I realised I had got badly behind in some modern advances because I was too busy. I was seeing 40–50 patients daily, delivering about two or more babies a week, and giving anaesthetics about three mornings a week too. Clearly I was neglecting both my academic work and my family. I was in my mid-forties and they were growing up fast. It was time to stop. But how? Doctors were in short supply and no new ones were coming to Nelson. Despite this, I realised that I really wanted to do some upgrading and revision in general medicine. I would have liked to have taken a postgraduate degree in anaesthetics, but the three-year course was quite beyond me financially. The Health Department would not help, despite strong suport from Dr Brunette with whom, by then, I had an armistice.

Another area of interest I had found in general practice was that of skin diseases, having been introduced to this speciality by Dr Ralph Park years before at Wellington Hospital. I made enquiries and found that there was a very good course at Sydney University which included good basic medical science revisions as well as a large amount of specialist general medicine and radiation physics. The problem was to find someone to look after my practice. Then Dr Brian Neill remembered that a friend of his, Dr Bryan Hardie Boys, had been doing some postgraduate study in child health and obstetrics in Britain and might be willing to return. And so he did. His family took over our house and Bryan ran my practice wonderfully well for me.

In sorting out the legal side of this locum arrangement Bryan advised me to contact his judge father, Michael Hardie Boys (now Sir Michael). It was an eye-opener working with this fine gentleman. Bryan had told him of our verbal agreement and when I asked the judge if I should see my lawyer and have a document drawn up to this effect he replied, 'No, that would be a waste of money.'

He went on to say he spent nearly all his working life in court trying to decide the exact meaning of legal documents and agreements and the best method was a simple exchange of letters. He advised me to write to him outlining the details of Bryan's and my verbal agreement. He then annotated it, saying that he agreed to all the conditions as outlined and signed it on behalf of Bryan. That was our legal agreement.

At the beginning of 1966 we packed up and headed over to Sydney, where we were met by a medical friend, Dr Dick Climie, who with wife Pat had been at Wellington Hospital during my time there. They had found us a semi-detached flat at Randwick, close to Centennial Park, and had us to stay at their home until we could get installed. They also introduced us to various aspects of Australian life, especially the beaches with their beautiful surf. Our flat was only minutes away from a number of beaches and we often used to go for a swim before breakfast.

It was a wonderful year. We were short of money but we managed to buy an elderly Ford and explored the whole area, with picnics almost every weekend. We economised on almost everything except petrol.

My work was most stimulating, with lectures most mornings and hospital work and clinics for the rest of the time. I saw literally hundreds of cases of skin disease as well as a lot of medical cases with senior specialists. I thrived on it all and the local specialists were great to us. They invited us out to their homes for barbecues, and tried to find some source of income for me in any spare weekend time. Dr Geoffrey Finley was a senior specialist and also senior medical officer to the army. He arranged many jobs for me interviewing and examining new recruits in the weekends, without which I don't know how we would have survived.

The children did well at their schools, with Tim becoming dux at Randwick Public School. We all made lifelong friends whom we still meet from time to time.

Jill in particular distinguished herself. She had a Bachelor of Music degree already but, being at a loose end, she decided she would like to do some postgraduate study herself. Typically, she set about this with great zeal, even sending all of us away camping one weekend before her examinations near the end of the year. She passed her A.Mus.TCL with flying colours, eclipsing us all.

Australian lifestyles and standards were interesting. We found the most incredible snobbishness and class distinction there. It was unheard of for professionals like us to send their children to state schools as we did. Status was crucial and one's motor vehicle even played a part in this. It was very much looked down on for a doctor, and particularly a specialist, to own a car for more than a year if it was a Ford or Holden. A Chrysler Valiant was okay for two to three years. If one had a Mercedes or Jaguar it was seemly to keep it for many years, likewise a Volvo. It mattered not the condition or age of the car – only the make.

Dress was important too and they were all horrified to hear that all the Nelson Hospital house surgeons wore shorts and open-necked shirts during the summer; they were beside themselves. Nevertheless, they were not only tolerant of our funny Kiwi ways but very good to us.

It was a two-part course but I had always intended to stay only one year – we could not afford to stay longer. After that year's study I passed my exams and felt really refreshed and very much up to speed again academically. But my seniors were most upset when I said I was going home. Dr Adrian Johnson, one of Australia's leading authorities on skin disease, and Dr Fred Anderson, another Sydney specialist, persuaded me to stay on on my own for a few months more. They thought I should complete the full part one course of lectures and then go home, get more funds and return for the second part of the course. Dr Johnson offered me work as a clinical assistant in his Macqaurie Street rooms for five half days a week, with time off for lectures, on what seemed to me a very generous salary. So my family went home without me and I moved into a room at St Andrew's College.

Before they left we decided to go for a camping trip, so we hired a tent, borrowed some camping gear and a trailer and headed off into the unknown. This trip was a tremendous success. We drove to Canberra, around the south coast to Melbourne, on to Adelaide and back again through the inland, stopping at all sorts of odd places and setting up camp. We saw roads without a corner for 80 miles – with not a tree, hill, fence or house in sight in any direction. We saw swarms of locusts, we swam in water so salty that we floated, and even shot rabbits with a rifle I had taken.

We stopped in bigger towns for several days and looked at the sights, wondered what the smell at our Melbourne camping ground was until we found we were parked near a sewage farm, and had an hilarious time in Adelaide at the Brown Creek Reserve camping ground.

It was appallingly hot there on Christmas Day so, as there was a small stream running through the grounds, our family enterprisingly got rocks and dammed it to make a small swimming pool. It would have been a great success if Jill hadn't suddenly erupted from the water with a scream and some leeches attached to her legs! End of swimming.

That evening we were invited for dinner at the house of a local doctor friend, and in the course of conversation about the hot weather they said they were mystified that for the first time in their memory, their water supply had failed. We asked where they got their water from, and they said from a small stream known as Brown Hill Creek! We thought it better not to tell them that someone had dammed it up and next day we pulled all the rocks out. We set off back to Sydney via a different route in very hot conditions.

We had a small insight into some of the hardships endured by the farming folk. Tim had had a dose of flu and was still running a temperature and feeling rotten, the weather was still too hot and we'd run out of drinking water, so we decided to stop at the next house and ask if we could fill our water container. Just before we saw a house we ran into an enormous swarm of locusts – millions of them like a cloud. They must have devastated the surrounding countryside and I was worried that they would clog our radiator cooling system, but they appeared not to.

At the next house we stopped and asked the housewife if we could replenish our water. I was shattered to be refused, even though I said we had a sick boy with a temperature. She said they didn't have enough for their own purposes and were quite unable to spare even a bottle full!

Another small lesson on that drive was when we saw two chaps on a heavy motorcycle behaving strangely on a lonely stretch of road. We stopped and found out they had just run over a sizeable snake, which they were then riding over a few more times to ensure it was dead. After they rode off we had a look at this, our first snake, and I decided I would try to skin it later on and keep the skin as a trophy. I picked it up and tossed it into the trailer with all our camping gear and we continued on our way. Then one of our family said, 'What are you going to do if you can't find it in the trailer where you put it? How do you know it will not recover and get into our clothes or other gear?'

That made me think. We arrived at a nice spot on the bank of the Murray River and I unloaded the trailer exceedingly slowly and carefully, thankfully finding one dead snake exactly where I had put it. I skinned it, found a bit of wood and tacked the skin onto it, leaving it out overnight. In the morning it was soft, clean and supple, having been thoroughly cleaned by myriad ants and other insects. We had that skin for many years.

Working with Dr Adrian Johnson was an inspiration. He was a laconic individual and a natural leader. A very tall man, he had an outstanding war record. At a party in Sydney a New Zealand doctor friend of mine was talking to the Governor of New South Wales, Sir Roden Cutler VC, who lost a leg in the war. This friend of mine saw Adrian Johnson across the room and asked who he was. Sir Roden said, 'That is the man who should have got my VC.' Apparently when Sir Roden had been wounded it was Adrian Johnson who, as a medical officer, had crawled out under fire and dragged him to safety, saving his life.

Adrian taught me, took me out to lunch and dinner at times, and also helped me get a job as a clinical assistant (unpaid) at Sydney Hospital Outpatients with Dr John Rea. These clinics were very rewarding for the diversity of cases I saw, and also I was in touch with all the medical goings on as well as being able to attend clinical meetings in the evenings.

At Dr Johnson's rooms I met a lot of interesting people who came as patients, including one of Australia's prime ministers. When he heard I had been in practice in New Zealand he questioned me at length about our social security system.

Only once was I able to diagnose a condition the experts did not recognise, though any New Zealander could have done it. In came a young woman with itchy inflamed and swollen toes. It had them bluffed. Of course it was a case of chilblains, quite unrecognised and almost unknown in Sydney.

My course of lectures finished, and it was time to go home. Having been medical officer in Nelson for the New Zealand Shipping Company, the Blue Star Line and the Union Shipping Company, I thought it would be worthwhile trying to get a cheap trip home with my car so I wrote to my shipping contacts in Nelson. To my gratification they said that if I could get to Adelaide there was a ship that could take me to Bluff with my car, signed on as a ship's doctor at no salary.

I packed up, hopped into the Falcon and drove west as far as I could, covering about 400 miles on that first day, hitting one kookaburra and one white-crested cockatoo en route. I stopped for a meal and a sleep before covering another few hundred miles the next day to Adelaide. We sailed for New Zealand a few days later.

It was a cargo ship, quite small and perfectly comfortable. The captain was somewhat appalled at my casual dress for meals and asked me to dress more formally as he wanted to maintain a standard. Fair enough. We had an engine breakdown in mid-Tasman, stopping for about half a day. It was uncanny as there was not a breath of wind nor a sign of even the smallest ripple all day. I wanted to fish to fill in the time and tried to borrow a line, but the radio officer showed me the depth sounder, which was showing several thousand fathoms of depth.

We arrived in Bluff after a few days and Jill met me there, having arranged for someone to stay with the children. We drove home happily in the Falcon in a day and a half to a riotous welcome from the kids and Jasper, who ran round and round in circles in his delight.

It was exciting to get back into my own environment. Bryan Hardie Boys and his family had looked after my practice and our home very well. He was not only well liked by my patients, but also a welcome addition to the local medical population. His post-graduate Diploma of Child Health had got him a part-time position on the hospital staff as a paediatrician. I had made an agreement with Bryan that he could take over any patients of mine who wanted to continue attending him, and he set up practice next door to my surgery. We worked amicably together for several years, sharing telephone duty at night and looking after each other's patients when the other was away.

Now that I had had over a year's study in dermatology I was in demand for that, both at the hospital as well as in my practice, and was busier than ever. However, thank goodness, we now had an obstetrician, Dr Brian Neill, in Nelson, so I was able to phase out that part of my practice. In time, with the advent of a specialist anaesthetist, Dr Alan Bradford, I could let anaesthetics go as well. It was with mixed feelings that I ceased those aspects of my work. Both had been challenging, especially emergency anaesthetics, and maternity work was very rewarding with many life-long friendships made.

We also bought a new home during this period. I wonder how I had the courage as we were just so 'broke'. It happened thus. One night, another doctor's patient rang me to say that he had a bad migraine and could I come and give him an injection? His usual doctor was away and had asked me to help if needed. I gave him the injection, staying for a while to see that it was effective, and then went home.

It so happened that our two houses were on either side of a valley and when I walked back into our bedroom Jill was awake. She knew that I was returning because she saw the outside lights of the other house go out. She asked what the house was like and I told her it was a very nice home but on an undeveloped section with no garden or lawn. Would she like to live there? I jokingly asked. She said she wouldn't mind investigating – Princes Drive was a lovely area with superb views.

The owner of this property was a taxi driver and a former professional boxer. He had invested his winnings in this house, building it of the best possible materials, even using copper guttering and downpipes, but his wife and family had left him and he lived alone in this large four-bedroom house, quite unable to develop it further.

Next morning I was in town and saw him on the taxi rank, quite recovered. I said, 'Have you ever considered selling your house?' and he answered, 'No, but I would to you.' A day or two later he sent me a letter telling me all the details of the house and the two-acre section it was on, and offering it to me for a price that was quite impossible for us at the time, although actually cheap by market standards.

In the end, after discussing it with my friend, adviser and solicitor, Jim Glasgow, we decided to rake up the money by hook or by crook, borrowing to the hilt. Then we sold our former home, which got us out of a large proportion of our debt. We have lived here happily ever since.

Jasper came of course, caught lots of possums in his day, and was looked after in his old age until he died at 17, a much-loved friend. Of our several other pets two dogs and one or two of the cats developed serious illnesses. We found that parting from these loved family members was so painful that we decided not to have any more.

As I have said, the section at this new house was undeveloped and this gave us a lot of work. I put 34 cubic yards of topsoil on the lawn areas, carting it all by wheelbarrow, and then levelled and sowed it all. It so happened that I had a patient who was a motor vehicle dealer who occasionally dealt in agricultural machinery, so I rang and asked him if he had a front-end loader I could borrow. He did and said I could use it. I went around to their place after my afternoon surgery, had some lessons on how to work it, popped my medical bag on the seat and drove it home clad in my working suit! During the three-mile journey along busy city roads I met a traffic inspector whom I knew. He did a double take but just shook his head as I trundled past.

Near home I saw Linda coming down the road in our Mini so I stopped, lowered the bucket part way to hide me from her sight, and waited, blocking the narrow road. She stopped and I could tell she was most irritated at the obstacle so I lifted the bucket to let her see who was driving and she was flabbergasted.

The machine did wonderful work after I got the hang of scooping the topsoil up and spreading it around, as did a bunch of Nelson College boarders who came home with our sons to join the fun.

We acquired a few sheep as well as a wee orphaned wild goat and let them run on the undeveloped part of the section, which son Mark and I were clearing of gorse by hand. (Incidentally, we were mortified to find that Mark had got lice in his hair from cuddling the goat.) One night, Mark came from his bedroom and said that he could hear a possum on the drive outside his bedroom window. I went out with a rifle to deal with it and was astonished to find a very nice-looking young ram wandering around, trailing a rope. We led him into the fenced-off grazing area and turned him loose. After we'd advertised him for about a week the owner, from a nearby farm came to collect him.

It was some time before we noticed how plump our sheep were becoming and how well they were doing on our feed, until one day at my surgery I had a call from Jill to say that we had a lamb. In no time we had half a dozen. The unfortunate sequel to this was that our sheep and lambs became a target for some dogs and it was heartbreaking to see the devastation they caused. Two dogs were destroyed, but others soon turned up and worried the poor animals so we sold them all.

However, not long after this I saw an advertisement offering a pet lamb/sheep to a good home. I telephoned to find that the young lady had had this sheep since lambhood and was now going away overseas. She said he it was quite large. What an understatement that was! We went down with a trailer, met up with the most colossal sheep that ever was, trussed him up a bit and loaded him on the trailer. When we got him home and untied him it was hatred at first sight. He charged us with great force and speed, to the delight and hilarity of the watching womenfolk. It took a long time and a lot of cunning to get him behind the fence. We had to put a collar on him with a rope out to each side, and kept well away from him in this manner.

That was the start of a disastrous relationship. That darned animal had been castrated late in life but this had been botched, not being fully done. He was what is known as a 'rig', and turned out to be very dangerous. We gave him a large packing case for shelter but he smashed it to smithereens with his head in no time. We named him Bunty.

Trying to get to the incinerator was quite a dangerous exercise, especially for Jill. It was quite useless taking a stick as Bunty ignored all attempts to fend him off. Even setting up an electric fence did no good. He savaged the posts and ignored all the shocks. Anyone who went into the paddock with him also faced serious injury. Once, when trying to get some firewood I had to fend him off with the back of an axe or I think he would have broken my knee with the sideways hammer-like blows from his head.

One day he got through the fences and out onto the street, where he saw our neighbour's lady help and charged her. She ran for her life, followed into her house by a furious Bunty, who bailed her up in the kitchen from where she telephoned for help. I was telling this story to a former neighbour of ours who had always kept a few sheep and he said he would take him off our hands. He also said he would arrange for Bunty to be properly castrated as he had a friend who was skilled in this. A week or two later, having piled Bunty into the boot of his lovely Rover car, he and his friend attempted this operation. But Bunty was too cunning for them, knocked one of them down and savaged him, fracturing his sternum. End of story – and of poor Bunty, I'm afraid.

Inevitably, my Australian friends urged me to return to do the second part of my degree but I explained that I could not afford to, having used up all my savings in Australia the year before. Then Dr Adrian Johnson rang and told me that he would

*CLOCKWISE FROM TOP LEFT:* Jillian at Castaway Island, recuperating from near death; Jill playing the Wurlitzer organ at Len Southward's museum at Paraparaumu; our holiday home at Boundary Bay; doing a spot of landscaping at Princes Drive; Jasper; with a wild pig I shot on our property at Boundary Bay; 'The Beast' – a winch I made to haul the boat up the beach. It worked well but I was eventually banned from using it by my family who considered it too dangerous.

Spanning the generations. My mother at 88 and my father at 100 (top); and me with my granddaughters, Nicola and Fiona.

Celebrating our golden wedding anniversary in December 2000.

Our family (from the top): Mark with his daughter Kate; Linda and Bill with daughters Nicola and Fiona; Mark's wife Angela, with Kate; Tim and me.

The ultimate moment for me in my lifelong passion for flying: I shouted myself a flight in a WW2 Mustang fighter at Wanaka for my 80th birthday. It turned out I was easily the oldest person my pilot, Tom Middleton, had ever taken up in the Mustang, but he gave me a turn at the controls, anyway. Tragically, Tom Middleton was killed in an air accident early in 2001.

I still use my 1972 MG-B, owned since 1973, daily, as does Jillian – when she can get it.

Jill and I doing what we love: tramping in the hills above Nelson.

again employ me if I would return, offering once again a generous wage and ample time off for study and hospital work.

I was keen but there were many difficulties, the first being that I'd need someone to look after my practice because Bryan was busy enough with his own by now. The other was the wish not to interrupt our children's education. But by this time some of the local general practitioners had become used to having someone around who knew a bit about skin diseases and modern treatment of sun damage and cancers. Headed by Dr Keith Emanuel, they offered to look after my practice for me if I went to Sydney for the further year. This was a great offer and typified the way our medical community worked as a team.

As regards the children's education, Tim and Mark were boarding at Nelson College (by their own choice, I might say) and Linda, who was at Nelson College for Girls, was offered a home with our cousins John and Gwynneth Oliver. After family discussion it was agreed that Jill and I would head off to Sydney for another year, and that since I would now be earning enough, we would fly the children across to be with us for all school holidays.

The next piece of luck was when a close friend, our former Bishop of Nelson, Bishop Francis Hulme-Moir, who had gone to Sydney Cathedral after leaving Nelson, heard that we were coming over. He wrote to us offering their home with car supplied, at no cost – not even for power – provided we would look after their cat, dog, a young pregnant adolescent whom they had given a home, as well as his secretary who lived there too, while he and his wife went off to England. We let our own house to a group of young women to look after for us.

Thus it was all arranged. We all flew off at the end of 1967, being met in Sydney by the bishop's secretary, who drove us to his home at Killara on the North Shore.

I started work with Dr Adrian Johnson a few days later. He was a tremendous diagnostician with a large following, both professional and social. While I was there he was awarded a CBE. His consulting rooms were on the fifth floor of a building in Macquarie Street, overlooking the botanic gardens. I was given a small room overlooking the park and was one day astonished to see a possum climbing around in one of the palms alongside the road, there in the heart of Sydney. When I called Adrian to show him he was not at all surprised, telling me that they were treasured and protected. Perhaps we should sell ours back to them!

In my work I took histories and prepared patients for Adrian to see. He would then comment, advise and prescribe. I found out later that there was considerable conflict of opinion over my presence in this specialist practice, perhaps inspired by jealousy. I was the only postgraduate student thus employed. This conflict was to cost me dearly, perhaps brought to a head by my being left in sole charge of Adrian's practice while he went to an important meeting in the US for a week or so where he was to present a paper.

Jill wanted to get some work too, both for her own interest and to help with the budget. She naturally wished to utilise her musical degrees so she decided to try to find some private teaching. Despite approaches to a number of musical authorities she was quite unable to get any work. Perhaps it was because she was only temporarily in Australia, but it felt more like closing of the ranks. Eventually she took a part-time job for a short time in the postal department of a shipping company, which at least gave her some interest.

Every school holidays our children came over and we were very happy together. At our lovely residence we had quite a bit of fun, particularly with Buster, the dog. One boundary of the property was a golf course and Buster simply loved golf balls, as did Mark who liked to pull them to bits to get the rubber out of them to use in small model planes. Buster would stand at the back boundary watching for balls to appear, as they did quite frequently after being sliced into the rough and among the trees. He would then dart out, grab the errant ball and come home, almost with a smile. If we were around we would try to return it, but if not the poor golfers were out of luck.

I was away all day, either at the consulting rooms or at hospitals, and I studied every evening for some hours. One day at work I was dashing down the stairs to get my lunch when I tripped, fell and cracked an ankle. It was excruciatingly painful and I nearly 'flaked out'. Adrian arranged for me to see a specialist, have x-rays and so on, and the leg was plastered up. I had a day or two off and then resumed work, but was quite unable to walk to the railway station and had to drive in each day. I found that if I left by 7.30am it took me just under 20 minutes, whereas if I left after that time it took me an hour and a quarter or more because of the traffic, especially on the harbour bridge.

I was reading a medical journal one day when I saw an advertisement from a doctor in Victoria who wanted to buy a general practice. I rang him and told him about my practice in Nelson, whereupon Dr Malcolm Peacey and his wife Fran hopped on a bus and came through to Sydney to talk about it. I had a collection of photographic slides of the mountains, sea and surrounding area. They loved it and made arrangements to take over my practice, for which I made no charge, telling Malcolm that he could set up his own practice when I returned.

On Saturday mornings there was a clinical meeting at an outlying hospital run by an extraordinary man, Dr MacGuiness, a small, somewhat rotund man imbued with his own importance and love of an audience. He was a senior physician at Sydney Hospital and his character could be deduced by one of his little quirks. His private consulting rooms were in Macquarie Street a few hundred metres down the road. After he finished his ward rounds at the hospital he always had his medical registrar walk down the street with him while still ostentatiously wearing his white coat, something no doctor would normally do. It was a source of some amusement to those watching this performance from the windows of the other medical establishments along the route.

Nevertheless his Saturday morning clinics were excellent. He smoked incessantly, which was a bit off-putting to many of us, but we did learn a lot from these sessions. Unfortunately this man was one of our examiners and he obviously disliked New

Zealanders: I was warned about this by one of his registrars, with whom I was quite friendly, but I could sense it for myself. I could also sense opposition from some of Adrian's opponents in local medical politics, at least one of whom used to refer to those of us who had been in general practice as 'ageing GPs'.

Eventually my final examination came around and I was failed in pathology by one of these gentlemen. I passed in general medicine and came top in dermatology but I returned to New Zealand pretty shattered and down in the dumps. Letters I received from Australian friends subsequently told me about the dirty hand of politics. Apparently Dr Adrian Johnson, who was also an examiner, was told by another examiner that he would pass me if Adrian would pass a candidate who was a friend of this other chap's. But this latter candidate was known to be quite hopeless, and Adrian refused to bargain.

It was so unfair I decided to give it another go in a year's time, despite one of the most senior doctors in Sydney, Dr John Rae, who was a close friend, advising me against it. I studied hard for a further year but was failed again. This time I was told I had 'done very well in pathology' but failed in medicine by the aforementioned Dr Macguiness, who had given me a very rough time in the oral examination.

He eventually 'died with his boots on', I later heard, suffering a fatal heart attack when about to do some ward rounds at Sydney Hospital. Perhaps his smoking caught up with him.

My friends and supporters in Sydney advised me to come back only when the dermatologists of Australia and New Zealand had combined to form the Australasian College of Dermatologists, which was being talked about at that stage. This I did in 1971 and sat the same examinations again in dermatology, pathology and general medicine with most of the same examiners (with two notable exceptions, who shall remain nameless). I passed without difficulty and became the first New Zealander to enter the new college by examination.

# 19

*IT WAS A GREAT HOMECOMING* after that successful trip and good to get into practice again with no shadow over my head. I was given a lot of work at the hospital and also ran a clinic in Blenheim each fortnight. In fact there was such a backlog of dermatological work in Nelson and the surrounding district that I became very busy. The other doctors had supported me without complaint when I left my practice and although I wished to return their loyalty, in 1972 I gave up all general practice work.

Specialist practice was strange after so many years as a GP. I was used to getting to know whole families, seeing them at home and knowing all about them. As a specialist I still got to know many patients very well, and knew a large number from my GP days, but it was quite different. In a specialist practice a doctor knows a great deal about a small section of medicine, whereas a GP has a medium amount of knowledge about a great deal and a lot of knowledge about his own patients and their families.

After dealing with the initial backlog of cases, it was wonderful to have time for research, study and trips to conferences, which I found most stimulating. I felt really up to date with my general medicine as well as dermatology.

In 1973 Jill and I went to a conference in Australia. As we had never seen the Far North of New Zealand we decided to hire a camper-van on our return to Auckland and go for a tour. While we were away I found it strange that my usually exuberant and bubbly Jill did not seem to enjoy the trip and took little notice of a great deal. When we got home she confessed that she had a 'stingy pain' in her tummy at times, so I set investigations in motion. Her doctor could not find anything wrong but I was not convinced so I did a few tests myself. These two non specific tests (ESR and CRP) were both grossly disordered so I asked a surgeon friend to see her. After his examination and x-rays I was devastated to find that she had a large and advanced cancer of the bowel. She was 49.

Peter Low operated on her within days and removed a large infiltrating cancer from her bowel. But Jill did not recover from the operation as well as expected. As the days went by, her temperature soared, she could not eat, her bowel remained in the post-operative state of paralysis and she gradually sank into a semi-comatose state. We could find no reason for this.

Family, friends, relations and our church gave tremendous support until came the evening when I thought she would die in a matter of hours. Late that night another surgeon, Peter Meffan, rang me and said that he and Peter Low had decided that Jill probably had a subphrenic abscess and wished to operate at once. Would I give permission? The risk was high but she was almost moribund so of course I said yes.

She was so ill that almost no anaesthetic was necessary – in fact she heard some of the conversation during the operation. They removed parts of some ribs, found an enormous abscess hidden away under the diaphragm and drained a large volume of pus. After the operation they rang to tell me of their success and that her condition was not too bad. I managed to sleep for an hour or two.

Then next morning there occurred one of those magic and memorable moments a doctor rarely has the privilege of seeing. I walked into her room at about 8am to find her sitting in a chair, a grin from ear to ear across her chalk-white face, eating a plate of porridge. It was like a miracle. From then on she never looked back.

Subphrenic abscesses are rare and I had never previously seen one. And yet every doctor has been taught to beware of them, with a jingle drummed in time and time again: 'Pus somewhere, pus nowhere, pus under the diaphragm'. Translated, what this says is that if there are signs of infection and abscess formation, swinging temperatures and failing health (pus somewhere), and this infection cannot be found (pus nowhere), then it is probably subphrenic (under the diaphragm).

Jill came home as weak as a kitten, all skin and bone, but in good heart. Our three kids were wonderful. Tim came home from South-East Asia to housekeep, and the others gave tremendous support. However, Jill is an outgoing and giving person and became tired with all the visitors, so I booked a trip to Castaway Island in Fiji. Mark was given leave from school and between us, the airline folk and the Fijians, we helped and carried her all that way. I shall never forget the look of bliss on her face when we deposited her on the beach under a palm tree. She walked a small distance along the beach each day and by the time we left she was able to walk right around the island.

As so many readers will know from their own experience, this sort of hurdle can cause one to re-assess one's life and priorities, and so it did with us. We took to the outdoors, to the bush, rivers, hills and mountains, tracks and tranquillity. We embarked on a campaign of getting fit by walking and climbing hills, of which there are plenty in the Nelson district. We got to the stage where we did a half-day's walk midweek and a whole day in the weekend, carrying reasonably heavy packs. And then I put my Jilly to the test and booked her to walk the Routeburn Track, some seven months after her operation. She fairly flew through this, as well as other side-trips. She has since done the Milford Track twice (once as a 'freedom walker' carrying a heavy pack), the Wangapeka Track, St James Walkway and numerous other lesser known tramps. She still plays tennis at 75 years, as well as going on vigorous day walks. My message is this: 'Don't give up.'

In that same year I became quite ill myself with encephalitis, a brain infection. I was in bed for some time with blinding headaches, vomiting and one period of about 12 hours of complete memory loss. But it passed.

I found that tramping was a wonderful means of recharging one's batteries and have spent a lot of time in the hills, mountains and river valleys over the years. I always have one major trip away with a friend. In later years this has been Ernest Farquhar, a small, vigorous man imported from Scotland as a child, who has tramped nearly every hill and track in the province and a lot of others as well.

I like travelling alone, even though it is not advised, and have done a number of solo trips without mishap. I always advise a ranger where I am going and take no risks. I had a dramatic experience one day. I was by myself in the Kahurangi National Park (formerly North-West Nelson Forest Park) on a six-day trip. At one stage I went well off the track to go to the toilet and saw a large bird on a sloping branch about four or five metres above the ground. It looked like a very large parrot and I was so astonished I said to it, 'What are you doing here?' I then noticed that it had an untidy fringe of feathers around its face – in fact it rather reminded me of my grandmother, whose hair was always like that around her head.

Gradually, as we gazed at each other, I began to think that it must be a kakapo. These had been common in that region many years earlier and signs of them had been reported not long before this. So I decided to try to make it fly to see what it was like, and also to check that it was not an old man kea. I approached and shooed it, whereupon it made a bumbling descending flight into tangled bush further away. It had no red under the wings and so was not a kea.

When I came out of the bush two days later I reported this to the ranger and the Internal Affairs Department in Wellington. My sighting has been investigated and may have been the last sighting of a kakapo in the Kahurangi National Park.

My dermatology practice became more and more absorbing with a backlog of interesting and some rare cases.

The porphyrias are a group of metabolic disorders and a good example of how a serious medical condition can first show as a skin disorder. There are various types and degrees, some of which also show serious mental disorders of the type that affected the English royal family some hundreds of years ago. They are fairly rare, but while training in Sydney I had seen a number of different forms.

Not long after I set up my practice a young woman from Blenheim came to see me. She gave a history of recurring patches of inflamed and sometimes blistered skin on exposed areas. She had consulted a number of doctors, including a specialist physician, but none of their treatments or prescriptions had helped her problem. Examination showed significant scarring on some exposed skin areas, with evidence of blistering having occurred. I suspected a type of porphyria and this was confirmed by a simple urine test (urine exposed to screened ultraviolet light fluoresces a bright red if the condition is present). The condition in susceptible individuals can be triggered or made worse by exposure to direct sunlight or other sources of ultraviolet light, as well as the taking of barbiturate sedatives, sulpha drugs, alcohol or oestrogenic hormones, including 'the pill'. I advised my patient to avoid these substances, told her how to care for the condition, then referred her back to her own doctor, who reported that she did well.

Some 27 years later there was a reunion of nurses who had trained at Nelson Hospital, with about 600 from all over the world attending. Since I used to lecture many of them, Jill and I and some other doctors were invited to the dinner. One of the first people to come to our table and greet me was the above woman. I did not recognise her name tag but as soon as she said, 'You diagnosed my porphyria,' it all came back. She had done marvellously, with little scarring evident.

I also met another woman there who as a teenage nurse had come to me with a skin cancer on her back, which is quite rare at that age. She was of Irish extraction, a race prone to sun damage, and said she had been sunburnt as an infant when accidentally left out without clothing. She later went to Britain where she developed another skin cancer, but because these were so rare there and because she was so young the physicians would not believe her diagnosis. She wrote to me and I sent a letter with her history, which apparently convinced them.

In my practice I saw a large number of superficial skin cancers as well as a great deal of lesser skin damage and gradually noted that I seemed to be seeing more cases of the potentially serious tumour, melanoma, than I had seen in Sydney. I wondered if we had a higher-than-average incidence of this, so decided to do some research. This was a fascinating exercise, taking some years. Since we had only one pathology department for the whole Nelson-Marlborough district I arranged, with appropriate consents, to see the analysis of every reported melanoma and classified each one into about 15 different categories according to age, sex, and type etc.

After three years I found to my astonishment that the incidence was greater than any previously reported from any other area in the world – which is not to say we necessarily had the highest incidence, but the highest *reported* incidence up to that time. I wrote it all up, presented it at an international conference and had it published in a medical journal. This caused a mini-storm as Queenslanders and Californians thought they had the greatest incidence and could not believe that a place as far south could have more cases. Some overseas experts even visited. My results were examined in detail and the pathology reports and microscopic slides checked, but the results were confirmed. The Nelson-Marlborough region has one of the clearest atmospheres in New Zealand and also the greatest number of sunshine hours. It is probable that these are the factors causing such a high incidence of melanoma.

Some years later I carried out a further survey, which confirmed my previous findings and was also published in a medical journal and presented at an international conference. Over time I had 14 papers on a number of subjects published in various journals around the world. I also became very involved with the New Zealand Dermatological Society, initially as secretary for some years and later as president.

The downside of the latter was that I had to represent New Zealand as delegate to the Australasian meetings. This was a black time for New Zealand dermatologists as the Australians objected to our admitting any new skin specialists who were not trained in Australia, no matter how well trained they were elsewhere. There was some pretty bad blood at that time and when I went over to Australia for council meetings I soon found out who my real friends were. It was quite unbelievable at times and one incident sticks in my mind. Staying at a hotel in Adelaide, I came out of my room to go to a meeting at the same time as one of the Aussie delegates came out of his. We walked to the lift at the same time from opposite directions but he would not turn to face me or say a word.

I survived with help from my true Oz mates and thankfully, as the 'old guard' disappeared, due to 'natural attrition', younger and newer graduates repaired the damage. Our Australasian meetings now have a great spirit of co-operation.

One of the most difficult skin conditions specialists have to deal with or diagnose with certainty is dermatitis artefacta, which is the name given to self-inflicted skin damage. Skin is a strange and awesome material. It is the largest organ in the body, regulates heat, protects vital organs, sheds rain, helps synthesise vitamins, grows hair and nails, senses heat, pressure, touch and pain, and repairs quickly when physically damaged. It is a complex organ without which we could not stay alive.

A senior Nelson specialist asked me to see his teenage son who had deformities of his thumbnails which his father thought might be due to a fungal infection. I examined him and noted that the nails had ridging from the base to the tip, but there was no sign of crumbling or infection. I could not see any cause for such a condition except repetitive injury to the bases.

Nailbeds are extremely sensitive growth areas, damage to which shows in the nails after a week or two, remaining until it grows right out to the tip. When questioned the young man admitted that when he was studying each evening he had the habit of scratching the base of his thumbnails with the nail of another finger. I advised him to try to stop this because it was almost certainly causing the damage, but his father was sceptical and flatly refused to believe me. It took weeks for the undamaged nail to grow out from the base but it did eventually, to prove the diagnosis.

In another case a young businessman whom I had known since childhood came with a peculiar rash on the lower forehead between his eyes. He said he had had it for months and it would not heal, despite all sorts of ointments being applied. Examination showed that the so-called rash consisted of small parallel vertical lines, about 2cm long. Some were quite new and raw, while others were healing or had scarred. Now, skin is funny stuff and when it forms rashes or diseases, these follow certain patterns and lines in the skin. If these lines are not followed one's suspicion is raised and these ones were quite bizarre. I suspected he was scratching himself, repeatedly and seriously, so questioned him about his job and home life to find that he was having serious trouble with both.

Eventually we developed a rapport and although he did not admit that he was graunching his skin, he knew that I knew, and similarly I knew that he now accepted this. He managed to stop the habit and his so-called rash cleared.

It is interesting to look back on photographic evidence of these cases. Skin reacts to minor injury by growing thicker, which can cause all sorts of bother. If someone gets a minor itchy spot on, say, a leg, and scratches it repeatedly, the skin may not only grow thicker but can become more itchy and even develop a low-grade infection. We call this 'lichenification' and it is often seen on the legs or back of the scalp where people have been compulsively scratching. Anyone who has a tendency to eczema is likely to get patches of lichenification if they scratch too much. It can take months to reverse the process.

A local GP once asked me to see his father, who was visiting from another town. He had a dark lump under a fingernail which had been present for some months. I instantly recognised it as a melanoma, and a very dangerous form at that. I advised him that the finger should be amputated as soon as possible since it was impossible to remove the growth safely by any other means. I found out later that another son, a medical specialist in another town, did not agree, and had the tumour alone removed. The patient, his father, died of secondary spread of the melanoma.

Misconceptions abound about skin rashes and diseases. One of the common misconceptions one meets in general as well as dermatological practice is with the disease known as shingles (herpes zoster). This is characterised by small blisters on the skin, usually in a crop around the chest. It is itchy to start with and can become very painful. Almost invariably when one diagnoses a case of shingles someone, usually a relative of the patient, remarks that this is due to 'nerves', implying that it is a stress-induced or psychological condition. This is not so. Shingles is a viral infection that gets into the nerve trunks leading to the skin, travelling to the surface where it shows as a blister. It is exactly the same virus as that which causes chickenpox. When a child has had an attack of chickenpox the virus remains dormant in the body, close to the spinal column. In adult life it can reactivate for a variety of reasons, including lowered immunity, and show as shingles. I have seen two cases occurring in lowered immunity: both were in patients who had some form of previous malignant disease that had recurred. In one of these cases the onset of shingles was the first sign of recurrence of the malignant disease. It is an exceedingly unpleasant and painful condition, as all sufferers will agree, and we are now lucky to have a drug that will largely arrest it if taken early enough.

I was unfortunate enough to suffer an attack of shingles and it led to one of the many hilarious incidents in our married life. We were away camping in our small caravan in the Lewis Pass area of the South Island and called in for a hot swim at a small open-air hot pool well known to campers. After we stripped off we found that the sandflies and mosquitoes were more ferocious and plentiful than we had ever previously known. At one stage my back was absolutely black with them and we had to finish our hot bath rapidly. That night I was very itchy on the back and this gradually worsened over the next week. I went to see my colleague skin specialist, who confirmed that I had developed shingles.

One day, my wife was at some female gathering and when politely asked, 'How is Miles?' she replied, 'Not too well: the poor man has got syphilis.' Consternation and dead silence. Thank goodness someone was able to put the record straight!

There were not nearly as many arresting or curious incidents in a specialist practice as there were in family medicine, but one of the most bizarre happened the night George and Des and I, with our wives, went for a celebratory dinner at a hotel which was about the best dining place at that time. After dining and wining well we were at the checkout desk when the man immediately ahead of us suddenly fell to the floor. We did not immediately realise the seriousness of the situation and one of us said that if his bill gave him such a shock we had better be prepared.

However, I soon realised he had suffered a cardiac arrest and was clinically dead. The staff shooed everyone away while we three men carried him into the adjacent lounge, where I attempted to revive him with external cardiac massage but to no avail. I advised the manager and arranged for an ambulance to come and remove the poor fellow.

The ambulance driver, whom I knew well, arrived and took me aside to say that the lift was not big enough to take the stretcher, so I said we would carry him on the stretcher down the stairs. But the stairs turned out to be too narrow for the stretcher to get around the corners. There was nothing for it but to carry him down in the lift without the stretcher.

So Des, George and I supported him upright and took him down. The khaki yellow lining in the brightly lit lift did nothing to improve the poor chap's pallor. When we arrived at the ground floor a couple of guests were waiting to go up in the lift, both fairly well wined. One of them looked at our patient and said, 'Hell, he looks crook.' To which one of my friends, who had also had his measure of wine, replied, 'Never crooker, mate.'

My specialist practice became far too busy for one practitioner with long waiting lists, and I tried for some time to obtain assistance, with no success. Then I heard of a relatively new graduate, Dr Peter Sears. He used to live in Nelson and I remembered him as a lad because of an early morning call when I sent him to hospital with an apparent acute appendicitis. By this time he was married with a family and I finally persuaded him to come and practise with me – not as a financial partner, but building up and running his own practice, while utilising the existing facilities which were altered to accommodate him. Later, he looked up his own records at the hospital to find that he had not had appendicitis, but another condition which mimics it closely, is rare, just as serious and mostly impossible to diagnose except at operation. I never saw another case of it. He teased me mercilessly about it.

We got on exceedingly well, having similar philosophies in regard to medical practice, and I gradually reduced my workload as he increased his. It was great to have another dermatologist on hand with whom to discuss cases and obtain second opinions. We would simply buzz the other on the intercom and advice and opinion was then freely exchanged in front of the patient, who was also usually grateful for this second opinion, especially as no extra charge was ever made.

As the years passed Peter's workload increased due to his own abilities and to my easing up and taking time off to indulge my passions for trout fishing and tramping. I eventually retired from practice in 1989 at the age of 69, leaving it all to Peter. We always got on well and still do. I cannot remember one single difference between us in all the years we worked together, and that is really something.

One must always remember the role that a receptionist plays in the life of a busy doctor, especially that of a GP. She (it always seems to be a 'she') can make or break a practice and is a very special person. She has to reassure patients, assist the doctor with minor operations, change dressings, give first aid, keep the books for accounts and appointments, send out accounts, clean the premises, sterilise instruments and make morning and afternoon teas.

I was blessed with a series of excellent helpers, many of whom were with me for only a year or two, usually leaving to get married. Most have remained firm friends.

My first receptionist, Mary, who came when I did not have a single patient, was a registered nurse who wanted a change. She worked for peanuts at first, with gradual increases in her pay as the practice expanded. She was a corker person.

After she left to get married I had a lovely girl, Rosemary, who was the daughter of our new bank manager. She stayed with me for many years until she up and married one of my closest friends. Her bank manager father was a great help to me too, and he gave me financial advice and training as well as personal help at times. When he found out that Jill had a music degree but no piano he was appalled. I told him I simply could not afford one and he told me that he would advance the money on two conditions: first, it had to be a grand piano, and second, he had to help choose it. He was a keen and able pianist with a grand piano in his home. And so he made me advertise for a grand piano, came to see all those who replied, and recommended the one we should buy, advancing the funds to do so. We never regretted that.

Anne, a very fast typist, and Esmé, a former school teacher, were both also with me for many years. And so it went on.

A good doctor's receptionist knows all the patients – and a lot about them – but does not ever try to give medical advice, is never rude or short with the patient, and has enormous patience, tolerance and understanding. I remember a new one once who came in with a roar and a flourish, boasting that she could handle anything and was a whizz with the books and accounts. It became quite apparent that her previous experience was in a quiet office job and did not involve the constant influx of the public or her employer frequently interrupting her nice orderly paperwork. On her fourth day she said to me, 'This is total bedlam – I simply cannot stand it another day,' and she left.

Then there was an attractive, apparently demure young woman who was well qualified for typing and who was a member of a religious sect known for their industry and dedication to work, as well as their exceedingly moral behaviour. She did a good job but left unexpectedly without giving any particular reason and I later found out that she had become pregnant. She left her religious group and the next time I saw her she was working in a large metropolitan department store with her hair cut off and looking most glamorous.

Shortly after I came back from Australia I employed a new nurse, a young American woman named Marti, who seemed well qualified. She was outstandingly quick and wonderful with the patients and picked up the nursing side of things so rapidly and so well that I came to the reluctant conclusion that she was really wasted in the work she was doing. I persuaded her that she should be doing full-time nursing. She applied to train at Christchurch Hospital and had an outstanding career, winning the Florence Nightingale Award in the process.

# 20

WHEN I RETIRED I HAD plenty of interests: restoring and riding classic motorcycles, motoring, amateur radio, boating, fishing, reading, gardening and tramping as well as keeping close to my grown-up family and holidaying at Boundary Bay.

I have scarcely mentioned my love of motorcycles and motorcycling. One of the world's greatest names in this regard is Vincent. These machines were made in England and held several world records, some of them set by New Zealanders. Their slogan was: 'The world's fastest standard motorcycle,' and it was true. They ceased production in about 1954.

I was keen to get one, and after advertising all over Australia and New Zealand in 1972 I managed to get a 1951 model from England. It was an awful mess, so I dismantled it to the last nut and bolt, restoring it slowly. It was a lovely machine – a dream to ride – and on my first New Zealand vintage rally it won the Concours d'Elegance prize. Incidentally, the then Minister of Transport had a somewhat shapely wife who presented me with my trophy and asked for a ride around the Addington Show Grounds where the competitions were held. She was quite a sight on the back.

Jill and I loved getting out on the bike and I did quite a lot of mileage all over New Zealand. I finally sold it as my neck would not tolerate prolonged wearing of a heavy helmet as a result of an old injury. I packed it up and sent it to Sotheby's where it sold for a goodly sum.

I still felt a hankering to keep a foot in the health scene so I decided to stand as a candidate for election to the local hospital board. I could not be bothered with advertising or campaign meetings but I was elected anyway.

Because of my high polling I was asked to stand as chairman of the newly elected board but I decided against it as the previous chairperson, Dorothy Matthews, had done such a good job and she was up for re-election. I also did not think it wise for the board to have as chairman someone new to hospital board work.

The role of the board was important. We could and did put a brake on the bureaucrats who were even then invading the health scene with expensive new ideas. Under the then Labour government I can fairly say that we had a great health service in Nelson: certainly Helen Clark thought so at the time, she being the Minister of Health. Then a National government was elected, introduced major new philosophies and sacked the elected hospital board. It has been amazing to see the proliferation of administrative offices in the hospital buildings since then, associated with the closing down of wards and bed space.

Sadly, general medical practice and health services generally have fallen into some disrepute and disrepair in the last few years. One of the most telling remarks I have ever heard about this was made to my wife and me when we recently met up with one of my longstanding patients, a registered nurse who had done a great deal of work in the public health service. She said, 'Years ago, when we women used to gossip as nurses and later as family people, we used to skite about our doctor to the others. But now when we talk about these matters we each tell the others of how poor our doctors are and the troubles and errors we have.' What an indictment. Why is it?

There seems to have been a major change in attitude. There is no doubt that in my generation we were cruelly overworked and underpaid in hospital work, and very much overworked in a successful general practice. But now there seems to have occurred a backlash in some respects. As I write this, in August 2000, junior hospital doctors are giving strike notice, wanting a 20 per cent rise in pay because they say that too many doctors are going overseas because of higher wages.

What a laugh – what a disgrace. Disregard the patients and the extra discomforts they will endure, disregard the Hippocratic oath, disregard the extra workload put onto nurses and doctors who are not on strike. How could they do it?

We hear that these new doctors have large student loans to pay off. Of course they do. So does everyone who spends a long time training as an apprentice. From what we hear of the salary levels of junior doctors they should still have plenty left on which to live after paying off their loans. Well done those who have refused to join the strike and walk out on the patients. I fear that it all comes down to a lack of dedication, lack of compassion, a lack of the spirit of service and feeling of responsibility. This has gradually crept into the profession along with an expectation of a large income and limited working hours.

I think that if a survey were done we would find that almost all GPs expect at least a half day and sometimes a whole day off work during the week, as well as most weekends and nights off. They expect their patients to be attended by some emergency service – yet they expect to be paid as if they were working a full and busy week.

Then there is the vexed and oft-voiced question of the apparent reluctance of GPs nowadays to do house calls. So often sick people, and even small miserable children with high temperatures, have to be taken to medical rooms instead of being visited at home. Little do these doctors know what they are missing by not going to the patients' homes.

Another frequently heard complaint is that doctors nowadays don't follow up their patients. They see them at the surgery, give some advice and/or treatment and leave it at that, without any attempt to find out the progress of the complaint. I remember getting a severe pain in my chest on one occasion shortly before I retired. I went to a doctor whom I had asked to look after me and my wife after our GP had retired. He listened to my heart, pulling up my clothing (but did not get me to disrobe or lie down), took my blood pressure and declared me quite fit. He did no other tests, x-rays or examination but pronounced that it was probably stress, and sent me on my way. Nor did he ever follow up my complaint (which incidentally was not stress but spinal damage from an old injury). He did not remain our family's medical adviser.

It is true that present-day doctors have an awful time with bureaucracy. Accident Compensation claims are a nightmare and I realise they have a lot more paperwork and fear of litigation than we ever had, but they also have a lot more staff to help with this. They seem to spend a lot of the consultation time looking at computers and picking at the keys in an unskilled fashion rather than looking at and talking to the patient.

When newly graduated doctors come on the scene who are highly motivated, regarding patients with compassion and displaying a desire to cure and enough interest to find out how these patients respond, they will once again be held in the high regard that was once their due for the dedication and service they enjoy giving. I know that practitioners of this type are in our community, thank goodness.

Fully retired now, Jill and I still find ourselves with plenty of interests and more than enough to do. We are lucky to have good health and a fair amount of energy. Jill is organist at All Saints Church where she plays every Sunday and she also involves herself with other church activities. She plays the organ for funerals and weddings, spends a lot of time doing watercolour painting, and enjoys some success in selling her work.

I like to visit elderly or ill friends when I can, and am involved with the Stoke Tahunanui Probus Club, especially their tramping group and a discussion group I managed to get started. A group of us meet regularly to discuss predetermined subjects of common interest. We have covered many weighty matters such as corporal punishment and the justice system and are about to discuss the proposed Golden Bay-West Coast road link.

Our large garden takes a lot of care and I enjoy maintaining this, but I am also still keen on motoring, trout fishing and tramping. We hope to continue to do these sorts of things for years to come. A trip to and tramp around Lake Waikaremoana is high on our list, as is another trip to Glade House at the beginning of the Milford Track. Jill loves the painting opportunities in such areas.

Our three children are very close to us. They all had their primary and secondary schooling in Nelson (apart from the year in Sydney), and all went to Otago University for a spell. None wished to study medicine perhaps because of having experienced the disadvantages of this as a career.

Linda interrupted her late schooling at Nelson College for Girls when she was selected to serve overseas for a year with Volunteer Service Abroad. She went off to Western Samoa to help with teaching at a school near Apia and made lots of friends there. We paid her a visit, had an hilarious time and met large numbers of relations descended from a Norman Hursthouse Macdonald who settled there many years ago and married a Samoan woman. Linda went on to Otago University to do a BSc. in microbiology, had jobs in Auckland for some time, married solicitor Bill Ralph, and has two lovely daughters. She and her family continue to live in Auckland where she now has a part-time office management job. She achieved an ambition when she

still keen on sailing and all forms of boating. He married Angela de Zwart, who has a masters degree in public health, and they live on a 'lifestyle' property with lots of animals. They also have two lovely daughters.

Our children are all musical, and are extremely good to Jill and me, keeping in close touch by e-mail and regular visits. They all turned up for my 80th birthday, each making an incredibly amusing speech. They give us a lot of joy. We like to spend January and February at our cottage, where we often have family come to stay. Grandchildren sometimes bring their friends with them, which is great. I guess it would be fair to say that our family is still our major interest in life.

Private medical practice is a hard mistress for those who choose it, but it is a wonderful career for those who can adapt to it. I loved it, and if I were to have my life again I could think of absolutely nothing I would sooner do than be a private medical practitioner in a medium-sized town.

In such a life there is a lot of laughter, occasional tears – of joy as well as of sadness – and the most enormous pleasure as well as a lot of hard work. It is worth every moment.

and Bill bought a keeler in which they go sailing at every opportunity. She is active in various clubs and pushes her parents around mercilessly – but always fondly.

Tim boarded at Nelson College for a few years at his own request, but came home each weekend. He was a strong-minded lad with strong ideas on human rights, which became evident when he once refused to allow a prefect to cane him for some misdemeanour. He insisted instead on seeing the headmaster, despite knowing that the caning would be administered by him, which it was. Tim had no trouble academically but did not feel it was worth putting in too much effort if he could pass his exams with a lesser amount of study. He went to Otago University to study architecture but gave it up and went on the wander overseas. Back in Nelson he set up a successful vegetarian restaurant in partnership with two friends and the three of them also wrote and published a book, *Fresh & Natural*, which has sold well and been reprinted several times. He went away again after selling his business and finished up working in Tokyo for some years where he taught English, learnt to speak Japanese and worked in translating pamphlets into English. We visited him there.

After some years he settled in Sydney as the manager of a Japanese company that had hotel and golf club interests there, then he left that job and started studying accountancy, qualifying at about 43. He is now in business in Sydney as a private accountant and visits all his New Zealand family at least once a year. Tim is still a passionate campaigner for human rights and the anti-racist movement. Linda and Tim were both dux at their primary schools.

Mark also went to Nelson College, first to the preparatory school and then, at his own request, as a boarder to the secondary school. He was mad keen on model planes and kite flying. Home for weekends or for a day, the first thing he used to do was to hoist a kite in the air and leave the end of the long line tied to a pipe in the garden. As we live on top of a ridge 500 feet above the airport, his kite used to be very prominent. Eventually the airport controller rang me to say that pilots of aircraft on approach to Nelson Airport were complaining. He pointed out that it was illegal to fly kites at that height so close to an airport.

Mark excelled academically at college so that he and another lad, who happened to be a close friend, were asked by the headmaster to have a shot at a scholarship. Mark asked us our opinion and we said we would back whatever decision he made. He studied as I have not seen many do before and he and his friend both got scholarships. I believe Mark topped New Zealand in mathematics. At the end of the year they were made equal dux of Nelson College – a first.

Mark went to Otago University and then Canterbury University to take a degree in engineering, but he suffered 'burnout' after a year or so and got permission from his professor to take a year off, a lot of which he spent working and playing on the South Island skifields. Having obtained his degree he had various jobs, and currently is with 3M, a large American firm.

Always keen on boating, he became an expert windsurfer, almost up to Olympic standard, competing in New Zealand and world championship events. He manufactured his own design of board, marketed as Bullet Boards. He is a keen fisherman and